To Dorothy
with much love
from Phyllis

1974

first edit

Lit

AC81.

£8-50

no jacket

The Joy of the Snow

Books by Elizabeth Goudge

Novels

ISLAND MAGIC
A CITY OF BELLS
TOWERS IN THE MIST
THE MIDDLE WINDOW
THE BIRD IN THE TREE
THE CASTLE ON THE
   HILL
GREEN DOLPHIN
   COUNTRY
THE HERB OF GRACE
THE HEART OF THE
   FAMILY
GENTIAN HILL
THE ROSEMARY TREE
THE WHITE WITCH
THE DEAN'S WATCH
THE SCENT OF WATER
THE CHILD FROM THE
   SEA

Short Stories

WHITE WINGS
THE REWARD OF FAITH
THE WELL OF THE
   STAR
THE PEDLAR'S PACK
THE GOLDEN SKYLARK
THE IKON ON THE
   WALL
THE LOST ANGEL

Novelette

THE SISTER OF THE
   ANGELS

Juveniles

SMOKY HOUSE
HENRIETTA'S HOUSE
THE LITTLE WHITE
   HORSE
MAKE-BELIEVE
THE VALLEY OF SONG

Non-Fiction

GOD SO LOVED THE
   WORLD
ST. FRANCIS OF ASSISI
A DAY OF PRAYER

Anthology

AT THE SIGN OF THE
   DOLPHIN
A BOOK OF COMFORT
A CHRISTMAS BOOK
THE TEN GIFTS

Omnibus

THE ELIOTS OF
   DAMEROSEHAY
THREE CITIES OF BELLS

The Joy of the Snow

AN AUTOBIOGRAPHY
by

ELIZABETH GOUDGE

HODDER AND STOUGHTON
LONDON SYDNEY AUCKLAND TORONTO

The extract from 'Little Gidding' by T. S. Eliot is reproduced by kind permission of Faber and Faber Ltd.; the extract from a tenth-century Irish poem by kind permission of Professor Brendan Kennelly whose adaptation is reproduced; and the extract from the Bhaganad-Gita, *translated by Christopher Isherwood and Swami Prabhavanda by permission of the Vedanta Society of Southern California.*

For
Alan Walton
and the other friends
who wanted me to write
this book.

I would like to express my gratitude, love and thanks to two friends. To Elsie Herron of Hodder and Stoughton who has edited this book for me, helped and encouraged and reassured me along the way, and to Kathleen Ault who for nearly forty years has typed my books, helped me with the proofs and the grammar, and never failed to read my handwriting.

Contents

Illustrations

Wells

Have you seen but a white lily grow before rude hands
had touched it?
Have you seen but the fall of the snow before the earth
hath smutched it?
Have you felt the wool of beaver, or swan's down ever?
Have you smelt of the bud of the briar or the nard
in the fire?
Have you tasted the bag of the bee?

I

THE BEGINNING OF BEN JONSON'S LOVE SONG COULD BE THE
opening of a happy nunc dimittis. Have you seen, felt, smelt,
tasted the beauty of this world? If your life has been lived in
such pleasant places that you can answer, yes, then you are
one of the lucky ones. I am one of the fortunate for I have
never lived in a place that was not beautiful, and if at the
end of my life I appreciate roses more than snow that was not
the case at the beginning. Then, in company with all children
and most dogs, I thought snow the wonder of the world. The
snow-light filling the house with magic as the white flakes
drifted down in windless silence, the splendour when the sun
came out and hills and fields and trees sparkled under the arc
of blue sky, the thought of the things one did in the snow,
tobogganing and snowballing and building a snowman; it
was all ecstasy. And somewhere tucked away at the back of
one's mind was the knowledge that every crystal in the vast
whiteness, though too small for the human eye to see, was
fashioned like a flower or a star. How could snow not be the
wonder of the world?

It was not myself as a child but the daughter of a friend of

mine who gave me the title for this book. Her mother,
accompanied by the dog Coach, had ploughed her way
through a deep fall of snow to fetch her youngest home from
nursery school. The hard going had been a weariness, the cold
a misery to the flesh. Ploughing back again, her youngest
attached, a small voice sang out beside her, "Look, Mummy!
Look at Coach and the joy of the snow!" Coach was leaping
and rolling in the snow, his eyes like stars, his tail a banner.
The little girl's eyes were as bright as his, her face pink inside
her hood. She glowed like a flame. Coach glowed. The
mother for a few moments looked at the snow through their
eyes and the earth had not smutched it.

Old age, I find, is a time when you start doing all the
things that in earlier years you reprobated in older people,
and were quite certain you would never do yourself, and if
there was one thing more than another that I was determined
not to do it was to write an autobiography. But the request
that I should do so came from a few of those people to whom
one can only say, in the words of Philip Sidney, "Your desire
to my heart is an absolute commandment." And so I obeyed.
Yet this book is hardly an autobiography, it is more an
attempt to recapture happy memories and with them some
of the joy in places and people that I have known, and to
share them. And to share, too, some of the conclusions I have
come to about work and life. Neither will be in the least
exciting and so my hope for this book is that it will be a good
bedside book, and keep nobody awake.

To find that one has reached and passed the biblical
three-score years and ten has a sobering effect upon anyone
brought up on the Bible, for the Bible thinks you have about
had it by then. And so you have. You have almost closed the
circle and like a ship that has sailed round the world you see
the last stretch of water narrowing at a startling pace. But
the coast of the country to which you sail is obscured by the
spray of breaking waves, and the rainbows in them show you

the shapes and the colours of your own childhood. What the poets say is true. The beginning is the end and the end is the beginning.

What do I remember first of the rainbow days? Someone years ago told me with great seriousness that our first memory is significant; it tells us much about ourselves. I remember I listened with polite unbelief, since my first memory is concerned with raspberries, and apart from the fact that I do not like them there seemed no significance at all. Yet now that I take a good look at that memory I am not so sure. It is a vivid one. I must have been very young at the time because the raspberries grew in the old walled garden of the house where I was born, Tower House at Wells in Somerset, and we left that house when I was two years old. I was standing on a pathway in a forest and on either side of me towered green trees. I looked at them with awe. The pathway stretched before me straight as a ruler, the trees converging to a mysterious vanishing point. My ambulatory powers at that period were those of a very ancient crone. One swayed on the feet, balanced precariously, then gathered courage and staggered forward. But I was not afraid either of my own unbalanced state nor of the towering raspberry canes on either side, nor of the mysterious vanishing point, because ahead of me on the path was my father picking the raspberries.

He took no notice of me and I had probably staggered after him without his knowledge; but he was there, just ahead of me, and so I was safe. A slim, upright, agile young man, he picked the raspberries with concentration, for he disliked domestic chores and when cajoled into them (my mother was always in complete control throughout their blissful married life) got them out of the way as quickly as possible. His figure grew smaller and I lurched forward, for I must keep him in sight. And then suddenly he had reached the vanishing point and was gone. Actually of course only round the corner into the next raspberry aisle, but for me totally gone. The one I had to follow, the one without whom I was lost, had vanished. The darkness of total fear fell upon me, and falls also upon the memory. Just as I do not remember how I got into that green aisle I do not remember how I got out. I would like to think that I was a brave child and turning round found my own courageous way back to Nanny sewing under the mulberry tree, but I know myself and my cowardice too well for that. Without remembering what I did I know perfectly well that I sat down suddenly and howled blue murder until rescued.

That memory gives me an accurate and humbling bit of self-knowledge; a woman full of irrational fears and always preferring to be rescued by others in my predicaments rather than tackle them myself; and it also puts into perspective my relationship to my father. This always was the one I wanted to follow, this was the shining example. But he was always so far ahead, moving so quickly and with such agility. A time did come when we were close to each other; not because I progressed but because in a time of trouble for me he turned round and came back to meet me. Then he turned away again, moving to the vanishing point. I am able now to read a happy symbolism into that memory. He appeared to vanish but he was actually only on the other side of the green barrier that separates one mode of living from another. I have heard this described by someone who had entered it, and had been brought back to life again, as 'a green peace'.

Equally vivid is my first memory of my lovely mother. It is a little later in date for it is a memory of our next home, the house across the road to which we moved when my father, at the time of my birth Vice-Principal of the Theological College, became Principal. Standing on one of those typical woolly Edwardian hearthrugs she was holding me in her arms, showing me a vase of flowers on the drawing-room mantelpiece, trying to make me say the word 'pretty'. I tried and failed. P followed by r was quite impossible. That memory goes out like a blown candle flame and there is another. The three of us were on the same hearthrug together, our arms about each other and my mother was saying in her clear voice, "A three-fold cord shall not be broken."

2

No child can have lived in lovelier houses than my first two homes, or in a more enchanted city than Wells at the beginning of the century. Since the world became the noisy and noisome place it now is I have not returned because I have a phobia about going back to places where I have lived and that I have loved. I cannot bear to see them changed; an idiotic phobia since change is almost another name for life itself.

As I look back on my life I realise that together with the beauty of the world that holds them I have loved places too much and people not enough. Old age should enable us to redress, as far as possible, the imbalance of a life; in the case of earth lovers like myself, to detach ourselves as much as we can from the soil and wood and stone that will not endure, and to live more deeply in eternal human beings. But there is no reason why grateful memories should not accompany detachment and memories of Wells are mixed up with my gratitude that I was born when I was, and can remember the place in the days when the passage of the water cart, spraying cool refreshment in the dust of Chamberlain Street, was an earth-shaking event; as exciting as the passage down St Thomas's street of the lamplighter, and the sound of the muffin man's bell.

We are probably better off without the white summer dust, yet I remember it gratefully. It could be so thick in the country lanes about Wells in high summer that the slow trot of the pony's feet, pulling a governess cart full of children to Wookey Hole for a picnic, could hardly be heard. Quietness was complete in the countryside. If you stood and listened in the lanes in those days it was so still that you could hear a dog barking a mile off, and at times it could be complete in the streets of the city. And sound, when it came, was much the same as it had always been; children coming out of school, bells pealing, dogs barking, the baker's boy whistling, someone singing within a house at evening, the sound drifting through an open window. It had hardly changed for centuries.

Even the houses had hardly changed. There must have been a few Victorian villas built here and there on the edge of the old city but I do not remember them. I only remember the changelessness of the place and the sense of safety that it gave, its only contacts with the outside world the few trains that slithered slowly and peacefully as earthworms through the valleys, stopping every ten minutes to pick up milk churns from under the lilac bushes on the station platforms, and to deposit in their place two sleepy passengers and a crate of hens.

The two houses seemed as impregnable as the place. To enter Tower House, down steps into a cool dark hall was like going into a cave and it had, as its name implies, a stone tower with little rooms like monastic cells leading from the spiral stone staircase. It was my parents' first married home and when they went there, young and agile, they would drag a mattress up to the highest of the little rooms, lay it on the stone floor and sleep there on hot summer nights. I can imagine them laughing together when the spiders ran over their faces, and listening to the bats squeaking. The garden was enclosed within high stone walls and that too gave a sense of safety as well as privacy. I think Edwardians must have loved privacy more than we do today for if they had no stone walls they would shut themselves in with ramparts of shrubbery. The Principal's House, across the road, had no walls, only railings, but there was a great deal of shrubbery which I remember as dark and dense as a forest, so much so that when I had been playing there for some while alone a numinous dread would suddenly fall upon me and I would make a hasty exit out into the sunlight again.

The sunny south side of the Principal's House had mullioned windows and the whole of its face, apart from the eyes, was covered with wistaria. Drawing-room, dining-room and study had french windows leading to the garden and the bedrooms upstairs were decorated with carved cherubs of stone or wood. When I wrote *A City of Bells* I placed my family in Tower House but fetched the cherub population from across the road to be with them.

This seems the place to apologise for a maddening habit of which I think most novelists are guilty. We give a story the setting of a place or countryside that we love but we are not accurate. Our memories go down into the subconscious, get overlaid with one thing and another and are fished up again anyhow and pieced together with the glue of sheer inventiveness. I know perfectly well that if we are writing of a real place we should get the map out and check up on our facts. But then we are not writing history, we are writing a story, and the temptation to alter or improve on the facts for the good of the story is impossible to resist. We give the real place a fictitious name but that does not prevent it from being recognised, and I have had in the course of my writing life many letters from irritated readers who have gone on pilgrimage to the setting of a book they have liked, and then found fields and woods either in the wrong place or not there at all. They have every right to be irritated and I am sorry.

I think the fictitious name may be at the bottom of the trouble. It is there because to use the real name might cause the inhabitants of a town or village to wonder if real people were being portrayed, and it is a matter of pride with us that we should portray entirely imaginary people. At least we think they are imaginary. My first novel was written about my mother's childhood and portrayed real people but otherwise, speaking for myself alone, while I am writing a story I think each character is my own creation; it is only when I read the finished book over afterwards I see that people I have known have all made their contribution to my characters. There is not a complete portrait of a real person but many shadows and reflections of real people.

And so the fictitious name and characters compel as it were an alteration of the furniture. In our hearts every one of us would like to create a new world, less terrible than this one, a world where there is at least a possibility that things may work out right. The greatest writers are able to do this. In the *Lord of the Rings* Professor Tolkien has created a world that is entirely new and if the book ends in haunting sadness Frodo and Sam do at least throw the ring in the fire; if it had been in this world that they embarked on their terrible journey they would have died half-way up the mountain. And so, even with lesser writers, a story is a groping attempt to make a new world, even if the attempt ends in nothing better than the rearrangement of the furniture.

Speaking of ideal worlds makes me ask myself, do I remember the world of my childhood actually as it was or do I rearrange my memories to make a more beautiful world than the one I really inhabited? Probably I do, since memory is never trustworthy, but if I do it is unwittingly. It is truth now and not fiction that I am at least trying to write.

3

I think I am correct in thinking that the garden of the Principal's House was a marvellous one. It was in those days large and as well as the shrubbery it had everything in it that a garden should have; grass and trees, flowers and vegetables, and it had something else in it which few gardens can boast; a cathedral for one of its walls. Beside the Cathedral, under an archway, a gate opened into a small graveyard and from there another archway led into the cloisters. Whenever I liked I could run through the green garth to the cloisters, and I often did. I liked being there alone and gazing out through the arches at the central square of green grass that seemed to breathe out cool quietness as a well does. Years later, when I lived at Oxford, I would escape in the same way to the small cloister at Magdalen College. It had the same sort of stillness.

From the Wells cloisters steps led down to a place of grass and tall trees, and beyond was the outer wall of the Bishop's Palace, and the drawbridge over the moat where the arrogant swans pulled a bell when they were hungry and bread was immediately thrown to them.

But I had a nearer way to the palace than that. On the south of our garden a low wall separated us from a peaceful curve of water, a kind of lake, with flowers growing beside it, that stretched out like a friendly arm from the main waterway of the moat. Beside it was a green watery place that was then an extension of our garden, but I think is separated from it now. It was reached through a low gate just the right size for a child. Some of the wells that gave Wells its name were half-hidden in the long grass. One, to me the most mysterious, was surrounded by bushes and barbed wire but a bigger one formed the large pool where we tried at one time to keep rainbow trout. But alas our pool was not still but living water, and the trout vanished down to the deep hidden place from which the water welled. It was a disaster that should have been foreseen, and worried me dreadfully, uncertain as I was as to the ultimate happiness of the trout. Irises grew in the long grass, and enormous blue periwinkles. I have never

seen such periwinkles, not even in Devon. A country name
for them is Joy of the Ground and I loved them dearly; not
least because of the fairy brooms that grew in their hearts.

The path that led through this wild green place ended at
a door that led into the palace gardens, and we had been given
a key of the door so that Nanny and I, and any visitors who
might be staying with us, could go into the palace gardens
whenever we liked, and my mother used to give me the key
and allow me to go by myself to visit Mrs Kennion in the
Long Gallery of the palace. And now I am sure I am remembering not what was there but what I thought was there. A
locked door and a key in one's hand, and the power to unlock
the door and pass from one world to another, is enough to
send any child's imagination off at the gallop. For it was
another world on the other side of the door. There was a
palace there, enchanted gardens and the ruins of a great
banqueting hall. And with the turn of a key I could enter this
kingdom.

Now what I am sure was not there was the thick dense
wood into which the door opened after I had turned the key.
Nor do I think that a door could have been set not in a stone
wall or wooden paling but in the living wall of the wood, a
dense wall of twisted briers and plaited branches, thickset
with crimson thorns and pointed leaves as firm and hard as
onyx and chrysoprase. One opened the door, went through
it and beyond was the darkness of the wood. I was often
frightened in the darkness of the very ordinary shrubbery in
our own garden but not in the wood that I am sure was not
there.

The darkness of that wood has fallen upon every memory
except one of the gardens through which I ran to reach Mrs
Kennion in the Long Gallery. I know that they were beautiful
but I have only that one memory. It is of a mossgrown garden
path arched over by nut trees in full leaf, the green moss a
soft carpet under the feet, the cool green leaves making the

place as secret as a shrine. There is no one to be seen but an ecstasy of joy is alive under the trees. But did I really run along that path?

My mother had told me that it was in the palace gardens that she had finally told my father she would marry him. When first proposed to she had said she would consider the matter. She had said, in the true Victorian manner, that it was very sudden, as indeed it was. She had been sent from her Channel Island home to college in England and there she had made friends with the daughters of one of the canons of Wells Cathedral, Canon Church, and sometimes in the holidays she went to stay with them. It was in their home that my father, then Chaplain of the Theological College, met her and fell in love with her. This to her was nothing new for she was vivacious and gay and according to her less attractive sisters she could be a heartless devastator. But she did not want to be married. She had doctors on both sides of her ancestry and she wanted to be one herself, the first woman doctor in the family. She scandalised people both by her ideas and the things that she did. Interested in anatomy as she naturally was she carried human bones about in her handbag and tipped them out upon the seats of railway carriages when looking for her ticket. She was an intrepid bicyclist and whirled downhill with her feet up like any errand boy. She was a keen fencer and practised the art in a very masculine costume. She was altogether shockingly modern.

My mother told me that she had to think hard when she was first proposed to by my father. She did not want to give up studying to be a doctor and if she had to marry the very last man she wanted to marry was a clergyman. Nevertheless before my father had seen her she had taken a good look at him. He had come one evening to see Canon Church in the house in the Liberty, after my mother had gone up to bed. With her bedroom door still half open she had heard his

voice in the hall, had whisked into her frilly dressing-gown
and run to lean over the banisters unseen. She had had a good
look at the young man below. He had just come from com-
pline in the chapel at the top of the Vicars Close and his
long black gown became his erect slenderness. He was good-
looking with dark hair and eyes. My mother herself was a
golden girl with fair hair and golden-brown eyes. She went
back to her room not only thoughtful but for the first time
considerably shaken, and when later she had to consider
what life would be like parted from this man she knew it
would only be dust and ashes. So at a palace party she had
beguiled him into a secluded part of the palace gardens and
said she would do it.

They were married as quickly as possible as my father
could not wait to start looking after her. For in spite of the
longing to be a doctor, the bicycling and the sparkling
vivacity, she was delicate. Just how delicate they were to
find out tragically soon.

And so I am not sure that as a child on my way to see Mrs
Kennion I really ran along that path under the nut trees. If
that was the place to which my mother beguiled my father
that she might be proposed to once again I may never even
have seen it, it may have been simply ancestral memory, I
do not know, but what I do know is that I can never find
myself on one of those mossgrown earth paths in the shade of
an old garden without being caught up once more by that
feeling of ecstasy. Is it the ecstasy of a man's love for a woman
or the ecstasy of the green places of nature, "annihilating
all that's made to a green thought in a green shade"? Or is
it a memory of God talking with Adam in the cool of the
evening in the age of innocence? "Why ask such questions?"
a common-sense friend replied to me once when I wondered
if a half-dream, half-vision, giving me the assurance that the
dead still live, could be true. "If you are starving and some-

one brings you food you don't wait to ask if it comes from the attic or the cellar. You merely eat it."

As I have no other memories of the palace gardens so I have no recollection of how I got inside the palace. There is just a fleeting memory of a stout child stumping up a large staircase behind the imposing back of a butler, so either I penetrated in through the servants' quarters or I stood on tiptoe and rang the front door bell in the approved manner. Whatever I did I arrived where I wanted to be and was sitting with Mrs Kennion in the Gallery, deep in conversation.

I was an inarticulate, frightened child but I loved Mrs Kennion too much to be frightened of her; so much so that I could brave the great palace just to be with her. I also loved my mother's friend Mrs Hollis but to her I could not say very much because her beauty awed me. So possibly Mrs Kennion was not beautiful. What I remember is an old lady with a soft face and grey hair neatly parted, wearing a plain dark dress and a gold chain round her neck and looking rather small and lost in the great shining expanse of the Long Gallery. Probably she was not old at all, merely elderly. She loved my mother very much, which was possibly why we were in possession of that magic key, and me for my mother's sake. But perhaps also she loved children in general with that painful love of a childless woman. She certainly knew how to talk to them in her soft Scottish voice, treating them as though there were no age barrier at all. I remember that once she had her brother staying with her. He had been away for a day or two to attend some dinner and came in to greet her while I was with her. He sat down and told her about the dinner, describing each course in great detail. Then seeing her engaged with a child he smiled at us both and went away again. Mrs Kennion turned to me with some anxiety, speaking as one woman to another. "My dear, I do not want you to think that my brother is a greedy man. He is not. It is just that ever since we were small children we have told each other what we had to eat at parties."

There was of course the Bishop somewhere in the background but too hardworked to be glimpsed more than occasionally. I have only one memory of him, talking to my mother in our garden, as natural and kind a person as his wife.

But the Dean made a great impression on my child's mind, unfortunately an impression that was a little too vivid, for as the years passed the originally fine and slightly theatrical figure became in memory no longer awe-inspiring but merely comic. Could he have been comic? I hardly think so for he had been headmaster of Rugby before he came to Wells and if headmasters were comic characters surely they would not last long. And so I mistrust my memory here. I only know that when I came to write *A City of Bells* the Dean of that story arrived instantly readymade, tall and handsome with white muttonchop whiskers, a high-pitched voice and a top hat a little on one side, a wealthy man who drove his tall dog-cart in a dashing manner and had an eye for horse-flesh and a pretty woman.

I wrote earlier in this chapter that only in my first novel did I deliberately try to portray real characters but I see now that was a half-truth. The Dean was in the book before I knew he was coming but when I did recognise him I am afraid I made no attempt at all to turn him out, and my father when he read the story could hardly forgive me. And he was justified in his dismay for though the Dean had been dead for many years, and we had lost all touch with his family, nevertheless one of his daughters was my very kind god-mother. But by that time it was too late to take the Dean out, for the book was published, and I am ashamed to say that at that time I was not penitent. But I am now, for not only was my godmother kind to me but the Dean was too, for he once

allowed me to drive with him in his dog-cart. The occasion
was one of these Edwardian driving picnics which the
dignitaries of the Cathedral, their wives and dependants so
much enjoyed. My young father was scarcely a dignitary
of the Cathedral and I can only suppose that I was one of the
distinguished company because my godmother had brought
me. The cavalcade had driven up into the Mendip Hills
and when the time came to drive down again the Dean said
I might be in his dog-cart. I was hoisted up and wedged in
between him and his daughter and we drove from the top
to the bottom of Cheddar Gorge. It was a magnificent and
electrifying experience. To this day I can see the high polished
dog-cart and hear the creak of the harness as the Dean drove
slowly down that precipitous place. He must have been a
skilful driver for as he drove he talked to his daughter. Far
over my head I heard their voices as though two enthroned
Olympian gods spoke to each other from cloud to cloud
across blue air. And so I think now that the Dean was probably a very fine old man and no one except such a twerp of a
child as I was would have found him funny.

CHAPTER II

Storytelling

I

THE ONLY PEOPLE WHO WILL READ THIS BOOK ARE THE people who read my stories and they have so often written to ask me, when did you begin to write? What is it like to write a book? Are writers inspired? Does it flow out of them like water from a tap or do they slog? Do they enjoy their work? Do they put themselves into their books? How long do writers have to be at it before they can earn a living? Do you mind what the critics say? Have there been other writers in your family? There have been other questions but these are the main ones and I will try to answer them. All writers get many letters which we answer to the best of our ability, with great affection and humble gratitude if the letters are complimentary, with less affection and an endeavour to be grateful (for criticism is helpful and salutary) if not, but lack of time means that we do not answer them as fully as we should like to do. I am conscious of having said a mere thank you very much, and no more, far too often and will try to make amends now.

I began to write as a child in the Principal's House at Wells and have scarcely left off since. I began with an interminable story that was intended to be funny but as the only character I can remember is a fat man stuck in a chimney it was probably only vulgar. This work was never finished because I became so absorbed in it that I forgot to feed my caterpillars, and they died. In grief and remorse I abandoned writing for the time being. When I took it up again I kept to short pieces, poems and fairy stories, perhaps feeling they would be less dangerous to the life of others.

These works included an epic poem on the death of Roland, Charlemagne's heroic knight, but it proved unworthy of the hero and has not survived.

Writing a book is much the same as any other kind of creative work, painting or carpentry or embroidery or having a baby, an act compounded of love, imagination and physical labour. And if a mother were to tell me that you do not need imagination to produce a baby I should answer that love and imagination cannot be separated. When a woman falls in love with a man it is as though she opened Pandora's box; all her longings and imaginings fly up and he is gilded with her dreams. And when the man's child is conceived it is the same; her love spins all sorts of golden imaginings about it. When neither turns out to be as ideally perfect as had been expected, well, by that time she is immersed in domesticity and hard work is full of comfort. A book begins with falling in love. You lose your heart to a place, a house, an avenue of trees, or with a character who walks in and takes sudden and complete possession of you. Imagination glows, and there is the seed of your book.

Some little while after I had moved into the Oxfordshire cottage where I live now I was trying hard to love it (a difficult process because my roots were still in the earth of Devonshire) when an impulse sent me to the window of the sitting room. It was spring, and cold, but the air had that special quality of a cold spring, the coldness of living water, and was scented with the wild violets that grew in clumps about the old garden. I was looking out at the garden, and over the sweetbrier hedge to the field beyond, and feeling the first twinges of love for the place, when a woman came down the narrow path in front of the window. She came from the place where the path ended abruptly in the hedge and I was told later that there used to be a gate there leading to the lane. Her name was Froniga. Some while later, after I had had time to absorb the beauties of my new home, I

wrote something of her history and that of the cottage in a
book called *The White Witch*. How accurate it is I have no
means of knowing, since only the last sixty years of the life
of the cottage is known and Froniga lived here in the seventeenth century. It seems to me entirely accurate but I may
be mistaken. However that is the sort of way in which a
book begins for most storytellers; with a light in the mind.
But this glimmer is certainly not inspiration. As I understand
the great word only the great ones have it. Blake was
inspired. Wordsworth was inspired. But the great flood of
light which poets and mystics pour into the world has nothing
in common with the glowworm sparks of the small fry; except
for the fact that something, or some being, must have lit it
in the first place.

I have never tried to do carpentry but I am sure the process
is much the same. The love of the wood, the feel of it in the
hands, the glow in the mind and then the slow labour of
craftsmanship. With a book this labour is so slow that though
writers will tell you they love their work, yet they never want
to do it. A book existing in the mind is one thing, enclosed
there it is delightful company, but when the glow becomes an
explosive personality demanding to get out that is quite
another. It must be got out, or the writer will go mad, but
getting the thing down on paper is a grinding slog. The
thought of starting the process yet again fills one with dark
despair. Anything not to start. I heard Joyce Grenfell say
once in a broadcast that whenever she knew she must get
down to writing a sketch she remembered it was her duty
to do some very elaborate cooking, I have heard of writers
who had to be locked in their workrooms by their irritated
relatives before they could be induced to make a start.

I don't know what other writers do in this miserable
condition. I only know what I do. Sit down at the appointed
time for work and stare in terror at the empty sheet of paper
before me. How many of these blank white papers must be

covered with hideous black marks before the book is finished?
Hundreds of them. But what a crazy way to earn a living,
making dirty marks on clean paper. Of what use can they
be to anyone when made? None. Yet what else can I do?
What else am I fit for? Nothing. Better make a start, turn
the tap on (that means grip the pen with loathing) and see
what comes. Nothing comes. There is an airlock somewhere.
No good. Try again tomorrow. One tries again tomorrow for
several days and then the airlock suddenly yields and there's
a small trickle of water. A couple of pages are made a mess of.
Next day they are read over, found to be hopeless and torn
up. The process is repeated and then suddenly one happy day
the tap is running freely; unbelievably one is once more writing a book. For a short while that is. Then comes another airlock, and then another, until the first draft of a book is
finished at last. Now it is there, out of us, and we feel what the
carpenter feels when the chair is formed and in being. Now he
has only to correct his mistakes as well as he is able, to smooth
the wood and polish it. The rewriting of a book, and when
the time comes the correcting of the proofs, is pure joy.

Do we put ourselves in our books? Speaking for myself I
do not put the woman I am into them but after I had been
writing for years I noticed the regular appearance in story
after story of a tall graceful woman, well-balanced, intelligent, calm, capable and tactful. She is never flustered,
forgetful, frightened, irritable or nervy. She does not drop
bricks, say the opposite of what she means, let saucepans boil
over or smash her best teapot. She is all I long to be and all I
never will be. She is in complete reverse a portrait of myself.

How long do writers have to slog at it before they can
earn a living? An unanswerable question. Some (especially
very clever young men) succeed almost at once. Others
work for years before success comes. Some, richly deserving,
never have it. Others, undeserving, do. I have been told, and
I think it is true, that the worst thing that can happen to a

writer is to succeed too soon. Success too quickly attained is hard to hold. The longer you have been working when it comes the more likely you are to hold it. I was one of the latter lucky ones. I started writing in childhood, my first novel was published when I was thirty-two. I was forty-five before I found myself a best-seller on the strength of one book only. I think the reason for this is that writing is more a matter of practice than anyone realises. Words to a writer are the same as bricks to a builder. It is necessary to learn about their size and shape and how to put them in place. The imagination and vivid life of someone young, poured into a first book, or even a second or third, can sometimes shape the bricks into place by sheer instinct and good luck, but when the fire dies down a little the building is not so easy. But perhaps this is no more than conjecture. The process of creation, however humble it may be, is always mysterious.

Do I mind when the critics give me hard knocks or, as is more often the case, dismiss me with contempt? When I was younger I minded dreadfully, now that I am older and I hope more humble I think they are probably quite right and so I mind less; though I am still almost overcome by joy at the rare-good criticism and think the critic an extremely intelligent man or woman. I think the sensible writer should sit easy to adverse criticism. It is foolish to mind because if you work hard to the best of your ability, and with all the honesty of which you are capable, you have done all that the most brilliant writer alive could have done. The results unfortunately will not be as imposing, but no worker of integrity should consider results unless he has a wife and six children to support. If he has he is in a dreadful fix and only he can sort it out. But such is the contrariness of life that so often the lone wolf, setting out upon the trail in the happy knowledge that he has only the one mouth to feed, finds himself to his astonishment earning enough to fill half a dozen. Then he too is in a fix but what he does about it is nothing to do with minding what the critics say.

Another reason for not minding is that you are not writing to please the critics but to please yourself and your readers. Yourself first, because basically we all write because we must and all other reasons are subsidiary to the need for self-expression, but for our readers with all our hearts because without them we are lost and we love them more than they know. For we have to earn our living by doing this work and how could we do it if these beloved people did not buy our books?

I think it is a part of our gratitude that, perhaps unconsciously, and without knowing it, we want to share our faith and what it has done for us and to make contact with those who think as we do. I say unconsciously because in my own case when a book comes into my mind it comes simply as a story; personal belief is something that comes in apparently without my knowledge or contriving. But I think it is this latter unintended thing that makes the strongest link between reader and writer. We all hold our faith with a certain amount of fear and trembling (even Blake wrote, "My hand trembles exceedingly upon the Rock of Ages.") and to find that others share our faith has a steadying influence, especially in these days when the Rock of Ages himself is for ever being prodded and sounded to see if he is still there. To those of us who think the tapping hammers would not sound so loudly if he was not there the likemindedness is a very special joy.

And so if it is your readers you are writing for why mind about the critics? They are highly intelligent people and you could only please them if you and your readers were as intelligent as they are. Yet that sentence as it stands is not entirely true since some of my readers have intellects that make me tremble with awe. They read me, I imagine, because of this likemindedness that has nothing to do with the intellect. And this brings me to something which I have a great wish to say. I owe my readers an incalculable debt, which I shall never be able to pay. I am not only grateful that they need me at all, I am even more grateful for the affection which for forty years they have expressed in so many delightful ways. From among them have come some of my greatest friends. And there is one more thing, which humbles me to the ground. Sometimes, and there is one reader in particular of whom I think, there comes to me an anonymous gift, and I always have a conviction that the gift comes from someone who cannot easily afford it. But that is the way things are in the kingdom of heaven, whose presence with us here on earth is shown in such ways as these.

2

I come to the last question my readers ask me, have there been other writers in your family?

The only writer was my father but the single likeness between us was an inability to compose on a typewriter; neither of us could think without actually holding a pen in the hand. My father was a theologian, and his books were works of scholarship. I had written only four books before he died and though paternity demanded of him that he should read them he found the first three very hard going indeed, but though I begged him not to waste his time he persevered, taking a chapter a day with determined patience. A fourth, a book about sixteenth century Oxford called *Towers in the Mist* that I dedicated to him, he liked better, because he was interested to see to what use I had put the historical books he had borrowed for me from the Christ Church library at Oxford, where we were then living. "You have a wonderful gift," he said, but before my head had time to swell, he went on, "you can make a very little knowledge go such a long way."

Yet though both of us found the books of the other hard going, he because he had too much intellect for mine and I because I had too little for his, we were in sympathy with each other. I can remember with what joy we sat on the floor together packing up the typescript of his last book for despatch to his publisher. The task completed we sat back on our heels and contemplated the neat parcel (the floor is the only place where anyone can make a neat parcel of a big bundle of typescript) with hearts swelling with thankfulness. Months of dogged perseverance had brought a creative act round full circle to its completion. A book was written. It was going out into the world. Our eyes met and we smiled. "They are our children, aren't they?" said my father. The humility and gentleness with which he spoke seemed to gather his books and mine into one family. I had never felt so close to him or so happy.

My mother was a wonderful storyteller and a witty, fascinating conversationalist but she was no good with her pen. That a woman who talked so delightfully and so fluently should have written such uninspired letters is perhaps not so surprising for the two gifts seem to belong to different types of people. "My tongue is the pen of a ready writer," said the Psalmist and one imagines that a scribe, and not himself, wrote down his songs. He sang and danced his joy, he was ready with his tongue and feet but not with his pen. He had the older, the lovelier and more enviable gift. Lovelier because more fleeting, enviable because it is the actual breathing magic of the person. Men danced and sang and told stories long before they wrote and the story sung before the fire by the ready tongue, the eyes of the singer darkening or shining with the alternate joy and sorrow of the tale, was in comparison to a written story as the living butterfly to one pinned out flat upon a collector's board. It was

soon gone, vanished in the smoke of the fire, living only in
memory, but living as the word that is merely read can never
live. We can read a poem with pleasure but it does not really
come alive to us unless we read it aloud. Even then it is not
the fullest life of which it is capable. It needs the authentic
voice of its creator.

My mother was one of these authentic voices, because the
stories she told were never secondhand, they were her own.
It is true that she often told me stories of her childhood in the
Channel Islands, and the old Guernsey legends with which
she had grown up, but these things were a part of her and
her vivid imagination wove them into a single web that was
her own creation entirely.

In summer my mother told me stories by the open french
window of the drawing room, but in winter she had her
sofa by the fire and I sat on the white woolly hearthrug to
listen to them. The soft wool was as comforting to bare legs
as the warmth of the fire. And I needed comforting because
that magic hour with her, between tea and bedtime, often
came as the reward and climax of a constantly recurring
purgatorial experience endured by all Edwardian children
and called 'going to the drawing room'. When nursery tea
was over the jam was washed from their faces, the tangles
wrenched out of their hair, the comfortable old holland
smocks were removed and starched, frilly horrors took their
place. I speak of the little girls. I think the boys wore sailor
suits and had the comfort of a whistle. A good child stood
still to be prepared for sacrifice and went bravely downstairs
to face the ordeal. Others revolted and had to be dragged
downstairs forcibly by Nanny and propelled towards the
drawing room door by a vigorous shove between the
shoulders. I know I was often guilty of atrocious screaming
and kicking behind the green baize door of the nursery
wing, but must have calmed down later for what I remember
best is standing outside the drawing room door alone in a

state of sick misery. On the other side of the hard slab of wood which reared up within an inch of my face was the sound of tinkling teacups and the hum of what Nanny and the servants called 'company'. And I had to turn the handle and go in. It was just one of those things that confront one again and again in life. It is impossible yet you have got to do it. You can't go back so you must go forward, and the only way forward is through this thing. Better get on with it.

The moment of opening the door I do not remember. Possibly one never remembers these moments of actual commitment to ordeal. Why was it so awful? All I had to do was to perform the ritual my mother had taught me, go round the circle shaking hands with each one, trying to look into each face and smile and whisper yes or no to the questions put to me. Yet it was so awful that it seemed always to take place in semi-darkness, and of those people in the half-light I remember only one; a young man who was as acutely wretched and embarrassed as I was myself. I knew he was the moment our clammy hands touched each other. And he knew I was. I hardly remember his face, only the sudden spasm of sympathy between us. And yet I was not afraid to visit Mrs Kennion in that great palace. Truly children are extraordinary creatures.

It did not happen every day for though my mother loved to entertain my father did not, and a party looming on the horizon cast over him the same shadow of impending doom as it still does over me. Yet he was not, like his daughter, devoid of social graces; he had charm and could be both a delightful host and a delightful guest; but he was essentially a shy and reserved man and it is our essential character that creates our dooms for us. Yet I early realised that there are two sorts of social intercourse. In our home one sort went on behind the drawing room door and another behind the study door which faced it across the passage. From behind the study door came roars of laughter, and under the door and through the keyhole seeped a strong smell of tobacco. I would stand in the passage outside and sniff and I thought it a joyous smell. Part of the joy of course was the bliss of not being of the company. Yet that in there was not 'company', it was just men. I could not solve the riddle. The nearest I could get was to realise one of the undoubted facts of life; 'company' is always predominantly female.

Yet storytelling in front of the fire, after I had survived my mother's tea party, revealed another of the facts of life; heaven grows out of doom endured. The rug seemed softer, the fire warmer, and my mother's stories more marvellous if preceded by a tea party. The stories had a flower-like quality. They had colours that shone and she unwound them one after the other like silks coming off the reel. She never raised her voice or used her hands. The drama was in the inflection of her voice and in the hidden power that was a part of her personality.

There was a second storyteller in the house, Sarah our cook, and she also reigned supreme beside a fire and a woolly hearthrug. The rug spread before the kitchen range was black, not white, but just as comforting to bare legs. I believe that in her own way she was as fine a storyteller as my mother, though their styles were perhaps as different as those of Ellen Terry and Mrs Patrick Campbell. Going about her work Sarah was a gentle, sweet-voiced little old woman, a marvellous cook, utterly selfless, her only object in life to work for her family, but like my mother she must have had power for when she was enthroned in her rocking chair, a clean white apron tied round her waist over her print frock, she seemed to grow in stature. Her stories were taken from the Old Testament and all the fire packed up within her gentleness flowed out in them. She used her eyes and hands with wonderful dramatic effect and as the story gathered momentum she would rock faster and faster. One day she told me the story of Elijah going up into heaven in his fiery chariot. It grew more and more exciting and when the climax was reached and Elijah was whirled to meet his God she urged the rocker to its utmost speed, crying out loudly, "The chariots of fire and the horsemen thereof!" and flung her apron over her head. I was terrified. I scrambled up from the hearthrug and fled from the lightnings and thunders that filled the big old kitchen.

3

Storytellers, writers, readers aloud, I think they come in that order, for until the story is written down the readers aloud cannot come into action. But theirs is a splendid gift, akin to that of the actor; and perhaps the actor came upon the stage of history very early indeed and was acting out in song and dance the splendour of war and the glory of the beasts even before the painters portrayed them in line and colour on the walls of their caves. However it came into being reading aloud is one of the arts, and proficiency in it is something that children have always demanded from their elders; even today if the telly happens to be out of order. My mother never read aloud. There was no need. Had she done so it would have been as though William Blake (whom she loved deeply) had set himself down with his delicate brush and pen to copy other people's visions instead of revealing his own. Certainly Sarah never read the Bible aloud. I doubt if she had even read it; though she must have listened with her whole being when she had heard it read by some master of the art in her village church, some reader of the calibre of my father, who would make every character in the books he read to my mother and me as alive as though they were living with us in the house.

Mrs Hollis was also a reader aloud. My mother's two great friends in her college days, Margaret Hollis and Lily Church,

at whose home she had met my father, were still her great
friends at Wells. Lily Church did not marry and in Wells
days was Aunt Lily to many children; as were my mother's
sisters, Marie-Louise, Emily and Irene. There are no aunts
today and I sometimes think that is partly what is the matter
with us. There are sisters of a child's mother or father,
kindly at times but too wrapped up in themselves and their
careers to be aunts. An Edwardian aunt was by definition
selfless and unattached; or sufficiently loosely attached to
get free from what she was doing when wanted. When a
crisis blew up, a real tragedy or a minor difficulty, an unmarried aunt was almost at once upon the doorstep. As I
remember them they were competent as well as selfless.
They came aboard a distressed household like a pilot and
brought the ship safe to port.

When my father became Principal of the Theological
College and moved across the road to the Principal's House
his friend Arthur Hollis, afterwards Bishop of Taunton,
became Vice-Principal and I think three of his distinguished
sons were born at Tower House. Mrs Hollis was not only
lovely to look at but she had a serenity surprising in the
mother of a family of small boys, and a good reader aloud
should always have serenity; it casts a spell. I have two
memories of her that especially shine out, just as certain
paradisial dreams do, clear and bright against the darkness
of much forgetfulness. The first is of her reading aloud to a
group of children in the panelled drawing room at Tower
House, a small beautiful room half-way up the stairs. The
sun was warm on the panelling, for it was summer, and there
were flowers in the room and a sweet smell. Perhaps they
were Mrs Simpkins pinks, or syringa or Dolly Perkins roses.
The children sat on the floor and Mrs Hollis sat on a low
chair, her wide skirts spread about her. She had a beautiful
voice and I think the sweetest face of any woman I have
ever seen. I had hard work to admit to myself that she was

lovelier than my mother but I had to in the end. She was. She lacked my mother's vivacity but she was more serene and serenity, I believe, is the first essential for lasting beauty as well as for reading aloud. The book she was reading was called *The Cocky Olly Bird*. I do not know if I have spelt this bird's name correctly, and I do not know certainly who wrote the book, and I have never been able to find it. I do not remember anything definite about *The Cocky Olly Bird* yet he is with me today, and is I think the original of a bird who seems to fly in and out of my mind whenever I am writing, and was especially with me when I was writing *The Bird in the Tree*. Perhaps I could find a copy of *The Cocky Olly Bird* in the world if I looked a bit harder, but I think I am rather afraid, if I found it, of finding him perhaps not so wonderful after all. The book might have owed the whole of its magic to the charm of the woman who read it aloud.

My second memory of her was when I was taken by her two older sons to visit the third on the day when he was one week old. It was an occasion of great solemnity and I can remember how my heart beat as the three small children approached the door in procession and the eldest knocked. I had not seen the baby yet, indeed I do not think that I had ever seen any very small baby at close quarters before, and the whole thing was fraught with magic and mystery. We were bidden to enter, and went in, and facing us was a nurse seated in a chair with the baby enthroned on her lap. And babies were indeed enthroned in those days. Their lace-trimmed long robes flowed almost to the ground and their royalty was awe-aspiring. The sight of that baby was for me one of those moments of dumbfounded astonishment that a child never forgets. He was so small and yet he was so royal. He had not been with us a short while ago and now here he was. What could anyone be expected to make of such an astonishing occurrence? The younger of the little boys pointed out the baby's excellent points but I hardly listened, and then suddenly I remembered that a person I loved was in some way very much concerned in this and I looked round for Mrs Hollis. She was also enthroned, in a billowy-white bed only a few feet from me, watching the children at the window. Our eyes met, she smiled at me and I was in heaven. And there the memory abruptly vanishes. There would be sadness in such memories but for the remembrance that being true they are eternal.

For practical purposes the event had repercussions when I returned to my own home across the road. Every morning I ran to my mother's room hoping and expecting that she had a small brother for me. He was intensely real to me and I was convinced he would come. I did not ask for him, merely looked around, leaving my poor mother completely mystified as to what I wanted. He did not come and having been told that if you can't have the best you should make do with the second best I demanded a baby doll, and was told I must wait. I was angry and frustrated.

At Christmas I got the baby, a wax one in a long robe that cascaded over a variety of undergarments, and over all a long cloak with bonnet and cape attached. He was such a feminine doll, that I decided to change his sex and called her Ida after my mother. I loved that doll with all the passion of which I was capable and she was with me until I was approaching middle age, when I felt it my duty to part with her to a child whose need seemed greater than mine. I read somewhere that the deeds of our life which we regret most deeply are the good deeds. The cynical remark is perfectly true. I wish I had Ida still. I wish she was still lying in my drawer, wrapped in tissue paper, and that I could take her out and look once more at her homely and scratched, yet angelic, pink wax face. She was such a cuddly doll, and her face was soft to kiss.

The doll I still possess, Madame d'Anvers, is too distinguished to be homely. I do not remember cuddling

Madame. The cold reserve of her aristocratic countenance forbade the liberty. But if I love her less than I loved the baby doll I can never part from her because she was the first gift of my Guernsey grandfather. He was in Paris when he heard the news of the birth of his first grandchild and he went straight out and bought Madame for me. And so she is as old as I am; but she has worn much better and before leaving her for my grandfather I will describe her, simply for the sake of my own pleasure in her. Her face is white china, delicately tinted, and there is not a wrinkle in it. Her hair, lying in curls on her shoulders, is as golden as ever it was and is surmounted by a tall headdress of stiffened lace ornamented with a large pink bow. Her dress, one of those wonderful striped eighteenth-century dresses so often seen in pictures of the period, is tightly laced over her bosom, fits close to her slender waist and then billows stiffly out like an umbrella. From gold chains at her waist hang two little watches painted with flowers, and she used to have pearl rings in her ears and a tiny golden cross on a bit of black velvet round her neck, but these have mysteriously disappeared and I cannot find them anywhere. The loss is tragic. She has a purple silk apron with two large pockets. If anyone should have sufficient temerity to lift her skirt lace-trimmed under-garments are revealed, white stockings on her shapely legs and wooden clogs on her feet. Her body and her hands are made of white kid and she is over one foot tall. Knowing my grandfather I am quite sure he chose for me the most beautiful doll in the whole of Paris. I am also sure that he could not afford it for he never had any money. But to write of my grandfather I must leave Wells and go to the Island.

CHAPTER III

The Island

I

HOW CAN I DESCRIBE WHAT MY GRANDFATHER WAS TO me as a small child? The odd thing is that I realise now that I have never talked to anyone about him. But I have tried once before to write about him. André and Rachel of *Island Magic* are my grandfather and grandmother but I think Rachel is the better portrait. The portrait of André is totally inadequate, as anything I can say about him in this chapter will be inadequate. He was a part of my life from the beginning, since I visited my grandparents in Guernsey almost every summer all through my childhood until the outbreak of the First World War. My mother, who left Guernsey for the first time when she was eighteen, was never able to visit her Island again for the birth of her only child, following too soon after a bicycle accident, made her an invalid for the rest of her life, and so we never went there together. I was a year old when one of my mother's sisters took me on my first visit, and a grim time she must have had of it for the sea passage from Weymouth to Guernsey in the small boats of those days could be a gruelling experience. I ache with sympathy now to think of that pretty girl, my Aunt Emily, lying prostrate on her bunk trying to keep hold of a vigorous baby in a ship that rolled and tossed like a cork.

The Channel Islands were proud of the roughness of the seas about their coasts and liked to relate how travellers who had sailed to India and back, and boasted of their powers of survival, had found themselves annihilated by the rough seas about the Casquet Rocks. I can remember the groans of relief that would arise from the prostrate bodies in the women's saloon, when a stewardess passed along the gangway between the bunks announcing cheerfully, "Ladies, we are now past the Casquets!" For those whose haven of hope was Guernsey the worst was now over. They roused a little and smiled wanly. Those bound for Jersey, with another hour of tossing to endure between the two islands, turned their faces from the light and black hatred of the Guernsey women filled their hearts. There was not much love lost between the two islands in those days, and I wonder now if the mutual lack of appreciation was rooted in that extra hour of hell which the Jersey people had to endure, through no fault whatever of their own. Children are usually good sailors and as soon as I could run I joined the other children in being a pestilential nuisance underfoot in the gangway. I remember being grabbed by an enraged stewardess and dumped in her special cubby hole, to be out of the way of whichever aunt it was I was driving out of her senses, until that great moment came when the cry went up, "We shall be in harbour in half an hour."

To climb up out of the stuffy saloon on to the wet deck and see the great waves racing by and be buffeted by the clean cold wind was great joy. And then came the excitement as the coast of Guernsey came into view and slipped slowly by to starboard. I have a little map of Guernsey drawn by my grandmother Marie-Louise Ozanne in the year 1865, a few years before she married. It is exquisitely drawn in Indian ink on a bit of handmade paper measuring only four and a half by three and a half inches, but with the tip of her fine pen she has portrayed trees and windmills, and it would seem every road and lane in the beloved little island, all clear and tiny as a map made in Lilliput.

I am looking now at the little map because I could not remember which came first along the coast; Vale Castle, Saint Sampson's Harbour or Mont Crevell. They were passed in that order. And then Soux Point was rounded and the little town of St Peter Port was in sight, the houses crowding up the hillside one behind the other, looking out to sea over each other's shoulders to watch the ships sailing in. One could see the spire of the town church, and the pier and Castle Cornet on its rock, and there at last was the harbour wall and the waiting people. As the boat drew slowly in to its mooring-place I would try to pick out my grandfather, and perhaps an aunt or even two aunts, who would probably be with him. The moment when I saw him and the moment when he saw me and lifted his hat in greeting were perfect moments. Then the perfection began to unwind itself, just as my mother's stories did, and became a thread of joy through the long business of the docking, making it not only bearable but beautiful.

The shouts of sailors and porters, the shrill whistles, the bangs and thuds of cargo being unloaded, the sound of the gangways being run out, the scream of the gulls overhead, the sound of the wind and the slap of the sea all made up a symphony of sound, the music of arrival in a happy haven.

I was in my grandfather's arms at last and then standing beside him holding his hand, speechless with the sudden shyness that would come upon me because I had not seen him for a year. Family news was shouted above the babel of noise and the special porter, who always attended our family arrivals and departures with as much interest as though the family were his own, collected the luggage and we pushed our way to where the cabs waited.

There was always a great deal of excitement when the steamer from England arrived, for it was the island's one link with the great world. It brought the mails, and sons and daughters and grandchildren returning perhaps from the other side of the world. The time of its arrival was always uncertain for it could be delayed for hours on end by bad weather, and upon one occasion, still remembered when I was a child, it did not arrive at all for a storm had driven it on the rocks and nearly all the passengers were drowned. "The boat's in!" was a cry that would echo through any Guernsey house that had a view of the harbour, and it was always a cry of relief. I can remember seeing the road that ran between the town church and the harbour empty and deserted, but when the boat came in it appeared to be the hub of the universe.

The vehicles that waited for travellers beyond the pier were a varied assortment; private carriages, cabs, brakes, and the enchanting little conveyances that were a specialty of the island. They were a cross between a bath-chair and a hansom cab, but low to the ground, with the driver sitting in front and not behind. But they held only two people, and such luggage as they could pile on their knees and feet, and were far too small to accommodate my grandfather, three aunts, myself and the luggage. And if it was Aunt Emily who had brought me from England there was a good deal of luggage; for she was not only pretty, she was dressy, and favoured very large hats trimmed with roses. We had to have a cab and just as there was a special porter who looked after the Collenette family there was a special cabby who drove us. I wish I could remember the names of these two kindly men, I can remember the face of the porter, but not of the cabby; though I remember the smell of horses and straw which pervaded his cab and which I thought a lovely smell. They were both, I think, bilingual. They knew enough English to make themselves understood by travellers and for the rest they spoke the French of the island patois that might not have been understood in the streets of Paris.

Those were still the good days when the island was orientated more towards France than England, but the change was coming. My grandparents grew up speaking French but by the time I knew them they had changed to English, which they spoke with a French intonation. I thought the change all wrong, for the Channel Islands have never belonged to England, but England to them. They originally formed part of the Duchy of Normandy and when their duke conquered England they naturally conquered it too. The situation has not been altered. Jersey and Guernsey have for years now tolerated an English Lieutenant-Governor on each island. But they keep him in his place. I once attended a meeting of the Guernsey Parliament. Before proceedings started the Lieutenant-Governor entered arrayed in full-dress military uniform with a sword by his side, and bowed to the assembly with a wonderful combination of dignity and humility. They acknowledged his existence with politeness and he seated himself on a throne-like chair. He was there as a representative of the King of England, but throughout the long proceedings he spoke not a word. He was not allowed to.

The Channel Islanders are a proud people and my mother's family were no exception to the rule. One of my aunts once said to me, "We think a lot of ourselves," and indeed they did. The founder of their family was William the Conqueror's cupbearer who fought at the Battle of Hastings and was of royal blood. (At least so my mother's family have always maintained but I am myself agnostic about this. If in a future life I am proved wrong none of my maternal ancestors will speak to me.) Although my mother was never able to go back to Guernsey after my birth she remained a staunch Channel Islander. She was a woman of strong feelings, wonderfully controlled. Only once do I remember an outburst of passion. It was at the beginning of the last war, when England was forced to abandon the islands to German occupation. My mother burst into a storm of grief and fury which shocked me speechless. "I will hate England till I die," she said. And she did.

And so for English people arrival at the island was like landing on a foreign shore. It must be some particular arrival that I remember when I think of clearing skies after rain and wind, and of wet cobbles shining in pale yellow sunlight as the cab rattled us away from the harbour. The tall houses of St Peter Port are built in the French fashion and the streets are steep and narrow. The streets of Wells slope gently so that St Peter Port seemed to me strangely exciting, more like a grey stone mountain rent with deep narrow chasms than a town. Here and there the chasms were so steep that instead of streets there were long flights of steps between the houses. In the lower part of the town were the exciting shops, dark and foreign, some of them fronting narrow cobbled lanes where only pedestrians could pass up and down. The big covered market was here, and the small stone houses where the poorer people lived. Then, as one climbed, came the bigger houses of the élite of the island. They had steps leading to elegant front doors flanked by tubs of blue hydrangeas or agapanthus, and behind them were gardens where palm trees grew in the mild climate, Guernsey lilies, fuchsias and escalonia. In England we know escalonia as a hedge, or a bush ornamented with rather small sparse sticky flowers, but in Guernsey it grows to a tree and the scent of the many pink blossoms after rain comes in great gusts of perfume.

My grandparents, after their children had grown up, had had a house in St Peter Port and from the high steep garden one could see the harbour, but I remember it only dimly, for they could not long afford it, and the house I remember so clearly and visited so often was a modern one, beyond and above St Peter Port. We reached it finally after a last slow drag up the hill and were out in the country, on the flat fields of the hilltop, in sunlight and sparkling air. I believe that hilltop is now completely urban but at the time the row of Victorian villas was lonely and stood out starkly as a sore thumb. But I did not think them ugly. I thought my grandparents' house perfect. The walls were of strong grey granite, and they needed to be for the wind up

there could be terrific, and there was nothing but the flat
fields between the houses and the cliff edge, and beyond
was the sea; and beyond that on clear days one could see a
blue smudge against the horizon that was the coast of France.
There was a small square of flower garden in front with a bed
of mignonette beneath the bay window of the drawing room.
Above was a balcony and a passion flower climbed over it and
covered the front of the house. It grew as luxuriantly as the
mignonette below and the smell of all those flowers in hot
sunshine would drift in through the open windows. There
was a larger bit of garden behind the house but this was
given over to a green lawn where stood the imposing array of
instruments used by my grandfather, who among many
other things was a meteorological expert, for measuring
rain and foretelling the weather.

The cab stopped at the front gate and my grandmother
came out to welcome us. Her face glowed with love but she
moved with her usual unimpaired dignity. Nothing ever
upset my grandmother's dignity. If her house had started to
fall upon her in an earthquake she would have moved out
from it in a serene and dignified manner. Had her dignity
cost her her life she would have considered death preferable
to unbecoming hurry. Like my mother she was a brave
woman; I do not think that either of them knew what fear
was. She was tall and beautiful, with fine dark eyes, and she
never lost her slim figure and upright carriage. In my
childhood her abundant hair was iron-grey but I have a
photo of her when she was very young, showing a mass of
dark hair piled in a high crown of plaits on top of her head.
She had great charm, and again like my mother no trouble
at all in getting her own way. She did not even have to try.
She dressed in long full-skirted graceful black dresses, with a
black coat and bonnet for out of doors. She always carried
an umbrella when she left the house. She had three, one for
wet weather, one for doubtful weather, and the third for use

on the days when her husband could assure her that it would not rain.

If it was Emily who had brought me over she was the first to be greeted, for she suffered cruelly at sea and must immediately be comforted. That done my grandmother and I greeted each other affectionately. We loved each other but not I think to any remarkable extent. I admired my grandmother but I found her a little intimidating. Though my mother had inherited her mother's strong character, in looks she was like her gentle father, and the velvet glove she wore disguised the iron determination better than my grandmother's height and dignity. I suspect that my grandmother thought me a shockingly spoilt child; in which opinion she was perfectly correct. And in nothing did I take after the Collenettes. I was entirely and distressingly English. When years later my grandmother had another granddaughter, the child of her younger son William, she had a grandchild after her own heart, a little creature dark-eyed and vivacious and strongminded as herself, and as brimful of charm.

My memories of that arrival stop with my grandmother's greeting. I recall only being in bed and marvelling at the extraordinary phenomenon of a bed that plunged and rose with the motion of a ship in a rough sea, even though it stood perfectly still on a flat floor.

2

The morning brought reunion with my grandfather in his study on the first floor above the front room. I made a point of standing at his elbow when he was working and if I drove him distracted his serene selflessness let no signs of irritation appear. In memory his little study is full of sunshine, with the scent of the passion flowers rioting over the

balcony outside coming in through the open window. It
would not even have occurred to me to stand at my father's
elbow while he worked; I doubt if he would have tolerated
me there. The difference between the two men was that my
father did not love children as children, though he did his
duty by them when related to him with admirable patience,
while my grandfather loved all children, clean or dirty,
good or bad, with equal devotion. He was an indulgent
father and the kind of husband tall, strong-minded women
so often marry. He was half a head shorter than his wife,
gentle and yielding. Yet possibly he yielded to my grandmother in the same way that my father yielded to my mother;
for love's sake and desiring peace; for I do not think he was a
weak man. No weak man could have been so undefeated in
adversity as he always was.

Following the family tradition he had chosen medicine
for his profession but after only a short period of work he
became ill with diabetes. There was no insulin then but
with determination and a strict diet he struggled on and
lived to be over eighty. But his sight was affected and though
he did not go completely blind until he was old, and with
strong glasses could continue to read and write, he could
not be a doctor. But he wanted to put his medical knowledge
to good use and so he opened a chemist's shop. In those days
a chemist was almost a doctor; his shop was not flooded with
cosmetics and cameras and was almost entirely used in
serving those with minor ailments and injuries who could
not afford the doctor. My grandfather was expert in help
but as he was just as dedicated to those who could not
pay as to those who could his business did not thrive financial-
ly. He could never succeed in any sort of business. He was
too conscientious and too compassionate. In the early days
of their marriage my grandmother had to help him by starting
a little dame's school in their home and teaching the neighbours' small children with her own.

They lived at that time in an old house called Le Hechet, that belonged to my grandmother's family. It had a yard with a pump in the centre, a good garden, and was surrounded by fields, and close to it, joy of joys for children, was a windmill. The house still exists though the fields have vanished. When I wrote *Island Magic* I did not keep the family at Le Hechet but moved them to a farmhouse which fascinated me. And that too still exists. The family were deeply united and loving, all the more so because life was not easy. The elder son Arnold died in childhood and neither of his parents ever quite recovered from the grief and shock of losing their firstborn. That was the only deep sorrow but there was an acerbation in the person of Aunt Marguerite.

In those days maiden ladies whose parents had died and who had not sufficient means to keep up an establishment on their own had to be supported by their brothers or nephews. The bliss of independence could not be theirs since it was not genteel for a gentlewoman to earn her own living. Lovers of Jane Austen's *Pride and Prejudice* will remember the anxiety among the males of her family when Charlotte did not marry. Which of them would have to have her? Mr Collins solved the problem. But there was no Mr Collins to solve the problem for Aunt Marguerite's brothers when her parents died. And then their nephew Adolphus, my grandfather, announced his impending marriage to Marie-Louise Ozanne. Magnificent! They should have Aunt Marguerite, and upon their return from their honeymoon they immediately had her. She lived to a great old age and her thwarted instincts found satisfaction in advising her niece by marriage in her domestic and maternal duties. Poor Marie-Louise. But also poor Aunt Marguerite, for what else had she to do?

When they had outgrown their mother's teaching the children were sent to a day school, the girls to Guernsey

Ladies' College, William first to the Gentlemen's College
and afterwards to a school in France, and the four girls
suffered deeply under the stigma of having a father in trade.
They were an old Island family, descended, they thought,
from William the Conqueror's cupbearer, but their father
was a chemist and they were made to suffer for it. Life in the
Victorian era was less violent and corrupt than ours but
at least in this age the distinction between a doctor and a
chemist causes no actual suffering, and the Aunt Marguerites
of that generation are in this one headmistresses and members of Parliament.

But apart from Aunt Marguerite and the chemist's shop
the children had an ideally happy childhood. They did
not have enough to eat and that left its mark upon them,
for they were none of them physically strong in later life,
but since bread with a smear of jam upon it is filling enough
without butter they were not aware of their deprivation and
they were given an unusual amount of freedom. They had
the cliffs and bays for their playground, the water lanes,
the fields and the windmill. Their parents loved them and
I think it can be said of my grandfather that he lived for
them and the wife he worshipped.

But he was a man of many interests. One was promoting
the teetotal cause. I do not know at what stage of his life he
became a purveyor of soft drinks, nor whether they were an
adjunct of the chemist's shop or superseded it, but I do know
that a large cart full of crates and rattling bottles, drawn by a
couple of horses and with A. Collenette inscribed upon it,
was a matter of pride to me since I had no sense of shame
in having a grandfather in trade; I did not at that time go to
school and no one jeered at me for it. It was also a matter of
pride to stand outside the library at St Peter Port and read
the weather forecast that hung on its wall framed in a glass
case, printed in large clear letters and signed A. Collenette.
And if a little group of people had gathered and were

attentively reading my grandfather's forecast I was in bliss.
Weather matters on an island. Those attentive people were
wondering if a crossing to Alderney in a small boat across a
strip of water famed for its choppiness would be possible
today. Others were anxious about a business trip to Le Havre,
and yet others who wanted to go sailing or fishing, or were
planning a picnic tomorrow, were bothered about the wind.
Would it rain? They stood in front of the library asking my
grandfather and their complete faith in him made my proud
heart beat almost to bursting point.

My grandfather was above all a man of science. It was
his first love, enthroned in his heart long before the age of
sixteen when he first proposed marriage to Marie-Louise
Ozanne. It was a tragedy that, failing medicine he was not
able to make it his profession. He was not a good man of
business but as a scientist he would have been happy. He
read every scientific book he could get hold of and the
amount of knowledge he amassed in a lifetime was very
great. Yet if science was his first love it was science that
brought him one of the great griefs of his life, for while he
was still young he completely lost the religious faith that
had meant so much to him. The scientific conclusions of his
day made it impossible for him to accept the book of Genesis
as literal truth. And if Genesis was not true then the Bible,
every word of which he had believed to be directly inspired
by God, could no longer be the basis for his faith. After an
agonising struggle the ground went from under his feet and
he fell into the darkness of unbelief, a darkness that shadowed
his whole life.

When I stood beside him in his study my grandfather
was writing scientific articles and pamphlets. When he
became aware of me he would patiently put down his pen
and smile. He had golden brown eyes like my mother's.
In appearance he was very French, with a pointed grey
beard and thick grey hair worn *en brosse*. He was the kindest

man I have ever known. I cannot believe that he ever had an unkind thought or spoke an unkind word in his life and his inner sadness was well hidden. He was a great tease and again like my mother he had a gift for merry repartee. He was driving the family out for a picnic one day and my mother, who had just become engaged, was sitting beside him on the box discoursing vivaciously on the marvels of this man she was to marry. Even in those days tourists had penetrated to the island, and native inhabitants able to provide them with the glories of an island tea would put a notice to that effect in the window, adding hopefully, *Ici on parle anglais.* As they passed such a notice, with my mother in full spate, my grandfather turned round to the rest of the family with twinkling eyes and ejaculated, "Ici on parle fiancé."

I think of the music of Mozart when I think of my grandfather. The great composers seem to represent different types of spiritual greatness in men. The Word speaks perhaps more clearly through music than through any other medium known to men, even the beauty of the world itself, but in different tones. Beethoven is a rock of strength and certainty; but there are times when you feel he speaks of something that could fall upon you and crush you to powder. Bach is less frightening. Beyond the dancing of his heavenly spirits, who whirl and spin and never put a foot wrong, are depths beyond depths of the unknowable, but when he writes of these he is happy about it. He believes with George Macdonald that "there is a secret too great to be told", and neither he nor Beethoven allow us to be afraid for long; in the midst of the thunders or the dancing they pause and let the mercy of God speak through them. Mozart too has his dancers moving in measure; but the dancers are sometimes ourselves, not always the heavenly spirits. He is so often gay and tender in those first movements of symphonies and concertos, as though delighting in us, and in the second movements, while we rest, he sings to us. It is often of himself he sings, and then delight is only on the surface; below is heartbreaking sadness. But he does not wish to break our hearts and the dancing comes again, but faster, as though urgent to cover up what was not intended should be revealed. I am reminded of my grandfather.

3

Driving picnics were still a feature of island life when I was a child. Those who did not possess a brake of their own hired one. If the father of the family could himself drive, he did so, if not a driver was hired with the brake, and the islanders being merry people he enjoyed the outing as much as anyone. Guernsey is a small island and the inhabitants of those days knew it like the palm of their hand. Yet to visit a favourite bay or clifftop six miles away for the fiftieth time brought no sense of stalemate. It was a visit to a well-loved friend and always there was something new to see. And the scenery is varied. The flat sands of l'Ancresse might be in a different country from the rocks of Le Gouffre, and there is no comparing the town church at St Peter Port with the little church at Le Forêt, where on one of the gateposts was an ancient stone figure of a heathen goddess. And Fermain Bay and Saints Bay have a totally different atmosphere. Fermain was the one the aunts and I visited most often because it was the nearest, but Saints Bay was the one I loved best.

A steep narrow road led down to a few of the bays but others could only be reached by leaving the brake on the clifftop above and climbing down one of the water lanes. I do not know if any of these remain now, and if they do they have probably been tamed and civilised. In my childhood they were steep stony paths, green tunnels arched over by trees, with a stream running down the side under a canopy of ferns. It was wonderful for a child to come out at the bottom and see the stream running across the sand, and run with it to the edge of the sea. Sometimes the picnic would be for both lunch and tea and then mountains of food would be brought and bathing things for everybody, and down in the rocky bay the family would take possession of a cave for the whole day. This sounds a selfish action but there were so few people then, and so many caves, that it was not selfish.

The cave was primarily for the bathers and getting undressed in a cave struck me, aged six, as a stupendous experience. It was also a dignified, leisurely and lengthy one. Edwardian undressing could never be done in a hurry, with dresses fastened up the back with many hooks, petticoats with buttons and tapes to be undone and laced corsets to be removed. And a bathing dress was not put on in a moment. It was an elaborate garment with frilled trousers to below the knee and a short full overskirt. There would be a monumental bathing cap, also frilled, and the whole outfit was frequently scarlet trimmed with white braid. It was a pity it had to get wet. If the mouth of the cave was rather large an elderly female relative who had accompanied the picnic sat at the entrance with a parasol up. Needless to say no gentleman, not even a brother, was allowed to set foot in the cave. They were sent off behind the rocks.

The caves were washed each day by the incoming tide and they had firm floors of silver sand. Frequently they had rockpools in which there were deep crimson anemones, delicate waving pale green seaweed and minute scurrying crabs. The seaweed, or vraic, that clothed the rocks in the bay and was washed up along the shore was lovely too. There was one special vraic called carrageen that was collected at certain seasons and made into jellies and moulds, and another kind used both as a fertiliser and as fuel. Collecting seaweed was called vraicking. A child could be endlessly happy in these enchanted bays, for when one had finished bathing and collecting seaweed and shells there was rock climbing. I was by nature a climber, having a good head for heights, but I liked to climb alone, having served my apprenticeship climbing the cedar tree in the garden at Wells where I was nearly always alone.

I am ashamed now when I think of my furious rages when my aunts interfered with rock climbing. Aunt Emily was easy to shake off for she was no more than a gripper of the ankle. Always so beautifully dressed, she was herself not partial to climbing. With a quick wrench and a quick scramble upwards one could get rid of her. But Aunt Marie, a spare agile person who could climb better than I could, was another matter. If she caught me starting to climb she did not grip my ankle but simply came after me to take care of me. She was the dearest of the aunts but I hated her, and said so, when she shared my rocks. The third aunt, Irene, was seldom in Guernsey for she spent her working life as nanny in royal families abroad. But I know quite well what her methods would have been with disobedient rock climbing children. She could not have climbed, for she was lame as the result of a broken thigh in her childhood, so she would have been an ankle-gripper, but being the most determined woman I have ever known in my whole life she could not have been shaken off. With her free hand twisted in the infant's jersey she would have got that child off that rock, and if there had been any incidents in the process she would have delivered a good spanking. These were her methods with her small royalties, for royal children, she would say, though always lovable and loving, have warm tempers to match. For this reason she liked working in continental palaces for they frequently had tiled floors, and it is easier to empty a jug of cold water over the head of a small boy in a rage than to spank him. He quiets instantly. But you need tiled floors.

My grandmother had yet another method with climbing children. She trusted in God. In early days she once took her young family for a picnic to one of the bays. They were old enough to be left to their own devices, she thought, and being very tired she sat down with a book and began to read. She was disturbed by a total stranger roughly shaking her shoulder. Outraged, she looked up. He was rather white about the gills and pointing with his finger to the cliff. "Are those your children?" he demanded. "If so, take proper care of them." They were climbing high up on the rock face, and they looked very small and were in considerable danger, but they were nearing the top and to shout at them at that juncture would have been the worst thing possible. My grandmother's serenity was inwardly slightly dented but this rude and total stranger must not know it. "I trust my children to God," she said, and returned to her book.

In her old age my grandmother found picnics tiring, but I remember one when she was present and it was illumined for me by the fact that we picked camomile daisies together on the clifftop for the camomile tea she loved. The Guernsey cliffs were always a paradise of wild flowers. In the spring they were fragrant with bluebells and primroses and in the summer came the honeysuckle and the foxgloves. A friend with a clifftop garden grew madonna lilies there and I remember how mysterious they looked just at twilight, tall and motionless, appearing and disappearing through the mist that was drifting in from the sea. It was from the same clifftop that I saw one of the most unearthly sights of my life. It was high summer and the sun was setting. The mother-of-pearl sea was calm and still, arched by a blue sky scattered all over with small pink clouds like feathers. Slowly, as the sun set, the sea changed colour and became a deep amethyst. I understood then the phrase, 'the wine-dark sea'. I stood where I was, unable to move, until with the sun down the colours slowly faded into the glimmering dimness of twilight.

I have seen, but only once upon the coast of Pembrokeshire, the green flash that comes when in a cloudless sky in a dead calm without a breath of mist, the sun dips below the horizon. That was unearthly too but the wine-dark sea was even lovelier.

But a dead calm can be frightening when a brewing storm is piling its thunderheads of cloud on the horizon. Heavy and menacing, they climb from the sea so slowly that they seem not to move, and out there the sea itself seems not to move, yet below it is sucking over the rocks and booming in and out of the caves as though a wind were blowing. Yet there is not a breath of wind. A tremor of fear seems to be running all along the coast, through the earth beneath one's feet as well as through one's body.

I had other happy times with my grandmother besides the picking of camomile daisies. When we were alone she often sang to me. She had a clear and pretty voice even in old age and she knew the ballads of the day by heart. The one I loved best was 'Gaily the Troubadour Touched his Guitar as he came Hastening Home from the War'. There was another about a lady called Clementine whose feet were so large that herring boxes were the only footwear she could get on. But this one worried me, I was so sorry for her, and I would ask to go back to the troubadour.

The only time my grandfather was really annoyed with me was over my grandmother's singing. It was Sunday evening, the aunts had gone to church, I was in bed and he was enjoying a peaceful and precious evening alone with Marie-Louise. But I had measles, was covered with spots and fractious, and from the top of the stairs I called to my grandmother to come and sing 'Gaily the Troubadour'. She obediently came rustling upstairs in her Sunday silk but would have nothing to do with the Troubadour because it was the sabbath. However she found a hymnbook and sitting in the armchair in Emily's room, where I also slept, she sang hymns to me. I was enchanted for she had never sung hymns before. In matters of religion she stood midway between her husband's agnosticism and her daughters' faith. I think she was nearer to him than to them, but she did sometimes go to the town church and she did not think it right to sing ballads on Sunday; and she did always just hope that she and Adolphus would not be parted at death. I think I was wrong to describe my grandfather as an agnostic, for even at the end of his life he was still convinced that beyond death there was nothing but darkness and the end of it all. He was perhaps an atheist and my grandmother an agnostic. But atheism is an ugly word, with a finality about it that no scientist should tolerate, and I prefer agnostic to describe them both. Only to my mother and my youngest aunt, who of all her children were the only ones to inherit the strong streak of extra-sensory perception that ran in her family, was my grandmother able to communicate after her death her discovery of the fact that 'it is all true'. To my mother especially she was able to convey her joy with overwhelming conviction. And so, uncertain as she was in life, she had forgotten the words of the hymns of her childhood, though she remembered the tunes, and had to find a hymnbook that evening when she sang to me.

My granfather down below was displeased. Not only were hymns reverberating over his agnostic head but he had lost his quiet time with Marie-Louise. Once or twice he came to the bottom of the stairs and called out, "Marie-Louise, come down." But she was not accustomed to being ordered about by Adolphus and replied sweetly but firmly, "Dolph, I must sing this child to sleep. I will join you presently."

I do not know how long it took her to sing me to sleep but I remember my dismay that my grandfather of all people should not have been on my side. Spoilt little brat that I was I thought everyone should always be on my side. Especially with measles upon me.

My grandparents, their four daughters and their son, were

all fascinating individuals, but the family charm gave them
a likeness to each other. It had a sparkle like light on water.
In one daughter only was it lacking. Emily had been born
soon after the death of the elder son Arnold and her parents'
grief had affected her with a pre-natal sadness. She was the
only one to have blue eyes and was considered the prettiest
of the daughters, but she was never happy and she died in
middle age. Her mother yearned over her with painful love,
as though in apology, and loved her the best of her daughters.

My grandfather's favourite was Marie. My father and I
thought his partiality correct for we too thought Marie a
wonderful person; I because she adored children and spoilt
me even more shockingly than my mother did, and he
because of her goodness and her intellect. My father excelled
in the in-law relationship and his house and his purse were
always ungrudgingly at the service of his wife's family, who
were too charming and unworldly ever to keep firm hold of a
penny. He loved them in a truly Christian way but when it
came to Marie he forgot about being a Christian and just
loved her. I do not think that my mother was jealous for
Marie had none of the feminine graces with which my mother
brimmed over. She was vivacious and talkative but her talk
was a man's talk since, my father maintained, she had a
man's mind. It was her father's mind, but her consuming
passion was mathematics. Yet she understood enough science
to be able to talk as an equal with her father, just as she could
talk theology with my father. All the aunts could perform the
duty known as 'doing the Obs.', but to her it was not only a
duty but a joy.

'Obs.' was an abbreviation of the words meteorological
observations. Twice daily the instruments in the garden had
to be consulted. Among other matters the velocity of the
wind had to be noted, the rainfall measured, and the hours
of sunshine. To measure the sun one left the garden for the
cliff and climbed a slender wooden tower to a small platform,

and consulted a miraculous instrument where the sun had
actually burned a path on a curved piece of cardboard. My
grandfather did the rounds himself whenever possible, but
there were occasions when someone else had to do them for
him. My grandmother had, at the very beginning of Obs.,
declared herself incapable of doing them; she said she was
not sufficiently intelligent; so if a daughter was not handy a
neighbour had to do them. This remark of hers was an
absolute lie and everyone knew it. 'Doing the Obs.' was
perfectly easy, and my grandmother had great intelligence,
but she knew better than to land herself with an incubus of
this kind for the rest of her life, and the mere suggestion that
she should 'just this once do the Obs.' made her feel very
unwell. By the age of eight I could have done the Obs. myself
if only they would have trusted me. I adored Obs. and would
tag after anyone who was doing them in what must have
seemed an intolerable manner. "To measure the sun." It
sounded like a fairy tale. If only they would have let me climb
alone to the platform of the sun and measure his footpath by
myself. But they wouldn't.

Marie was so clever as a child that every available penny
was saved and she was sent to the Cheltenham Ladies'
College, to study under the revered Miss Buss and Miss
Beale. It was a fellow student, and not Marie, who wrote the
famous verse.

> Miss Buss and Miss Beale
> Cupids darts do not feel,
> How different from us
> Are Miss Beale and Miss Buss

but she could have written it for she was a very witty person.
Men delighted in her friendship but I never heard of any
dart wounds. She dressed deplorably, and could not see to do
her hair properly because her looking-glass had the letters
of the Greek alphabet stuck round it and on it (she taught

herself Greek as she dressed) but she was not unfeminine in appearance for she was small and slender. I think she was just not interested in Cupid. Combined with a strong will and occasional explosions of a fiery temper she had the greatest power of selfless loving of any person I have ever known, and since she spent her whole life teaching mathematics to children she needed the lot. It was Miss Buss and Miss Beale who taught her the deep and enduring religious faith that she afterwards handed on to her sisters.

I cannot leave this enchanting family without recording a small incident which lights up in my mind a picture so vivid that I feel I am there, looking on in the old disused stable at Le Hechet where the children used to play. It concerned the facts of life, which were not taught to little girls at that date. They either found out for themselves, or not, as the case might be. These little girls could not find out, and as they were very intelligent it worried them. Or at least it worried the three youngest. I cannot believe that it worried Marie, indifferent as I think she was to anything even remotely connected with Cupid. It was the youngest who found out. She was not intellectual like Marie but she had a needle-sharp mind. They had I suppose been told by someone, not their father, to apply to the Bible when in need of guidance. So she went through it with eyes as sharp as her mind, noting down everything relevant to the subject, until the day came when she could say to her three elder sisters, "I've got it! Come to the stable." So carrying the Bible they trooped to the stable, four little girls wearing frilly white pinafores over dark dresses, and quiet and undisturbed in the cobwebby shadows and slanting sunshine all was (more or less) revealed.

4

I must leave the island where I entered it, at St Peter Port. There were frequent shopping expeditions to what was grandly known as Town (with a capital T as though the little rocky place were London) but before anyone left the island there was a final expedition to buy gifts to take back to England. Early in the morning the aunts and I set out laden with baskets. We caught what we called the bus at the end of the road. It was not a bus at all but a large open brake drawn by two bony horses. I was sorry for the horses, perpetually travelling up and down that steep hill with the added bitterness that going down the shopping baskets of the passengers were empty while coming up they were full of heavy parcels, with live shell-fish down at the bottom. This was the custom and no one seemed to realise its cruelty. The crabs and lobsters were still alive when taken from their beds of seaweed in the market and were imprisoned for fear they should get out of the basket and walk up and down the bus.

The moment when I first discovered that crabs and lobsters are boiled alive was what in modern parlance is called a moment of truth. My grandmother had sent one of the aunts and myself to Town one day to call at the library and to buy a lobster for tomorrow's lunch. This we did and the lobster was placed beneath the library books in the basket. It must have been a very quiescent one for I thought it was dead. After we got home I went to the kitchen to talk to Sophie, my grandmother's maid who did the cooking. I opened the door and saw the lobster frantically trying to climb out of the pan of boiling water. Sophie pushed it down and put the lid on top. I shut the door and ran away. I do not remember where I hid myself and after the fashion of children I kept what I had seen to myself. I did not seek for comfort, not even from my mother when I got back to Wells. I have never been able to eat shell-fish from that day to this.

Yet if one could turn one's mind from the fate of shell-fish the market was a wonderful place, almost a cathedral of a place, with stone aisles and a high echoing roof. The country-women in their black shawls and bonnets came from all over the island with their produce, eggs and yellow butter, curds, vegetables, fruit and flowers. Oh the flowers! They were piled up in great banks of colour and their perfume scented the whole place. The fish on the other hand had no smell. For one thing they were too fresh and for another the beds of seaweed on which their bodies lay sent a breath of the sea to mingle with the scent of the flowers. The aunts bought butter and eggs and always without fail a canful of curds. A bowl of Guernsey curds is delectable food. Yogurt cannot hold a candle to it. The making of curds is a very complicated matter and is best done by those with hereditary skill in a cool farmhouse dairy. They were eaten with sugar and grated nutmeg in the same religious silence that used to attend the eating of shell-fish at a Guernsey high tea. Such a silence was remarkable for whether they talk patois or English true Channel Islanders are equally voluble. My aunts talked so constantly and so rapidly that English heads went round.

We did not buy goche in the market but in a bakery in one of the narrow, paved shopping lanes. There is no cake in the world like the Guernsey goche. It is a lard cake packed full of fruit and delicately spiced, and crisp and crackly on top. A wonderful cake, but digestible, for my uncle in his youth could eat a pound at a sitting with no ill effects. It is still made but I have heard to my sorrow that it is not now what it was, and that Guernsey biscuits have disappeared altogether. This is a tragedy. They were not biscuits, they were like circular rolls to look at but they were not rolls. They cannot be described. Whenever my mother was more ill than usual, and nothing the doctor could do seemed to help her, we would send for Guernsey biscuits. When presented with one she was immediately very much better. A last shopping expedition had to include Guernsey biscuits, and boiled sweets from a little shop in a narrow alley. And then we would visit the verbena shop.

I think this was in the same alley as the sweet shop and

was even smaller and more mysterious. One was served by a
dark, gentle man who had some unearthly quality about him.
He might have been a fairy man in disguise and perhaps he
was. It was he who manufactured the Guernsey verbena
scent and it was a magic perfume. The monks of Caldey
Island now make something which very nearly reaches the
same perfection, but not quite. Verbena likes to grow facing
the sun, with its back against an old stone wall and its roots
where it can feel old stones below the earth. The fairy man
must have had a walled garden such as the monks have, and
I should guess that verbena likes to have sea air as well as
sun on its face. It will grow without sea air provided it has
old stones to its feet and its back, and sun on its face, but it will
not smell so sweet. And nor does mignonette, and the passion
flowers in my Oxfordshire garden do not have the scent they
had in my grandparents' garden. The Guernsey lilies on the
other hand, which have no scent, stand along the wall that
faces the sunrise as gaily and triumphantly as though they
thought they were in Guernsey.

If there was time between the buying of the verbena scent
and the catching of the home-going bus I might be allowed
what to me was a great treat, and that was a visit to Victor
Hugo's house. It had been kept just as he had left it as a
memorial to him, and was open to the public at certain hours
and very reverently visited, for the islanders were proud that
he had found refuge with them when he was exiled from
France. As a child I knew very little about him but I was
awed by the fact that the house had once belonged to my
great-grandfather Doctor Ozanne. He had sold it to Victor
Hugo and my grandmother had taken the great man round
the house on her eighteenth birthday. Children are dreadful
little snobs and the fact that my grandmother had talked with
Victor Hugo, and of all the houses in Guernsey hers had been
the one he had chosen for his home, seemed to me to shed a
very bright lustre indeed over our family. When I went there

I marched through the rooms that Victor Hugo had made so magnificent with tapestries, carvings, ornate marble clocks, inlaid tables, chandeliers, velvet draperies and much more, and had hard work not to call out to the other sightseers, "My family lived here. My grandmother talked to Victor Hugo. This is *my* house." I thought it beautiful. Now, how much I wish I had seen it in its original simplicity. But at the top of the house was a little room that Victor Hugo built out from the roof and this was comparatively simple. Here he would sit and work and on a clear day when he looked up he could look out over the steeply sloping garden and see the coast of France.

The last evening came, trunks were packed, the Obs. and my grandfather anxiously consulted as to tomorrow's weather. The morning came and we said good-bye to my grandmother and I think we all cried a little. The aunts had to survive another term of teaching in English boarding schools before they would see the island again, and I was returning to Wells where there was no bathing; you might not bathe in the moat. My grandfather came with us in the cab to see us off but though I remember the arrivals at the island so clearly I cannot remember any of the departures. Perhaps my grandfather standing alone waving to us as the ship drew away, and then the slow disappearance of St Peter Port and the ships at anchor and the circling gulls, and then the heading out into the open sea away from it all was too poignant to be remembered. For I would not be back for another year, and a year to a child can seem an eternity.

CHAPTER IV

Edwardians

I

BACK IN WELLS THE ISLAND AND ITS ENCHANTMENT RECEDED
from me as the busyness of home grew round me once more.
It was another sort of enchantment, remembered as a hum
almost like the busyness of bees. Deprived of (or not yet
burdened with) our modern labour-saving inventions there
was a great deal to do even in a modest home like ours. It
was a world in itself, self-contained to an extent it is hard to
realise today. Households were larger then than they are
now for as well as children they almost always contained
grandparents or an old retired governess or nanny as a
permanent member. People with adequate homes and
families did not take up room in the little hospitals, called in
a small town like Wells cottage hospitals, but were ill in their
own homes, and if the illness was serious that made work.
There was no old person living in our home for my father's
parents had died in his youth and my mother's, hating to
leave the Island, visited us at rare intervals and could never
have borne to live in England, but the aunts always came to
our home to be ill.

And then there was the cooking, a tremendous business.
The very size of the blackleaded kitchen range, taking up the
whole of one wall, the highly polished pots and pans and
rows of china plates on the dresser, the stir and bustle, the
comings and goings of tradesmen and servants and children
and dogs and cats, cried aloud of the enormous importance of
cooking to an age that had never set eyes on a tin opener.

Without it there were hams to be boiled, marmalade and
pickles and chutney to be made, plum puddings to be stirred

in large earthenware crocks, quantities of food to be bottled and preserved and stowed away, fruit that included such things as mulberries, medlars, apricots, nectarines, bullaces, the old-fashioned fruit that grew in the walled gardens which most houses seemed to possess in country towns; passing along a street, if the front door was wide open, you could sometimes look through the dark polished depths of an old house and see through the open garden door the rich glow of an autumn garden. These walled gardens trapped the sunlight and distilled it into golden wine, and the wine got into the fruit.

The comfortably-off ate far too much but with that kitchen range glowing like an altar at the centre of the house, and the garden packed with food that must not on any account be wasted, it was perhaps not surprising. Yet after a breakfast of porridge and bacon, followed by an adequate lunch and afternoon tea with homemade cakes, however did the adults of those days manage a three-course meal in the evening? Yet many did and though I remember very portly persons I remember too lovely ladies with willowy figures and tiny waists. Emily, for instance, and cousins who came to stay. I would look through the baize door that shut the nurseries off from the rest of the house and see them floating down to dinner in their long dresses; and one evening I remember they had each fastened an aster into their dress.

Asters were a favourite flower and so were sweet-scented geraniums, and the peonies I especially loved because their petals and leaves were always so wonderfully cool; but they were less useful than geraniums whose petals could be rubbed on cheeks that needed a little colour. Make-up was not considered proper for virtuous young ladies, only the other sort, but no one knew what you were doing with geranium petals.

That past age had many evils that were peculiarly its own and one of the worst was disregard of the misery existing

outside the self-centred home, beyond the quiet village or the
sleepy country town. "We lived in our own world," a friend
of my own age said to me not long ago. We did just that and
paid little attention to what went on in the world outside. At
least so it seems to me, looking back. The solidly based home,
the small communities with their songs and tales and dances,
were good things, but upon the other side of the coin was this
indifference. When told of conditions in the London slums,
or in the industrial North where the infernal machines were
spitting out their venom over blackened homes and lives,
we were very sorry but we had no means of picturing it to
ourselves, it all seemed very far away.

My parents were more aware of the suffering of the world
beyond the charmed circle than were many of their friends,
my father because he had been born in London and as a
young priest had worked in a factory town, and my mother
because she was deeply compassionate and had made it her
business to know. People went in to meals in our house past
two large collecting boxes which my mother kept on the hall
table. One was labelled S.P.G. and the other Waifs and
Strays, and the latter had a picture on it of two ragged
children. I do not know if anyone looked at them as they went
in to dinner but I do know that people who came to stay in
the house did not leave it until they had done their duty by
one box or the other. I do not know how my mother contrived
this but she was a clever woman and could contrive most
things. If the Waifs and Strays got more than the S.P.G.,
which they did, that would have been because my mother
cared more for waifs and strays than she did for the heathen.
They were less remote.

It is said that parents always try to give their children
what they have lacked themselves and so my mother,
remembering the austerity of her own childhood, allowed
me too many pretty clothes, too many toys, too much
spoiling, and ended by having a very nasty little spoilt brat

on her hands. But upon one piece of discipline she did insist. Every Christmas I was forced to choose from my multitude of toys a basketful that must be given away. No matter what the display of tears and temper the basket must be filled. Nanny then took me by the hand and led me to St Thomas's street, where lived children poorer than myself, and I had to go from house to house giving away my toys until the basket was empty. I suffered agonies of embarrassment but there was no escape for Nanny was with me and prodded from behind. I can remember only one of the many homes. The kitchen was dark and there seemed nothing in it except too many children. They sat still as statues as they suffered the indignity forced upon them, moving only to put out a hand and take the proffered cast-off toy from the rich little girl who wore a velvet bonnet. That scene of poverty must have burnt itself into my mind for I can see it vividly now, though at the time I think I felt more embarrassed than ashamed.

The affair was not without its effect upon me, though hardly the one that my mother intended, for I decided to give away the whole of the contents of our apple store, laid out upon slotted shelves in the garden room. It only took me about an hour, filling my basket with apples and running backwards and forwards from the apple room to the garden railings through which I pushed the apples to the delighted children outside. Just as the birds know by some mysterious instinct that you have put out crumbs for them, so did the children of St Thomas's street know about those apples. They gathered in flocks and there was no sullen indifference this time. They knew I was defying authority and there was ecstatic delight on both sides of the railings. I am happy to remember that the last apple had left the apple room before I was caught. I could not understand the ensuing row.

"But you told me we must give away our things," I said to my mother.

"*Your* things, I told you," retorted my mother. "Not my

things and your father's. Now we shall have no more apples until next autumn."

The thought of no apple dumplings was sobering and I wept. It was my first depressing realisation that an act of true self-sacrifice is not intended by God to leave you just as comfortable and well off as you were before. My mother was mollified and said we would plant an apple tree in my own little-patch of garden, which was situated in the midst of the vegetable garden and commanded a splendid view of Tor Hill, and every apple on it would be my own to do what I liked with. This was done but the devil saw to it that that tree never bore a single apple.

2

I come back once more to the hive of industry that was an Edwardian home and marvel that it cost so little to keep going. My father had an income of five hundred pounds a year and this supported a medium size house and garden, three maids (though the little one aged about fourteen only earned ten pounds a year) and Nanny and a gardener. There were always many mouths to feed and even when making allowances for what inflation has done to the currency how was it managed? As I think about it I realise that we spent practically nothing outside our home. We seldom went to a theatre and holidays, if taken at all, were a visit to relatives or a fortnight in lodgings at the nearest seaside resort, for only rich people went abroad. Light was cheap, consisting of oil lamps and candles. Coal was also cheap but was never used in bedrooms unless you were seriously ill. The houses were dark and cold but I think we hardly noticed the cold because we wore so many clothes, and these were cheap because mostly made at home and made to last practically for ever.

A great deal of time was expended on our clothes. They were lovely in our home and owed much of their beauty to the lady with no head who stood like a saint upon a pedestal in the day nursery. Her name was Dummy and she was much revered. She was red in colour and had a well-formed bosom and a tiny waist. Below the waist she expanded considerably but ended abruptly at the hips. Her only garment was Nanny's tape measure which when not in use was draped round her neck. Upon her serene and docile form Nanny and Emily, who often stayed with us and was clever with her needle, created Emily's and my mother's dresses and my mother's tea-gowns; though there is something of a mystery here because my mother and Emily were so slim and Dummy had such a well-developed bosom. I can only suppose that by the standards of the time Dummy had the correct measurements and my mother and Emily filled up the empty spaces with some sort of in-filling. Created is the right word for these garments were works of art. Yards of material formed their flowing lines and they were ornamented with lace insertions, tucks, ruffles and ribbon. Tea-gowns were a veritable froth of this and that and looked like the foam of the sea. They were never worn at tea time so far as I can remember but were put on when you felt poorly; something midway between a dressing-gown and a dress and indicating that though you were up you were only just up.

Female clothes were designed very much as an outward symbol of the passing years. As soon as ageing gentlewomen began to show their age rather badly they cashed in on it, wearing soft dresses of lavender and grey, a shawl or lace scarf round the shoulders and a lace cap to hide the place on the top of the head where hair tends to get thin. Having dressed for the part they sat down. On chilly days they sat by the drawing-room fire, on really warm days a basket chair was carried into the garden and they sat there and watched the grandchildren at play. That is all they really did about the grandchildren; watch them and occasionally sing them to sleep. What they would have thought about the overworked grandmothers of today I do not know. But whether or not they had grandchildren very little was expected of these ageing ladies. They had done their work, were revered for it and might now sit down. I suppose it is on balance a happy thing that old people are put on the shelf less early now; but I do have days when I hanker for a lace cap.

I also hanker after the hat-trimming box, for it was great fun. Edwardian hats were so elaborate that only the wealthy could afford a new one every season, the less wealthy bought what were called shapes, felt for winter, straw for summer, and these shapes went on year after year, retrimmed in spring and summer from the hat-trimming box. The placing of this large box upon the nursery table on the appropriate half-yearly date was almost a religious ritual. Everyone gathered round, the lid was lifted and the contents ceremoniously emptied out. There was practically nothing that could not be placed on an Edwardian hat; fur, flowers, cherries, jewelled buckles, velvet bows, ribbon rosettes, ostrich feathers, swansdown, cocks' feathers. And worst of all, wings of birds, big white wings that looked like wings of gulls and ducks' wings in all their lovely variety. A woman could look at times as though she wore a whole dead bird on her hat. The thought of it revolts me now but then I longed for wings or a swirl of ostrich feathers instead of just a swansdown edging to my bonnet. But if the winter headgear was sometimes an outrage the shady straw summer hats could be lovely with their wreaths of poppies and corn, cowslips, rosebuds or forget-me-nots. And sometimes a wreath of real flowers was worn with a matching posy tucked in at the waist, but this was not a good idea because they died so soon. A better notion was that adopted by the men at a garden party or wedding. A small silver or glass container with water in it was fastened under the lapel, how I cannot imagine, and a rose or carnation with appropriate greenery was stuck in the drink and remained fresh throughout the afternoon.

There was a lot of gladness in the clothes of that period. They swished and rustled and floated and swept, and chains and bracelets tinkled. My mother had few jewels but she tinkled because on the days when she was well enough to abandon her tea-gown and put on a dress she wore her chatelaine. It was fastened to her belt by a silver hook and from it depended on slender silver chains a pair of scissors in a silver sheath, a little purse of silver mesh to hold her thimble and a tiny notebook with silver covers and a pencil in a silver case.

Mothers get dressed so quickly in these days that their offspring cannot get much fun out of helping them do it. A zip-fastener, if it does not stick, is switched up the back in a moment but hooking your mother up the back when heaven alone knew how many hooks and eyes you had to manipulate was a work of art, and required much practice and heavy breathing on the part of the child and much patience on the part of the mother. Hair had to be brushed with a hundred strokes a day. When it was up it was coiled on top of the head like a crown, and when down it was a matter for pride if a child could boast that its mother could sit on her hair. My mother could and it was a joke between us that she could have emulated Lady Godiva. Her hair was brown with golden lights and so full of electricity that on frosty days it sprang about her head like snakes when it was brushed.

Washing long hair at home was quite an undertaking and so was washing bodies without the aid of bathrooms. There were large marble-topped washstands in each bedroom with patterned jugs and basins. Our nursery jug was ornamented with chilly storks standing in a pool, depressed bulrushes growing beside them, and in cold weather the water in the jug would be frozen hard by morning. Our home possessed bath tubs of two sorts, some round, some shaped like armchairs, and these were placed in the bedrooms at night, each with an early Christian beside it. These early Christians were a fascination to a child. I do not remember how they got their name. It was not a name known to the trade I am sure. Probably my mother invented it because they were supposed to encourage early rising. They were small brown wicker hampers, tubular shaped, lined with cotton wool and twill of a vivid shade of scarlet. At bedtime metal containers filled with hot water were put inside and they were carried upstairs one by one and placed in each bedroom beside the tub. I imagine you did what you liked with it, using the hot water then and there or keeping it till the morning when it would still be hot and could be used for shaving as well as washing. I say I imagine because I have no certain knowledge of these mysteries. Children and servants were the lucky ones. Children bathed in a tub before the day-nursery fire and the servants bathed beside the blessed warmth of the kitchen range.

Just before we left the Principal's House my mother, whose active mind was always well ahead of the times, lost patience and startled Wells by installing a bathroom. It was a nine days' wonder. I do not think it worked very well, and the only thing I really remember about it is that when the first wave of zero weather struck the bathroom all the pipes froze, and later burst, and the resultant display of icicles was so glorious that a professional photographer asked if he might come to take photographs.

I hope that bathroom eased the lot of our servants, for they were wonderful. In those days servants never left you except to get married or die. In a middle-class household they were members of the family, dearly loved and loving. Mostly the people they worked for were unworthy of them, it was very seldom that they were unworthy of their people. When their breed disappeared something extraordinarily sound and sweet went out of life. Sarah reigned in the kitchen all through the years of my childhood and Mary and Lilian, two beautiful sisters, were in turn our parlour-maid. But Mary was so incomparably beautiful that she did not last long and I had the honour to be her bridesmaid at her wedding at St Cuthbert's Church. Her sister Lilian was like a lily, with a perfect skin and smooth pale gold hair. The housemaid Araminta came to us as a small girl hardly more than a child. She was not a beauty, for she had a sallow skin and prominent teeth, but she was most attractive all the same. She had a trim little figure, curly black hair and sparkling black eyes. She also had one of those stout hearts that so often go with a very small body, and a loyalty to match her heart. When we left Somerset for Ely and the Cambridgeshire fens Sarah was too old to contemplate taking her roots out of Somerset, and she went to live in an alms-house, but those two brave girls Lilian and Araminta, because of the great love they bore my mother, said they must come too. They came but alas we did not keep them very long. Their soft West-country voices and their charming ways made havoc of the tough hearts of the Fen men and they both got married.

3

I think Nanny would never have got married however many men had asked her. From the time she came to us, when I was a month old, her life was centred on my mother. She was like a planet revolving round the sun. My mother possessed what I think is best described as a healing person-ality. She had slightly the charismatic gift in her hands and more strongly the telepathic knowledge of the spiritual needs of others. Nanny came to her a plain shy girl, very slow in all she did and with no self-confidence. Yet when my mother's sisters blamed her for choosing such a dull girl as Nanny she replied, "She is the one. She is kind." And how right she was. Shut behind the green baize door of the nursery wing the children of that period were entirely in the care of their nurse and at her mercy. Nanny was all mercy. But my mother saw in her more than kindness. She arranged for her to have sketching lessons and to her amazed joy Nanny found that she was a painter. Later she found that she was also an excellent photographer. To find herself an artist transformed her and she blossomed into a happy girl.

My mother had her reward for in all her illnesses she never needed a nurse. Nanny did everything for her. The love of the two women for each other and their reliance upon each other was extraordinary. When in the last war Nanny was killed in an air-raid something broke in my mother. She was not defeated but she carried on for the rest of the way without gaiety.

Nanny's parents lived at Bath and if there was an aunt handy to be with my mother Nanny would sometimes take me to stay with them for a short while. It was almost as good as going to the Island. They were the opposite of my grandparents for it was the old man who was tall and imposing while his wife was tiny, gentle and obedient. But Nanny-Daddy (surely I could have thought up a less obvious name for him) did not alarm me because he was grey-bearded like my grandfather. His considerable girth was contained in front by a large gold watch chain stretched across it. Picture to yourself King Edward the Seventh with the face of an exceptionally good and kind man and that was Nanny-Daddy. He was hospitable and liked to see the large dining-room table entirely surrounded, the guests doing justice to the superb cooking of his eldest daughter Mary. He did justice to it himself but he always kept a selfless eye on the progress of his guests and did not forget the children. I was never scolded for greediness in his house, as was sometimes the case at home, instead his voice would boom above the hum of conversation with the information that "Elizabeth's plate is empty." No wonder I loved him.

Nanny-Mummy did not sit round the table with the rest of us for she was frail. Dressed in black with a gold locket round her neck she sat by the fire and warmed her thin hands and said very little, but when she did speak it was lovingly in a soft musical voice, with a gentle nodding of her head that was somehow like a caress. I cannot remember that she ever embraced anyone but she called us all 'my dear', with a long lingering inflection of the last word that made one feel strangely protected. She must in her life have wept much for only three of her large family of children had survived and her eyes were pale and faded.

I do not know what Nanny-Daddy's life work had been, though I have the feeling it was the Great Western Railway, but I think he must have come from country stock for he had chosen for his retirement an old house that had once been a farmhouse, with a large rambling garden where he spent his days growing superb vegetables and rearing chickens. Once it had been right out in the country, and when I knew it there was still country on three sides, but on the fourth side it was attached to the City of Bath by streets of small Victorian houses. The old house looked as though attached to the stretch of grey streets as a ship is moored to a long grey harbour wall.

On arrival, having got out of the cab and paid the cabby, the traveller faced the high stone wall that surrounded the house and garden, but looking up one could see beyond the house green hills that rolled up to the sky. They were a sea of green waves that rolled for ever, never breaking and making no sound at all.

There was a strong door in the wall, an iron chain with a ring on it hanging to one side. This one pulled and a bell sounded far away in the depths of the house. Then came the extraordinary, amazing, magic moment. The door opened, one went through and there was nobody on the other side. It had opened by itself onto a short stone-paved path arched over by a curved iron roof green with age, supported by iron posts on each side. Then Mary, Nanny's older sister, appeared in the wide darkness at the open front door, smiling a welcome. Someone, probably Nanny-Daddy, with knowledge learned from the G.W.R., had contrived a mechanism which both rang the bell and opened the outer door without human help. It was a great marvel.

The hall was stone-floored, large and dark as a cave. Worn stone steps led up to the kitchen upon one side and upon the other was the large dining-room where everyone lived as well as ate. Meals were presided over by a very large framed engraving of the Last Judgment. The companion picture in the hall showed Christians being thrown to the lions; but it was mercifully so dark in the hall that you could not see it very clearly. Beyond the dining-room was an exquisite little parlour which was only used on Sundays. This contained a tinkling upright piano and lots of fascinating china ornaments and antimacassars. The whole house smelt of furniture polish and shone and sparkled with cleanliness. It was a tall house and there were exciting empty storerooms and attics that both scared and fascinated me.

But best of all were the cock and the hens. His hen houses occupied the same position of importance in Nanny-Daddy's garden and heart as the Obs. did in my grandfather's. The daily ritual of collecting the eggs, at which I assisted, had the same sort of religious importance as the ritual of 'doing the Obs.', and my wonder the first time my grandfather showed me the path of the sun on a crescent curve of burnt cardboard was equalled on the day Nanny-Daddy first put a fluffy chicken into my hands. How did these things come to be? How could a bit of cardboard measure the sun? How did the egg get under the hen and the chicken out of the egg? Where did the sun come from when it came up out of the sea looking like a painted Easter egg? In Wells we always had painted eggs for breakfast on Easter day. Why? Nanny was no good at answering questions and quick to say with a weary sigh, "Well, that's enough. How many more times am I to tell you that I don't know." Why did people not know? What was this mystery at the heart of things? To wake up in the dawn and hear the cock crowing in the garden filled me with ecstasy. Cocks and hens were not kept in the precincts of Wells and I heard the thrilling sound for the first time in Nanny's home. From visit to visit I looked forward to hearing it again and I shall never hear it without a thrill. When first I made acquaintance with *Hamlet* the phrase "The cock that is the trumpet to the morn" went right through me. That was what the triumphant cry was, a trumpet that celebrated the return of light. The answers to our clamorous questions are hidden in a light too blinding to be approached, but the cock agrees with George Macdonald that there is a secret too great to be told.

4

The short visit would end and Nanny and I would return to Wells. I was never homesick either on the Island or at Bath. I had begun visiting the Island before the beginning of memory, it was an extension of home, and in Bath I had Nanny. I was with her far more than I was with my mother, and it was she who satisfied the needs every child has for a trustworthy experience of security and love. In my earlier years I think I loved her more than I loved my mother, and I was afraid of my father. He was the very reverse of a harsh man but he was the one who was called upon to administer discipline when my behaviour passed all bounds. Discipline was my chief point of contact with him when I was small and his marvellous tenderness was something I discovered only in later years.

Though I remember my first foretaste of it. My mother became desperately ill with terrible pains in her head and so paralysed by some form of poisoning that she could hardly drag herself from her bed to her sofa. Our doctor had not the faintest idea what was the matter and was anxious that she should leave home and live in Bath for the winter, in the care of a doctor there who was reputed to be very clever, and of course Nanny had to go too to look after her. I was left in the care of Nanny's sister Mary, but even so to have both my mother and Nanny disappear at the same moment was for me a very traumatic experience. Spoilt little horror that I was I found comfort in resenting Mary and being as naughty as possible.

And then quite suddenly my father became for those few months the central figure in my world. He had as it were turned back upon the pathway where he was always in the distance. There would be many of these brief meetings before that final turning back, and this was the first of them. His days were an austere fixed routine of work and prayer, beginning at six in the morning and finishing at midnight, but somehow he found time to play with me as my mother had done before she became too ill. The playtimes with him were not story-telling sessions for he was not anchored to a sofa or a rocker as my mother and Sarah were. There were big wicker armchairs in the study, for the use of his students when they came to talk to him, and in these marvellous playtimes they were turned upside down and turned into caves inside which my father and I growled and prowled as lions and tigers. Or they became little huts in which such characters as Bruce and Alfred watched spiders and burned cakes. But on Sundays there were no games. For one thing my father had had a very stern, almost Calvinistic upbringing, with no storybooks or games allowed on Sundays for the children (except Noah's Ark because it came out of the Bible) and though for the rest of his life his mind became steadily broader and more tolerant he was at this time still a little shackled by it. And for another thing my Sunday scripture lesson, always given me by my mother, was now his task.

I think he had not the slightest idea how to set about instructing a small child. My mother had given me carefully prepared instructions which went in at one ear and out at the other. My father took me on his lap, with a cushion placed between his exceptionally bony knees and his child's tender posterior, and turned the pages of a New Testament picture book, commenting briefly on the pictures as we considered them one by one. At the pictures of the passion of Christ I refused to look. I had caught a glimpse of one and that was enough. My father was understanding about this and we turned them over in a lump, leaping straight from Palm Sunday to Easter day and ignoring the crux of the matter altogether. Yet now I think that turning the pages of that picture book with my father was the most important thing that ever happened to me, important because for the first time in my life the man in the picture book came out of it and was alive. It is probably simply my fancy that his arrival had been heralded by the crowing of the cock, but fancy or not the cock-thrill went through me all over again when I discovered the poetry of Gerald Manley Hopkins and found how often the thought of Christ would be linked with a bird symbol; there is 'The Windhover' dedicated to Christ our Lord, but the best of all to me is the ending of the sonnet on 'Patience'.

> And where is he who more and more distils
> Delicious kindness? He is patient. Patience fills
> His crisp combs, and that comes those ways we know.

The theophanies of children could be the subject of a book in themselves. I am sure most children have an awareness of God in very early childhood, though it can come so early and be so simple that later they forget it; or if they remember they do not wish to speak of it for fear of being laughed at. I am speaking of it now only because I am trying to tell the truth and believe that it was a valid experience and that I am lucky in remembering it so clearly. I owe the clearness perhaps partly to the loneliness of my childhood and to the beauty of my home. (How can a child in a slum experience God? Can it have a theophany with nothing to look at but dustbins and brick walls and never a moment of silence and loneliness? Yet sometimes perhaps in the mercy of God it comes.) And also without doubt to the fact that my father had in some way communicated his own conviction to me. He had made the Christ in the picture book a living person.

The winter passed and my mother came home, making a gallant pretence that the doctor at Bath had helped her, and even though my father receded from me again the spring world was full of joy. It was in a world of sunshine and bird-song that I had my first conviction of sin. So baldly stated it sounds a comic occurrence but I did not think so at the time. It overwhelmed me. I know the exact spot on a field path where I first knew the vileness of sin in myself; and can recapture the misery I felt because it has been repeated so many times since. What caused this first conviction? Was it because Christ had come alive? Or because I had come to know and love my father better and perhaps subconsciously compared myself to him? Partly perhaps the shock of joy caused by my mother's homecoming, because it was to her I ran when I got home and to her that I poured out the tale of my wickedness; and I hope that the way I had treated Nanny's sister, and also frequently treated my poor daily governess, came first on my list rather than stealing sugar from the nursery cupboard. The shock of realising what went on behind the green baize door of the nursery wing must have been a cruel one to my mother but I remember that she stood up to it well and was able to assure me of God's forgiveness.

A little later I was alone in the garden, at a spot where hyacinths and deep red wallflowers were in bloom against a grey stone wall, and God revealed himself in a shining world. Every flower flamed with the glory and every bird sang of it. It would be foolish to try and describe the experience; who can? Only the poets and mystics can capture something of the light, Traherne perhaps even more perfectly than Wordsworth.

All things were spotless and pure and glorious; and infinitely mine and joyful and precious... I was entertained like an angel with the works of God in their splendour and glory; I saw all in the peace of Eden; heaven and earth did sing my Creator's praises, and could not make more melody to Asam than to me ..... Is it not strange that an infant should be heir of the whole world and see those mysteries which the books of the learned never unfold?

I think of Laurie Lee's description of his own experience at the age of three:

The June grass, amongst which I stood, was taller than I was and I wept. I had never been so close to grass before. It towered above me and all around me, each blade tattooed with tiger skins of sunlight. It was knife-edged dark and a wicked green, thick as a forest and alive with grasshoppers that chirped and chattered and leapt through the air like monkeys. High overhead ran frenzied larks, screaming, as though the sky were tearing apart.

He felt fear as well as awe and he was right. In our weakness it can seem a terrible as well as a beautiful world, but I do not remember fear, only awed amazement. I picked some of the deep red wallflowers and a small hyacinth, and Nanny let me keep them in a pot of water beside my bed in the night nursery. The scent of wallflowers and hyacinths is now for me irretrievably mixed up with the reading of the Gospels. My godmother had given me a little copy of the New Testament and in the ungrateful way of spoilt children I had not bothered with it and had lost it. But now, I don't remember how, it came to light again and lived under my pillow. I woke up with the birds and read it every morning, not ceasing to read it until I had reached the end of the fourth gospel. I cannot have understood much of what I read but all through that reading time I continued in the amazement of peace and love. And that experience too has been described over and over again. "He looked us through the lattice of our flesh and he spoke us fair." Then the whole heavenly thing slipped away never to return.

Almost for a moment this child sounds a nice little girl but though these visitations of mercy may give direction to a life, may even store up some strength in us of which we are not aware until much later, they do not alter fundamental character. I have met many delightful untarnished only children but I was too spoilt to be one of them. I do not see how the spoiling could have been avoided. In my early years no one expected that my mother would live long. She herself was quite sure she would not, and like so many sensitive extroverts her own suffering caused her not only to be acutely aware of illness in others but even to imagine it was there when it was not. She considered me a delicate child who might not live long either. Whichever way she looked at it fear of being parted from this adored child, whom she had nearly died to bring into the world, was always a shadow upon her. And so she, who if she had been a well woman would have been a wise mother of many children, was in illness the reverse. Whenever I sneezed she sent for the doctor. Or if she did not Nanny did, for Nanny well or ill was a congenital spoiler. And so that child was and is a neurotic selfish little beast. I say is for she is with me still. All my life I have been waging war with her. I have a dim hope that I may get rid of her before I die, but it is very dim. If I do not, and beyond death find that she is with me still, the starting of the battle with her all over again will be my purgatory.

CHAPTER V

The Family of the Silk-Weaver

I

IF I FOUND IT DIFFICULT TO DESCRIBE MY GRANDFATHER HOW much more difficult will it be to write of my father. Mere facts are easy, they are the outlines of the picture, but to fill in outlines with the colour of reality is hardest of all with those who are nearest to you. They are too near. You feel rather than see their true quality and the feel of a person or a thing or a situation is hard to communicate. My father was born in Canonbury, North London, in 1866. He was the third son, but the only one to survive infancy. A few years later, after the birth of a little girl, the family moved to Blackheath. The house was actually on the heath, fresh and breezy above the roar of London but yet to my father's mind a part of it. Though at heart a countryman he loved London and was proud to call himself a Londoner.

Love of London is perhaps hereditary in the family for so many of us have seemed to love the place. The first ancestor of whom I have any knowledge is William Gooueds, a Flemish Huguenot weaver whose family came to England and settled in London. He established himself in business and did well, becoming a flourishing silk merchant, and was admitted to the Freedom of the City of London and Worshipful Company of Weavers. I wish I knew more about him. I think of him living with his wife and family in some low-ceilinged old house, with plenty of space in it for the clacking looms where his daughters would sit and work, singing as the shuttle sped from hand to hand; weaving was one of my greatest joys when I was young and I know from personal experience that you cannot work at a hand-loom without singing. Behind the house there would have been a quiet garden, shaded by a mulberry tree for the silkworms. I have been told that until recently it was quite common to find old mulberry trees tucked away here and there in London, and that they marked the dwellings of the silk merchants.

My grandfather spent his days going backwards and for-wards to the Bank of England and cultivating his garden in his free time. I know that he, like William Gooueds, was good at business, that he was a religious man and a fine gardener, but that is all I know, and his portrait, showing a dark handsome man with side whiskers, does not tell me anything more, and I am not helped by the fact that his son and daughter gave such contradictory accounts of him. That perhaps is natural since my grandfather did not get on with his son but dearly loved his little daughter. The fact that father and son were not compatible is also not surprising. My father, though he delighted in the beauty of his garden and would stand lost in delight as autumn by autumn he watched the butterflies on the michaelmas daisies, could never be in-duced to do anything in it. And when it came to business his brilliant mind closed down altogether. He hated money as much as he hated gardening and was scarcely able to ascer-tain if the right change had been given him when he bought a railway ticket.

Even oneness in religion soon failed father and son. My grandparents were stern Protestant Evangelicals and when a Roman Catholic missal was found in the bedroom of their schoolboy son they were appalled. If my father had shown any inclination towards penitence things might have been better but when he stood upon the mat he was not penitent. "I don't want to *be* one," he insisted, "I just want to know how other people worship God, and why shouldn't I know?" In that rather sad household fun was suspect; theatres were considered wicked and no stockings might be hung up on Christmas Eve. My father reacted, for gentle though he was he had all his life a streak of the rebel in him. He developed a strong sense of humour, became a champion of the ecumenical cause, a high churchman and a devotee of the theatre. We become what our upbringing makes us, we are told, and this is true, but I think quite as many minds are formed by rebellion as by conformity.

My grandmother Elizabeth Bennet was very delicate and through almost the whole of her children's memory of her she suffered from asthma, and from the melancholia that is the skeleton in our family cupboard. Her little daughter remembered her in later life as very often enthroned inside her fourposter, "writing letters to everyone else but shut away from me". The words conjure up an unhappy picture of a sick woman drawing her sadness around her as she draws her bedcurtains, and too absorbed in it to notice the presence of a small daughter in need of love. At the period in my life when I began to succeed as a writer I was seized with an absurd longing for a fourposter, not with heavy Victorian curtains but gay chintz ones. The longing was acute for some years and my mother complained that my stories were full of fourposters and she was thoroughly tired of them. I fought the addiction for two reasons, firstly my politics were anti-fourposter; to spend so much money on oneself would have been a crime of the worst order for a socialist; and secondly I feared I might start behaving like my grandmother. My beloved Great-aunt Emma, my grandmother's sister, had told me that I was the exact reproduction of my grandmother. "Just like my dear Bessie." Well, I had inherited Bessie's tendency to melancholy, though not, thank God, her asthma, and I was not going to risk a fourposter. Now, when

I think it might be safe to risk one, though my politics remain what they were, I no longer want it; such is the contrariness of life.

Between my father and his mother there was a great love. He looked after her devotedly and perhaps it was her suffering that developed the tenderness that was so characteristic of him. If it was his fate to be beset with delicate females at least he had the refreshment of contrast. My grandmother's photo shows sadness and resignation but my mother was never either sad or resigned. She was never so ill that she could not make other people laugh, and was far too good a fighter to be resigned to anything whatever that she disliked. Greatly though he loved his mother perhaps my father's marriage too had in it, deep down, something of reaction.

He went to a school called the Blackheath Proprietary School. It was a day school, and boys of all ages tramped there from every corner of the heath. It was certainly not a public school nor was it a grammar school. I do not really know what sort of a school it was except that it was a bad one. The teaching must have been good for it turned out some distinguished men, but the tortures inflicted upon small boys were the type known as refined. The big boys would lift the little ones up above a stone floor passage and put them with their shoulders pressed against one wall and their feet against the other, in danger of serious injury should they relax the pressure and fall to the stones below, and leave them there until it was their pleasure to take them down again. These and similar bullyings my father apparently took as a matter of course, though as a small and delicate boy he was a popular victim. He set himself to work hard and grow fast and won the comparative immunity of the sixth form at an unusually early age. Then he won a scholarship and left that abominable school, and the restrictions and sadness of his home, and went to University College, Oxford, and happiness.

2

When my father spoke of his undergraduate days he conjured up a picture of idyllic bliss. A quiet city of exquisite beauty, not much changed in those days from the Duns Scotus' Oxford of Gerald Manley Hopkins' poem.

Towery city and branchy between towers;
Cuckoo-echoing, bell-swarmèd,
Lark-charmèd, rock-racked, river-rounded. . . .

Towers and spires, bells and bird-song, a green and quiet countryside lapping like the sea right up to the city, 'the streamlike windings' of The High disturbed only by the occasional passing of wheeled traffic and the voices of the young men who strolled up and down it discussing and arguing in the way of youth for ever. The slow passing of the seasons, spring with fritillaries in the meadows and bluebells in Bagley Wood, summer and sculling on the upper river, the sound of oars in the water and the flash of kingfishers' wings. Autumn and the virginia creeper scarlet on old grey walls, gold leaves floating down from the tall motionless trees in Christ Church Meadow, bonfires in the gardens. Winter and groups of enthusiastic young men gathered together in college rooms before a roaring fire, reading the fashionable poet Robert Browning. They were ideally cared for, those fortunate young. They dined in Hall at candlelit tables, fatherly Scouts looked after their health and their morals with all possible solicitude, old ladies in black bonnets called 'bedders' came in to make their beds and clean their rooms and when they wanted to work alone they 'sported their oak'; that is, closed the outer of the two doors that separated their rooms from the rest of the college, as a sign that in no circumstances whatsoever, except the college on fire or the Day of Judgment, could they be disturbed.

I imagine that my father, with his passion for reading

half the night, must have sported his oak a good deal. In
later life, when the blessing of double doors was denied him
he worked out for himself the best equivalent he could
manage. The artist-craftsman of a cabinet-maker who made
much of my parents' furniture constructed for him a double
bookcase. It was about six feet long and five feet high, was
lined with bookshelves on each side and placed at right
angles to the door. My father had his chair and writing table
upon the other side of it and with books at his back and books
to right and left sat in a protected nook, unseen by anyone
entering the room. This excellent piece of furniture accompanied him from study to study wherever he lived. Its value
was greater than may appear at first sight. As a priest my
father had to be at any time cheerfully available to anyone
who wanted him, but as a writer he hated to be disturbed.
At the sound of a knock at the study door exasperation would
rise within him, and was sometimes apparent in the tone of
his 'come in', but the time it took the visitor to get round to
the other side of the bookcase gave him time to compose his
features, and take a firmer grip of his Christianity. There
was nothing to be seen on his face when the intruder reached
him but an expression of angelic patience, and the warmest
of welcomes was always apparent in his smile and voice. I
know, for I had to intrude myself so many times. But the
bookcase had yet another value. To knock at the door, to
hear that 'come in' and then have to walk around that bookcase, was intimidating. One did not intrude upon my father
on merely trivial matters.

At Oxford he was one of a group of brilliant young men
one of whom, Clavel Parmiter, afterwards became his
brother-in-law. Another friend, in later years Professor de
Burgh, Vice-Chancellor of Reading University, wrote for me
after my father's death a description of the young man he
remembered.

What made the strongest impression on myself and on others, both at the time and afterwards, was his winning, radiant personality. Its influence spread around him without conscious effort on his part and largely without conscious appreciation on ours. It was not merely or mainly the brightness and vitality of youth, it was something less transient and more firmly rooted in his nature, something that sprang from constant communion with the supernatural spring of joy and hope, that reflected the light that was its source. He was so entirely free from any form of egoism, whether self-indulgence or self-assertion or self-righteousness. . . I never saw him show contempt for anyone or anything; though he could when occasion required express strong disapproval and even indignation. With his real modesty and simplicity of heart went a personal dignity that no one would lightly venture to offend. . . . Above all he was keenly interested in persons of all sorts and conditions and was ever ready to share wholeheartedly in their interests and activities. The easiness and optimism of his nature was never dimmed by his realisation of the evil and suffering of the world, for they sprang not from ignorance of the stern facts but from knowledge; from the vision that he had already seen in his youth of a city that hath foundations, of an abiding reality above and beyond the changes and chances of this earthly life.

This extract goes deeper than anything I could say and yet it is astonishing because even this close friend did not put his finger upon what was the keynote of my father's character, and that was his courage. Because he was not an optimist. While my mother was always quite sure that everything would turn out all right he was privately very much afraid that it would not; yet he was able nevertheless to place disaster in God's hands and leave it there; a condition of mind that he described as being 'an optimistic pessimist'. His courage lay in the fact that he could present this gay face to the world whatever his private grief and despair. For he knew grief even in his Oxford days, for both his parents died while he was there and the death of his mother especially hit him hard. He knew about despair. After a period of strain or overwork darkness could fall upon him suddenly out of the blue and last for weeks. My mother and I knew when this happened, for you cannot live in the same house with a soul in darkness and not know it, but not from anything he said or any alteration in his loving manner towards us. I doubt if anyone else knew. His attitude to this lifelong anguish could be perfectly expressed in the words of Leslie Weatherhead's prayer.

> Help me, O Lord, so to strive and so to act, that those things which cloud my own way may not darken the path which others have to tread. Give me unselfish courage so that I am ready always to share my bread and wine yet able to hide my hunger and my thirst.

Yet it is true that he could be wonderfully happy for he possessed the three most necessary ingredients for happiness; the power of delighting to the utmost in any sight or sound of beauty, a keen sense of humour and a humble love for God and man. Every human being had his profound reverence and he criticised no one.

The happy Oxford days must have passed all too quickly. He read Honour Mods and Greats and went down in a blaze of glory with a Double First; due he said to a diet of Bath Oliver biscuits and Cooper's Oxford marmalade. In the last frantic weeks of revision there was no time to dine in Hall. Dr Oliver and Mr Cooper alone sustained him.

He was ordained Deacon and Priest and for four years worked in a big working-class parish in Leicester. Then he turned to the work of teaching that was his vocation. For a year he was Chaplain at Salisbury Theological College and then he moved to Wells, to find my mother and the West-country and the sixteen years of work that were the happiest of his life. All his life long his pupils had a great affection for him but I think the devotion of his Wells men was greater than any. I can remember how vital he was in those days. His early physical delicacy had been left behind, he played games hard, he tramped for miles over the Mendip hills and he bicycled with incredible speed; generally holding forth enthusiastically upon some favourite topic while his companions, faint but pursuing, tried to keep near enough to him to hear what he was saying.

One of his Wells pupils has told me how sometimes the unregenerate, when reading their papers to him, would expound heresies in the hope of shocking him. But no one could get a rise out of my father. Very seriously, with a twinkle in the eye, he would wax very enthusiastic over the heresy in question, point out everything that could be said for it and only then knock it to bits.

He hated slackness. Mentally and spiritually as well as physically he was always taut and vigorous and controlled. He had a temper but he seldom lost it. Looking back over the years I can only remember two occasions when he really blazed out; and then over somebody's intolerable slackness. He could at times seem hard on his men. The first Office of the day was said in the College Chapel at some extremely early hour, and those who dared to creep in late on a cold winter's morning were in danger of being awakened the next day by the Principal wrenching the bedclothes off them. And the same sort of cold douche could be applied to a badly prepared sermon; for those unfortunate men had to read their sermons aloud to the Principal before they were allowed to preach them in the little mission churches in the Mendip hills where they tried themselves out on Sundays. "Will it do?" asked a poor young man one day when the reading of his composition was received in stony silence. "Do what?" asked my father. And yet they loved him.

3

I did not feel the loss of paternal grandparents because
their place was taken by Uncle James and Aunt Emma, who
became father and mother to my father and his sister when
their own parents died, and grandparents to their children.
They might have walked out of one of Galsworthy's novels;
indeed my father's delight in the early part of the *Forsyte Saga*
was partly due to the fact that the Forsyte uncles and aunts
were so like his own. I remember them perhaps too vividly
for truth because for me they were figures so august that they
took something of a fairy-tale quality, and as soon as the
golden glow of a fairy tale starts to gild the facts the latter tend
to lose something of their validity. But golden is a correct
adjective to apply to Uncle James and Aunt Emma for they
had both kinds of gold. They were goldenly good and they
were also wealthy. They possessed a town house in Portland
Place and a country house in Sussex. When Uncle James,
who was a doctor, drove out to visit his patients it was in a
smart brougham with his hat poised at an elegant angle.
Aunt Emma, who was delicate, mostly sat at home. A
violet-coloured velvet bow adorned the lace cap she wore
on her smooth white hair and she had jewels in her ears, and
on the rare occasions when she accompanied her husband in
the brougham she wore her sables. I am certain about the
sables since the remnants of them, incorporated with humbler
remnants from the small sable tie of my Guernsey grandmother, are now a source of moral support to me at the rare
times when I screw my courage to the agonising point of a
social occasion, but I am not certain about the earrings. I
may have invented them to match the sables and the soft
flowing dresses, and the gentle beauty and sad dignity of
Aunt Emma.

Her sadness, I believe, was caused in part by the heartbreaking severity of her religion, and in part by her husband's wealth. She did not like it. When she had married him he had been a perfectly ordinary young G.P. in the suburbs, with his way to make. My father was responsible for the marriage for as a small boy he had been very ill with pneumonia, and his young Aunt Emma had immediately gone to the help of her sister Bessie, as unmarried aunts always did in those days, and James Goodhart, his father's nephew, was also hurried to the rescue and in the opinion of the family saved my father's life with Emma's assistance. Naturally they fell in love, their marriage yet another of the happy unions that shone around my childhood like warm beacons. This particular happy marriage, when my father's aunt upon one side married his first cousin on the other, meant an extraordinary interweaving of double relationships throughout the family. As far as I know only one member of the family ever tried to work it out, but upon coming to the conclusion that he was his own uncle he gave up in despair.

Having saved my father's life Uncle James went on from there to save the lives of many other children, for it was with children that he was as a doctor so specially gifted, and in what must have seemed to Aunt Emma no time at all they were living in Portland Place, and some years later her husband was a baronet. What she felt about being Lady Goodhart and wearing sables was, I think, expressed by what she did every Saturday night. She tipped the contents of her purse, from the sovereigns to the farthings, into her washhand basin and she scrubbed every single coin clean. Her religion had taught her that money is the root of all evil and I am sure that whether she knew it or not she was trying to scrub the evil off hers before Sunday. At least the coins she put in the plate should be clean.

I don't think Uncle James had any guilty qualms about his income. He had worked hard for it, he worked hard till

the end, he was generous with it and he would have enjoyed
it if Aunt Emma had let him. Indeed I think that in spite of
her he did enjoy it a little for I remember him as a cheery
man of great charm, with a dark silky beard streaked with
white and a lock of hair falling artistically over his forehead,
beautifully dressed in dark clothes with a big black tie.
Indeed he looked far more like a fashionable portrait-painter
than a doctor. He was a wonderful host and loved entertain-
ing but I doubt if Aunt Emma did, though for love of him
she could be a charming hostess too. Yet the effort it cost her
was always apparent and when Uncle James stopped
laughing his face had a shadow of sadness over it.

I have said her religion was severe, the statement based not
only on the fact that the same religion clouded my father's
childhood but also on something my mother told me. As a
young bride she stayed with Uncle James and Aunt Emma
that she might watch the pageantry of Queen Victoria's
Diamond Jubilee. It was a glorious occasion and London
nearly went mad with excitement and jubilation. The aged
queen symbolised for her people England's greatness at that
time, and the glory of the Empire, and perhaps it was more
themselves than the old lady whom they were glorifying.
England considered herself the greatest country in the world.
Kings and princes had assembled to pay homage to her
queen, and no doubt every man, woman and urchin in the
streets felt more than human and rejoiced accordingly. Uncle
James rejoiced and insisted that Aunt Emma should come
with him in the brougham, just the two of them together,
that they might drive round London and look at the decora-
tions and see the happy people. It would do her good, he
insisted. It would cheer her up. To please him she went and
my mother ran eagerly downstairs when she heard the
brougham's return to welcome them home. To her dismay
they came in silently with unsmiling faces.

"Didn't you enjoy it, Auntie?" she asked.

Aunt Emma shook her head sadly. "How could I enjoy it, dear? All those thousands of people. It was for me a sight to break my heart."

"But why?" pursued my puzzled mother.

"They looked so unrepentant, dear. I could only ask myself how many of them were lost souls. To think of them in hell, I could hardly bear it."

My mother looked at Uncle James, saddened and distressed at the total failure of his attempt to cheer up Aunt Emma, and what she could hardly bear was his bitter disappointment. Dearly though she loved her my mother did not forgive Aunt Emma for that. Whatever her private conviction as to the final destination of the Jubilee crowds Aunt Emma should, for her husband's sake, at least have looked and laughed and smiled as though she thought it was heaven for all. My mother forgot that Aunt Emma was not the excellent actress that she was herself. Though she had a sharply truthful tongue my mother could send any expression she chose rippling over her animated face. My father, who enjoyed reading aloud, read aloud to her indefatigably for forty-two years, not only novels, plays and poetry for her supposed entertainment but also all his lectures and sermons and books, for she was an excellent and unbiased critic and she appeared to enjoy it as much as he did. I could hardly believe my ears when years later she told me that if there was one thing she hated it was being read aloud to. But Aunt Emma had no French blood in her and was incapable of deception.

We did not stay with Aunt Emma and Uncle James very often; only I think when my father brought my mother to London in search of some relief from her suffering. Uncle James could do nothing to help her himself but was only too anxious that she should see other doctors, though without

X-rays to help them they could diagnose neither her dislocated coccyx nor the fact that she was suffering from arthritis
caused by acute poisoning from sinusitis.

I cannot imagine why my parents took me with them on
these visits, unless it was because Aunt Emma so enjoyed
brushing my hair ("so exactly like my Bessie's hair. The
likeness of this child to my darling Bessie is something
extraordinary"), for my neurotic hatred of all large towns
made me nothing but an exasperating incubus. From my
babyhood all noise reduced me to an extremity of terror. I
was taken protesting to children's parties and sat through
the festive teas cold and shaking in dread of the banging of
the crackers. School sports with the pop of pistols terrified me,
and so did fireworks, thunderstorms and the noise of London.
I think my mind has not often reached such a pitch of terror
as was produced by a drive down Regent Street in an open
victoria, sitting on the small seat with my back to the horses.
It would have given delight to any sensible, normal child but
the rush of noise coming from behind me, and the claustro-
phobia produced by crowds and pressure, were sheer hell.
The ridiculous terror had no connection with physical
danger; what I was afraid of I did not know. And yet driving
in a hansom cab brought a sort of trembling bliss; even such
a little fool as I was could not help rejoicing in such a magic
equipage. And I could bear the top of a horse bus. Perhaps
both conveyances gave me a sense of height and of removal
from noise, and I have always loved heights; especially if it is
quiet up there on top. To make matters even more annoying
for my exasperated relatives I was always physically ill in
London. Uncle James, appealed to, could find nothing
whatever the matter with the maddening child, and must I
think have indicated that it would be preferable to all
concerned if I visited himself and Aunt Emma in the country
only.

Their lovely country home was a very different kettle of

fish. It was bliss. They had a large garden that in my memory basks always in hot sunshine. I have only to think of it to have in my nose the scent of the giant sweetpeas that grew there, and the smell of the azaleas and rhododendrons that separated the garden from the open country. By crawling through the bushes I could reach a certain secret place I knew of. There no one could see me from the house and I could sit cross-legged in a bower of apricot and golden azaleas, and see the world stretching away from me in mile after mile of blue shining heat mist. This hidden place was almost as wonderful to me as the cloisters at Wells, or Saints Bay in Guernsey; and at night in the deep stillness of the Sussex countryside the nightingales sang.

4

There was another garden where I was happy. My father's only sister was now living at Uppingham, where her husband Clavel Parmiter was a housemaster and Nanny and I sometimes visited them. There were four children and they had a large sunny nursery in a big house and a Nanny who, like mine, had been trained at the Norland Institute in the arduous business of coping with 'the modern child' of that age. I suppose children always have been and always will be naughty, the rare moments when they trail clouds of glory being for those who look after them mere fitful gleams of sunshine in a long stormy day, but I think we behaved better then than the little demons do now, for I remember the two Nannies reigning very serenely over the five children in that nursery. And I remember these children dressed in their Sunday best, one small boy in a sailor suit and four little girls in white muslin dresses with coloured sashes, sitting good as gold and still as mice in the drawing room after tea while my uncle read aloud to us from (I think) *The Child's Book of*

Saints. Like my father he read aloud extremely well, trained to
it as part of his parental duty, but even so the picture of even
temporarily good and quiet children listening to a Sunday
story with hands folded in muslin laps is distinctly a period
piece.

I admired my cousins because they were so clever; they
could catch a ball without dropping it and play card games
well, and they never shamed their father by the clumsiness
and speechlessness of desperate shyness as I shamed mine,
and they made fairy houses beautifully.

It was the fairy houses that made me love their garden so
much. I may be wrong about the garden but as I remember
it the lawn sloped down to a hollow where narrow paths
wound among flowerbeds and under the shade of bushes and
low trees. It seemed a secret, mysterious place to me, just
the place to build houses for the fairies. Somehow, though of
course I believéd absolutely in fairies, I had never thought of
building houses for them in the Wells garden. As an only
child I had been more aware of the need for human than for
fairy companionship and had found for myself a boy of my
own age called Charlie. I do not know if that was his real
name because I do not know what sort of boy he was,
whether he was the creation of my imagination or whether he
really had some mysterious, inexplicable life of his own. He
was, in either case, completely real to me, and we played
happily together for hours. Also he was useful. When I did
not want to go to one of the hated parties I said Charlie
was coming to tea with me. If I did not want to do my lessons
I said Charlie was coming to play with me. The boy became
a perfect nuisance to everyone except myself, and finally my
mother lost patience and spoke terrible words. "Once for all,
child, there *is* no Charlie." It was a death sentence and the
boy left me. I cried bitterly but he never came back.

But my cousins, having each other, thought fairies in the

garden would be preferable to more children and taught me how to build houses for them. The roofs and walls of these mansions were constructed of twigs and leaves, and inside were beds for the little creatures made of flower petals and on the floors were carpets made of more flower petals arranged in patterns. We would see who could make the prettiest house but we never knew if they gave pleasure because we never managed to see a fairy inside.

We were so sheltered in our nurseries that children then did not grow up so quickly as they do now, yet to reach the age of ten years gave us a grown-up feeling. One's age now had two figures instead of one. Ten candles on a cake went all the way round it. At ten years old I decided that I no longer wanted to be called Beth. I told my family it was a babyish name. I was ten years old and must now be called Elizabeth. Having delivered my ultimatum I banged the door shut on my childhood and thought it gone. But my father opened the door again. He obstinately refused to call me anything but Beth.

5

I find it impossible to think of the family of the silk merchant without thinking of what they believed, for their faith was so much a part of themselves that they cannot be separated from it. It has been said of Victorians and Edwardians that they were frequently hypocritical in their religion, and I think this is probably true, for even in my childhood to be an agnostic, like my Guernsey grandfather, was to be slightly suspect. A doctor or lawyer who did not go to church would not have so many patients or clients, as one who did. Therefore nearly everyone did go to church and Sunday was a day set apart, entirely different from other days, with a different flavour to it.

In town and city alike one awoke to a sense of serenity and quietness, unbroken until the bell-ringers got going in every tower and steeple in the land. But it was not noise they made, it was music. In the country the wind carried the sound of the bells over the fields from one village to the other, and in the towns there seemed to be bell-song at every street's end. Sunday was a dedicated day, sacred to the bells, to top hats, rustling silk dresses, kid gloves, roast beef and Yorkshire pudding; and God. To what extent God himself mattered to each one only that one could have told you. Or perhaps he could not have told you, since sincerity finds it hard to find the right words and hypocrisy, being so often a form of self-deception, finds it only too easy. But for the many I do believe that faith in God was deep and strong, and so his law as they conceived it was important, and sin mattered, and the discipline of their moral code was as binding as their faith and gave strength to the nation.

I do not think there were any hypocrites in my father's family; they did not have Huguenot blood in them for nothing; and I think of them with great respect. If they were too stern, too obsessed with thoughts of sin and death and judgment, I believe they had paradoxically a basic happiness that we have largely lost today because we no longer have their discipline.

Certainly they were much too tied up in the minutiae of sin. When I had to go through my father's books after his death I found a little book of devotions that he must have used in his very early days. It made my heart ache, for the lists of sins for which the penitent must search his conscience made it seem that one could hardly breathe without sin, and if my father was using this little book in the early days of his marriage I can understand the exasperated cry which some-times broke from my mother, "Why can't people realise that God has common sense?" Yet in the practice of a strict discipline of penance there is joy. There are few joys so great as the joy of a sense of forgiveness and without a sense of sin one cannot know it.

But I will say for us today that we get ourselves dead, and our bodies disposed of, with less fuss and bother than our ancestors did. The funeral elaborations of those days were tremendous, and yet I think our ancestors were not so afraid of death as many people are today. I think it had a kinder face. Since those days two great wars have scored their wounds across the body of our shared humanity, and in our individual lives we see daily on the TV pictures of death by violence, torture or famine, and road accidents are always with us. This face of death is too hideous to be seen without fear and horror but it is the one we see most often, for normal deaths from illness or old age take place almost always in hospital. Very often even the nearest relatives do not see them; or if they do it is in the atmosphere of a hospital ward, fraught with an accumulation of pain and distress. And so how can people not be afraid?

But in those pre-war days people mostly died in their own homes and a death in the house was as normal as a birth. Even the children knew all about it. You came into the world and you went out again, the children were told. You took off your body as though it were an old coat and went through the door of death into another world. Both birth and death could be painful, and death was hard to bear for the people left behind, but there are other things in life which are hard to bear, we are told; life is not a bed of roses and heartbreak is to be expected.

"You must expect that," was the constant and lugubrious remark of an old servant of ours. She said it of every disaster, from death to smashing the best teapot, and the invariable remark could rouse hidden laughter in her hearers if the disaster was not too bad, but it represented a serenity of acceptance that took away the dread of death. I think we children grew up with little fear of it. Frightened person though I am I do not know yet what people mean when they say they fear death. Injury, disease, pain, these things that meet us on the way to death and test our courage to the utmost, yes, but not death itself. Yet I believe that the fear of death must come at some moment to every soul, and that it is right that it should. A sense of immunity is a bad thing, a separating thing. At the end of it all, perhaps at the end of many lives, there should be no human experience that we have not, all of us, shared with each other. How can we hope for union with God until we have come to regard unity with each other as the greatest treasure that we have as we journey to him?

But paradoxically what a fuss was made about this normal thing, death. The elaborate funeral procession with the black horses and the carriages following filled with mourners in inky garments, and afterwards all the letters of condolence that must be answered on black-bordered notepaper, and then the weekly Sunday visits to the grave with floral offerings, and to the dressmaker for new clothes, as black dresses were discarded for purple, and then purple for grey and heliotrope, and then finally (though with trembling and temerity) the thought of a pink dress could once more be entertained.

One is thankful so much fuss has passed into oblivion, but yet, had it a good side? The relief of tears was not only allowed but expected, and it relieved tension. Having so many things to do occupied the mind and provided death with pageantry and ritual, things that have always seemed to be two of the human hungers. And ritual is basically religious. Bereavement was easier to bear when faith upheld it, for in spite of their black garments everyone said, and most people believed, that departed members of their family had gone to heaven.

And yet they believed in hell too, and not all departed members of a family are equally virtuous; but of course for the black sheep of one's own family there were always extenuating circumstances. Dear Aunt Emma mourned over the probable destination of the crowds in the streets, but I don't think that she imagined for a moment that anyone related to *her* could share their fate. Human thinking always seems to get especially muddled when it has to do with religion and the old lady who said, "The Hand of God has been heavy upon me but there's One Above will see me righted," was quite representative. The basic thought at the bottom of each selfish mind is, "It can't happen to me," and that 'me' includes the relatives who seem a part of us. We felt that way in the last war and would confess it to each other. We might be racked with anxiety for husbands and lovers fighting overseas, our bodies would tremble and our mouths would go dry when bombs were falling close to us, yet down at the bottom was that strange sense of immunity. When it *did* happen to us I think the first reaction was one of stunned astonishment.

CHAPTER VI

Ely

I

RELIEF FOR MY MOTHER CAME AT LAST FOR UNCLE JAMES
sent her to a London surgeon who knew what was the matter.
Her sinusitis was so bad that it had caused an abscess pressing
on the brain. He was getting old and he told my father that
he himself had not the courage to operate, but he sent her to
a brilliant young Bristol surgeon whose name if I remember
correctly was Watson Williams. I expect that the operation he
performed then, and the others which followed later, are
now normal and commonplace, but they were not at that
time for surgeons came from France and Germany to watch
this first operation, while my father spent the time praying
in the chapel of the nursing home. My mother was delivered
from the worst of her pain, though still no one knew that she
had a dislocated coccyx, and after a long time away from
Wells she came home relieved but anxious. For even before
the sinusitis and arthritis attacked her the relaxing climate of
Wells in its hollow in the hills, combined with the dampness of the old house where we lived, a dampness which in
those days frequently meant water oozing up through the
floors, had not suited her and she was afraid of what would
happen when she returned to it.

Then deliverance came from this fear too for my father
was offered a canonry at Ely Cathedral, combined with the
Principalship of the Theological College. He went down to
Ely and found a little city built on a hill in the open breezy
fen country, and an airy dry house standing high with bay
windows facing south. Closer inspection revealed that the

roof was in bad repair and there was no bathroom. The new wonder, the Wells bath, would have to be left behind. There was however a well in the middle of the stone-floored apartment called the servants' hall. There were also drains, but the roots of the grand old garden trees had grown into them, and hindered them in the performance of their duties.

My young and hopeful parents in the first flush of their enthusiasm brushed these little matters aside as irrelevant. They wanted a climate that would be good for sinusitis and they wanted to do the will of God. There was sometimes a little difficulty between them because my father's more melancholy mind tended to think the will of God was what he didn't want to do, while my mother in her congenital optimism was generally certain that her will and God's coincided. But there was no friction this time because my mother had suffered so much in Wells that neither of them doubted that the sunny bay windows were the gift and will of God. Also my father loved Somerset so passionately that I am sure he knew that he would leave his heart behind him in its sacred earth and also that never again would he be so happy in his work as he had been at Wells. So there he had his slice of self-sacrifice to make him happy, and also the cheering thought that Queen Anne would help with the drains.

In those far-off days part of the normal duty of any priest of the Church of England was the upkeep of a large house, and larger garden, upon a salary insufficient for the purpose. It was what the poor man did because it was what he had always done, and whatever always has been done in the context of religion appears for conservative-minded lovers of tradition to be the will of God and so is not questioned; or was not questioned by past generations. Except perhaps by Queen Anne when she endowed the bounty from which poor clergymen in financial difficulties could borrow. And so we went to Ely in a state of euphoria and found that what Queen

Anne could lend us was insufficient for our needs. She could and did renovate the drainage system and place a modern floor over the stone flags and the well in our servants' sitting room; for even in those days families had ceased to like a well as a central ornament in a living room; but she could not mend the roof and my father had to sell his valuable collection of foreign stamps started in his boyhood, and his collection of coins and any other family treasures he could find. But even then he remained in debt for some while.

But he was rewarded by my mother's pleasure in Ely. As well as her sunny bay windows she rejoiced in the sense of being lifted up on the little Isle of Ely just as she had once been lifted up on her own Island. The fens were like the sea for one could look for miles over their ever-changing colours, green of the young wheat or gold of the harvest fields, and the great blue-shadowed stretches of white snow in winter, and see the magic point where the horizon meets the sky. As pleasure turned to joy her health improved, since joy is the greatest healer in the world, and at Ely she enjoyed more freedom from the miseries of the body than she knew at any other time between my birth and her death.

And so no wonder we loved Ely so intensely; even my father gradually put down some roots in fen-land earth and began to forget about the heart left behind in Somerset. And for me Ely was the home of all homes. We all have one home in particular which, as the years go on and we move from one to the other, seems to contain the other homes within itself. I have a Russian toy, a wooden painted egg-shaped box representing the figure of a peasant woman, a smiling protective mother-figure. Inside the box, one within the other, are four smaller peasant women, all delightful, but the one who holds them is the best of all. Five boxes, and I have had five homes, all of them lovely, but Ely is the mother-figure.

2

How can one describe the place? Wells was fairyland, in my memory a diaphanous cathedral and a city so hidden from the world that it seemed to have dropped out of the world, but Ely had the hard strength of reality. The cathedral had nothing diaphanous about it but was a great brooding presence that could at times be terrifying, so much so that at that time there were many people living in Ely who had never dared to go inside it. It leaped on you like a lion, taking you captive beyond hope of escape, but the lion was Aslan the divine lion and once the bondage had been accepted the pursuer became protector. When the winter gales came, or the great thunderstorms of summer roared in a darkening sky, the tall tower looked like a giant's mighty arm held up to keep the storm from falling on the city, and wherever one went on the sea of the fen one could always see the tower standing up like a lighthouse. Without it one might have felt lost and desolate in the vast flatness that lay so helplessly beneath the huge dome of sky, but with it one was safe; tied to it by an invisible cord through which a tremor ran when it was time to go home.

Visitors to the cathedral could approach it in two ways. In those days a flat road ran from the railway station to the foot of a hill so sudden and surprising that it seemed a precipice. At the top of the hill a stranger, choosing the first way, could go straight on to the Cathedral green and the west front. Entering the Cathedral under the tower he would get his first sight of the interior of the place looking from west to east along the whole stretch of the Norman nave. To enter the nave suddenly on a hot day is like diving into the sea; it is so cool inside, and so amazing, and so utterly another world from the one left behind only a few moments ago. The whole of history seems to fall upon you, and because of the great length of the place there is a sense of unendingness.

In the beginning a tower stood at the crossing of the transept, almost at the centre of the Cathedral. In the year 1322 this tower crashed down and the central portion of the Cathedral was in ruins. But two great men set themselves to bring resurrection out of disaster, the sacrist of the Benedictine monastery, Alan of Walsingham, and a master carpenter called William Hurley. Instead of rebuilding the tower Alan of Walsingham designed a stone octagon supported by four Norman columns, with above it a lantern sixty feet high built of oak wood, the outside covered with lead, suspended in mid air ninety-four feet above the Cathedral floor. It is a feat of engineering that takes the breath away. And so does the beauty of it. One looks up and up to where, at the highest point of the lantern, a carving of the triumphant Christ, head and shoulders surrounded by the rays of the sun, looks down with his hand raised in benediction.

But if you wish to come first to the octagon you approach the Cathedral another way, through the south door, and this is reached by turning right at the top of the steep hill and going in under the gateway known as the Porta. Again you are in another world, not this time of history and eternity but a place of green peace where in the season of blossom bees hum in the tall lime trees, and in the days of my childhood cows and sheep were pastured in grass and buttercups.

This green space is surrounded by the little city yet it looks so rural that it might be in the heart of the country. Both Wells and Ely are very individual places and scorn to call their cathedral precincts the Close, like most other cathedral cities. In Wells they are called the Liberty and in Ely the College. Grouped near the Cathedral are the bishop's palace, the deanery and the canons' houses. When we lived there the bishop's palace was on the green to the west of the Cathedral, but it was an enormous place and is now a hospital.

The deanery then became the palace and the house where we lived is now the deanery. It is not striking outside, for the Victorian addition has made it sunny but not beautiful, but the heart of the house is Norman. There was a famous Benedictine monastery at Ely, and our house enclosed part of the infirmary. The lower half of the pillared infirmary chapel formed part of our stone-floored kitchen regions, and if that sounds sacrilegious it is at least unique to have a Norman larder.

The upper part of the chapel had been divided off from the lower and formed a separate room which was my father's study, and if he never loved Ely as much as he loved Wells he loved this study with his whole heart. Here he prayed and worked on a level with the heads of the Norman arches, their capitals carved with the arrow-headed reeds that grow in the fens. The two windows looked east and west, east towards the fen, west down a narrow lane that ran between old canonical houses to the Cathedral. One went down steps to the narrow doorway of the study and on entering found a wall to the right and on the left the ominous darkness of that invaluable bookcase. Somewhere round on the other side of it was my father at work, but it was very dark between that wall and the bookcase. I was only eleven when we went to Ely and if I was entering the study conscious of my misdeeds I found that narrow dim place most alarming; especially with my father dead silent round the corner, no sound to be heard except perhaps the faint scratching of his pen.

If the study was a little frightening to a child my mother's upstairs drawing room, with three large sunny windows looking over the garden, was the warmest as well as the loveliest in the big, rambling, cold old house. For the house was remarkably cold, not with the penetrating dampness of Wells but with the east winds from the fen that caught it full blast on its little hill. Our predecessors in the house had fought the cold by installing in the hall a peculiar monster resembling those seen in pictures of prehistoric beasts. He was called the Tortoise Stove and had a tortoise sculptured somewhere on his iron mail. He also had a huge metal chimney that reared up like a proboscus and disappeared in a hole in the wall to go I know not where. In the winter a fire was lit in his belly and on calm days he shone with a soft glow and gurgled gently in his sleep, but on windy days he became red-hot all over and roared and bellowed. His temper was then considered to be dangerous, and we would approach him carrying bowls of cold water that we placed as propitiatory offerings at his feet and upon his scaly back. But he must have been a good monster at heart for he never exploded, never did us any harm at all, and served us faithfully through all the years we lived at Ely.

For me personally his chief use was not for warmth for I spent many happy hours making toffee on him. The accomplished cook who took the place of Sarah was too efficient a person to want children under foot in the kitchen, and the hours I had been used to spend toasting myself in front of the kitchen range at Wells I now spent making toffee with Tortoise. I loved him dearly. He had a distinct personality, hot-tempered but good-natured with it, a friendly sort of dragon, though friendlier when not red-hot. I was with him when I had to say good-bye to Nanny.

This good-bye was the one shadow on the move to Ely. I was to have a daily governess to prepare me for boarding school, my mother was now well enough to manage without a nurse and my father made a terrible decision. A man in debt to Queen Anne was not justified in keeping a Nanny permanently in his household for no reason except that she was beloved, and so Nanny must go. I was told about it but children do not understand the meaning of a grief that they have not as yet experienced, and I received the news with total incomprehension. How can a child understand that someone who has been the foundation of life from the beginning is not going to be there next week? It is the same as being told that the earth itself will not be there on Wednesday. The situation cannot be understood. It was not until she said goodbye to me in the hall, and for the first time in my life I saw her weeping, that I realised what was happening to us. I clung to her, but it was no good, she pulled herself away and blind with tears went out to the cab that was waiting at the door, got in and was driven away.

Then I knew. She was not just going away for a holiday, she was going for good. She might visit us but she would never live with us again. She was going to live with another mother and another child. She would love another mother and child, not us any more. Nanny had gone. I doubt if any of the partings of my life have plunged me into quite such total desolation as this one did. I stayed for a while in the hall with Tortoise and then went back mechanically to the unfortunate new governess from whom I was careful never to learn one single thing. Not only was my mind closed against her, it was closed in the face of learning for many years to come.

If my desolation was so great what could my mother's have been? Nanny had been with her when the flood of illness and pain had overwhelmed her youth, and it had perhaps been Nanny rather than her husband who had comforted her most as she struggled to find her feet and conquer her despair. My father was always a great strength to her, I know, but her instinct was always to spare him . . . I do not think anyone ever tried to spare Nanny . . . I wish I could say that my mother and I comforted each other but I cannot remember that we did. My mother was a very proud as well as a very brave woman and in the whole of our life together I never once saw her cry. When she wept she did it alone and no one would have dared intrude upon her. She faced the world in the manner laid down by King Alfred. "If thou hast a woe tell it not to the weakling, tell it to thy saddle-bow and ride singing forth." Any emotional display, any voicing of sentiment that was not entirely sincere, roused her anger. She would cheerfully deceive people for their good, as she did when she let my father think she enjoyed hearing him read aloud, but in the things of the human spirit she demanded truth.

3

The top floor of the tall rambling house was extraordinary. There were six rooms, the schoolroom and five bedrooms with steps leading up and down between them and a huge skylight in the roof above the landing. One felt as though on board ship, there was so much light and air up there, and when the wind blew from the fen such a turbulence of sound. Other small girls joined me daily in resistance to education. I do not think our poor governess enjoyed herself, but we did. The schoolroom was over the drawing room, a big room taking the curve of the roof. I had been allowed to choose the colour scheme and so the walls were white and the door, window and exposed beams were painted the bright corn-flower blue which at that period was my favourite colour. There was the usual big schoolroom table, uncomfortable chairs, a wooden cupboard, bookcases and an upright piano. There were two windows facing south and east and I remember the room was perpetually filled with sunshine. But then I have no memories of wet days in my childhood, I remember only the spectacular thunderstorms, great gales and the whiteness of snow, never dull drizzling rain. Yet I also remember the umbrella stands with metal trays to take the drips, and the enormous goloshes. So it must have rained.

The south window looked over the front garden and had a view of the old walnut tree surrounded in spring with hundreds of aconites growing in the grass. But the glory of the room was the east window. The tall house was at the summit of the little Isle of Ely and from the east window one looked out as from a tower over the vast stretch of the fen reaching to the distant line of the horizon. The colours of the fen, especially in the days of harvest, were lovely. They changed with every passing cloud and when the floods were out in winter they mirrored the sky. When later I went to boarding school and the schoolroom became my bedroom I had my bed by the east window, and could watch the sun come up over the horizon and paint a huge skyscape of clouds lilac and saffron and crimson and rose. I developed a love for Ruskin in those days, partly because he could paint a skyscape in words as it seemed to me that no one else could do.

If I had closed my mind to learning in the academic sense I had not closed it to books, for I did not consider that books were education, and if I learned nothing else in my schoolroom I learned to read. Flat on my stomach I read the Andrew Lang fairy books, the Waverley novels and Dickens, and later in an upright position much of Thackeray and Trollope and the Brontës, and last of all Jane Austen. I read them in that order, an order prescribed by my father. I read as children do, by suction. My sight was so good and my body so free from aches and pains that I did not know reading could have a physical side to it. A book just flowed in. But unfortunately it did not stay in, for no good fairy had given me the gift of a good memory at my christening, and a lifetime spent in learning poetry by heart has not supplied the lack. Because of it I am totally uneducated. If I have to study a subject for a book I want to write I forget all I have learnt as soon as the book is finished. If I need the same knowledge later for another book I have to go back to the beginning again.

But if I have no memory I have been blessed and cursed with a vivid and fertile imagination. It is no blessing to be

able to picture so clearly the fearful things that happen in the
world, and what I go through when those I love are flying the
Atlantic, driving on the roads in a fog, or even late for tea,
cannot be described. But for a writer imagination is certainly
a blessing, and in addition to my Channel Island heritage
I have not far to look for the cause of it. My first two homes
were enough to stimulate any child's imagination. They were
so unlike each other that they belonged to two different
countries of the mind. Wells, held in its benign and sheltered
cup in the hills felt very safe. Our house too I remember as
safe and cosy. Certainly one breathed in Wells the air of a
fourth dimension but it was the air of the fairy tales, or of a
peaceful book of saints and angels, and in that early garden
of Eden the snake was still safely asleep in the sun.

But Ely, though equally fourth dimensional, gave a sense
of safety that was the reverse of cosy. There was strength and
power there but it was an embattled power, and there was
an equal awareness of the strength of the enemy. For the
first time in my life I was aware of these things and afraid of
them, and nature in her stormy aspect seemed a warning
voice that trumpeted their coming. At evensong in the
Cathedral on a dark winter's night when the wind roared
round the walls, the candles guttered and the shadows of the
great place leaped and shuddered, I used to tremble.
Partly from the cold, of course, for the Cathedral was very
inadequately warmed by a contingent of Tortoises, but with
fear too. Though I could not have put what I feared into
words. On winter nights I was very afraid, coward that I was
and am, of the walk from home to the Cathedral, which when
my father was away or ill I had to take alone. If I went out
of the front door it was pitch dark and the trees of the park
were full of wind and whispers, but if I went out of the back
door and down the lane there was a haunted house on my
right and another on my left and either ghost might issue
out; not to mention our own ghost who had probably

walked out of the house behind me and at any moment might lay his hand on my shoulder as we went along. My parents never at any time forced church-going upon me and I faced these terrors because I wanted to. It was worth a few clammy shivers to be in the Cathedral.

The place had very soon taken me captive and it was by no means always frightening. On sunny days it was warm with colour, for the sun shone through the stained-glass windows and filled it with rainbows, but on the hottest days it remained cool. I have never been a lover of the hot days and I hope John Dunne was right when he said it will always be autumn in heaven. Spring is in such a hurry but autumn has the peace of fulfilment and a still warm autumn day, with a touch of cool frost night and morning, is the loveliest weather there is, and it was in the autumn, at the Feast of Saint Etheldreda, that the Cathedral was at its gentlest and loveliest.

Ely gave thanks that day not only for Etheldreda herself, queen and Abbess and patron saint, but for all benefactors of the Cathedral. On the evening of the feast we all stripped our gardens of their flowers and early next morning appeared in the Cathedral with arms full of michaelmas daisies, dahlias, Japanese anemones, the first chrysanthemums and the treasures of the last roses. All the morning we worked in the Cathedral and every tomb was decorated. The shrine of the Saint was always a bower of flowers but no one else was forgotten or neglected. I think there was a sort of hierarchy of decorators. The most accomplished ladies did the shrine, those who were gifted but not quite so gifted did the more important of the tombs and the children were given bunches of flowers and greenery and a few jampots and pushed to-wards obscure tombs and dark corners. I have a bright bit of memory of myself and some jampots and a bunch of left-over flowers alone with some nameless tomb. I do not re-member whereabouts in the Cathedral it was, but I remember that it was low to the ground and easy to reach and that arranging the flowers, atrociously I am quite sure, gave me a feeling of quiet rapture. There seemed something personal about it as though I were giving flowers to someone I knew quite well. In the afternoon there was a festival service and the choir processed all round the Cathedral, past the flower-laden tombs, singing 'For all the saints'. Afterwards I think there was a tea party somewhere, probably at the deanery, with a good deal to eat.

It was a great occasion and there was nothing to equal it except the festival evensong on Christmas Eve. The choir sang parts of Handel's *Messiah* under the lantern and I can never hear 'Wonderful, Counsellor, the Prince of Peace', without seeing again the shadowy height of the lantern soaring above our heads with the figure of Christ at its apex. When the service was over the big congregation passed down to the west end of the nave and sang 'Now Thank We All Our God'. Another year had passed and a new year would soon begin and when the singing was over the bishop blessed us.

4

After Christmas would come the season of the bitter cold, and chilblains. All children had chilblains in those days as a matter of course, not only on hands and feet but sometimes on noses and ears as well. Now most of them are spared the infliction. Was it the cold of the houses in those days that gave them to us, or were we fed wrongly? We were dressed warmly enough, in woollen combinations, flannel petti-coats, serge bloomers, reefer coats, gaiters, muffs and mittens, but something must have been lacking and when cold fingers and toes warmed up and came alive the irritation was agonising; though it could be relieved by rushing to the bathroom, if you had a bathroom, and holding feet and hands alternately under the cold tap and then under the hot.

But for the children there could be a wonderful compensation. The floods and the skating. Provided it rained hard enough before Christmas the dykes overflowed, and if the river Ouse, winding its way from Cambridge, overflowed too that was an added glory. If the floods were very bad indeed the fens could be under water almost as far as you could see. The little fen villages seated upon their small hills, the churches crowning the summits of the hills, and the windmills on their hillocks, rose up out of the water like the castle-crowned islets in Swiss lakes. For the villages and for those who lived in the lonely farms in the fen these floods could mean tragedy, but the Ely children were not concerned with this aspect of the floods. With intense anxiety we waited for the great freeze-up and it seldom failed us. The children, and grown-ups too, emptied themselves joyously out of the little city and down on to the ice, and the scene could almost equal for picturesque beauty the pictures of the Dutch masters. If the frost was hard enough and lasted long enough it was possible for the river Ouse itself to freeze over, and then the masters of the art could skate all the way to Cambridge. I have never managed to be proficient at any single outdoor sport but I remember floundering joyously along clinging to the back of a wooden chair, sliding and snowballing all in the glow of a great fen sunset flaming across the ice and snow. But there was always a nagging anxiety at the back of the mind. How long would the frost last? One day there would come a south wind and a cracking of the ice and the bliss would be over.

Then it was spring again and little girls were riding their ponies along the droves, under the branches of wild crabapple blossom, for small girls went mad about horses then as now, while their brothers preferred bicycles.

I had learned to ride at Wells on a Devonshire pony with a

long tail borrowed from an old lady who lived in the Liberty. It pulled the governess cart she kept for her grandchildren but it was a gay little pony and could gallop fast and well. I was taught to ride first by our gardener and then by one of my father's students, who took me up to a magic stretch of green turf above the Tor woods and taught me and the pony to go like the wind. At least the pony and I thought we were going like the wind, it felt that way to us, but if I looked up at the tall young man on a tall horse beside me they did not seem to be exerting themselves at all. While we were going at full stretch they were merely cantering easily. I remember I looked up at that young man as though he were one of the gods upon Olympus and I remember gratefully his great kindness to a small child, and the gentleness of his teaching. Never be afraid, he said. If you are afraid you communicate your fear to your horse. Fear is a dreadful thing, so easily communicated that it hurts others as well as yourself. Never be afraid of anything. I wish I had listened to him more attentively. I also remember of him that he seemed to love horses only a little less than he loved God. He wanted to be ordained to the priesthood, so he said, that he might go out to Australia and have there a parish so large that he would be obliged to spend his life in the saddle. One cannot think of a better way of combining love of God and horses and Saint Francis would have approved of it.

Riding at Ely was more restricted. The only pony I could get hold of was the milkman's, and he could only be borrowed at hours suitable to the milkman. He was a large stout pony with a very broad back and he could not be persuaded to go faster than he was accustomed to go when he took the milk round, in a cart shaped like a Roman chariot with rows of polished milk churns shining in the sun. Also he was old and he liked to stop now and then, to put the milk down and to rest. The other little girls rode rather similar mounts but we were not irked by our leisurely progress because the winding

narrow droves in spring were not places where one wished
to hurry. They were too beautiful.

The droves were the ancient roads through the fen, linking
the old farms and hamlets one to another. They were
grass tracks, perfect for horses and wheeled farm carts but
impossible for cars. They went on for mile after mile, a
network of communication that spread over the fen, and
one could ride or walk along them for hours and never come
across another human creature. They were bordered with
stunted trees, sloes and hawthorns and wild crab-apple. I
can shut my eyes now and smell that apple blossom and
am quite convinced that no other apple blossom in the world
ever has, or ever will, smell quite like it.

In the shade of these trees bordering the way grew enormous cowslips. There was much waste ground in the fen in
those days and whole fields would be cloth of gold from
hedge to hedge. In D. H. Lawrence's *Sons and Lovers* there is
a description of just such a field, a description so perfect that
when I read it I could have wept; for sheer joy at the marvel
of the poet's writing and also for sorrow, for the Ely cowslip
fields and the droves that do not exist any more. The old
ways still link the farms, it is true, but they are macadamised
and the trees have been cut down. It is right that there
should be no more waste land but could there not be a
cowslip sanctuary somewhere? A patch of them preserved
as fritillaries are preserved in Magdalen Meadows at Oxford;
to show a later generation what fields looked like once upon a
time.

In the droves we sometimes came upon encampments of
gypsies, real gypsies, living in dark tents like igloos with a
small painted wooden caravan drawn up against the hedge.
There would be a camp fire and horses grazing and round-
eyed children who gazed at us in utter astonishment, as
though we were creatures from another planet. Sometimes
they could return our greetings in halting English, some-

times they knew only the Romany tongue. Many of the gypsy women were beautiful.

In the early days of the 1914–18 war my father and I were out for a walk. He was an inveterate walker and however busy he was he hardly ever missed his daily tramp. He had taken me for walks as soon as I could stagger, suiting his pace to mine, but when it came to suiting my pace to his I could not face his sort of walk more than once a week, so great was the speed and the mileage. But that day we were far out in the fen down a long drove when a tall vigorous young gypsy leaped over the hedge and confronted us. But he was not there to rob, he only wanted information, and he could speak excellent English. "They say there's a war on, sir. What's it about? How's it going?" My father told him about it. He listened attentively and very seriously and seemed to understand. Then he thanked my father politely and went back over the hedge. I have often wondered about him. Did he merely want to know about it or did he want to fight? Did he afterwards enlist?

I was once told by a man who had commanded a regiment of fen men in the war that they made the finest possible soldiers. They had immense courage and toughness and if told to hold a position they would do so until they died there. It had never been easy to wrest a living out of the fen. In past years, if the dykes burst, winter floods could drown the stock and wreck their homes. If harvests were ruined they could face near starvation. Many of the farms were so isolated that the children would die, and mothers would die in childbirth, because the doctor could not get there in time. They knew the meaning of tragedy better than most. They were a dour and difficult people and when we first went to Ely we adjusted to them with difficulty.

In friendly Somerset, if you stopped at a lonely Mendip farm and asked for a drink of goat's milk, you were received with the utmost joy. You were taken into the parlour, a chair was dusted for you and you were made to feel that your arrival and yourself were the great events of the day. Should it be tea time the larger farms were always ready to regale you with homemade bread and wortleberry jam, and a lunch of bread and cheese at a country pub was the most delicious meal in the world, with beer for the menfolk and lemonade for the ladies and children. The lemonade bottles had large round marbles as stoppers, made of greenish glass. Sometimes even now, if you are lucky, you can find one digging in an old garden or among the pebbles on the beach.

But if you knocked on a door of a grim-looking little fen pub, or at a farm, and asked for nourishment, more than ready to pay for it, you might very well have the door slammed in your face. That is, if that was the way they happened to be feeling that day. They might of course, though that was rare, be feeling hospitable. They were truthful people and acted as they felt. I do not think that any Somerset man or woman, even though some grief or illness in the house had momentarily clouded their natural hospitality, would ever have banged a door in an expectant face however much they wanted to. Moving from one county to another it was necessary to get used to the change of temperament. It was rooted in the soil and the weather. The life of the poor in friendly west country valleys was never so starkly grim as it could be in the fen.

Though not in high summer. When I think of summer in the fen I think of the long summer holidays, of water and tall rushes and the sound of oars in the rowlocks. Water picnics were the delight of children in the hot days and we were for ever badgering our elders to take us up the river to the fen waterways, to bathe and picnic and see the swans and the herons. My father was a good oarsman and if he had a free day did not take much persuading. A couple of families would perhaps join together, would hire two or three boats and with sandwiches and bottles of lemonade would go out for the day. There would be a fairly long scull up the river and then we would turn aside up one of the quiet waterways, the fresh smell of water mint in our noses, the tall rushes rearing up like an army of spears on either side, and make our way slowly and peacefully to where we wanted to be.

There were patches of the fen that had purposely been kept in their original wild state; rare butterflies were to be found in them, and rare plants. It was a paradise for the botanically-minded, and for the historically-minded too for everything there was as it had always been. This was the fen as Hereward the Wake had known it, and Etheldreda and the monks of Ely. And for the children there was the fascination of the water birds. The herons, tall and meditative, had something in common with the windmills and the church towers. They broke the flatness of the grey-green sea of rushes and water with sharp notes of contrast. Something aspired upwards for once, instead of flowing on and on into eternity under the vast dome of the empty burning blue sky. It was possible to come home from these fen days more tired than from a similar sort of day spent on one of the beaches in the Island. There was no shade in the fen and if a storm came, no shelter. It was a place of great beauty but sometimes also of fear.

5

If the Ely days were for my mother and me the happiest days they were hard ones for my father. He only had three years of the teaching he loved and then the war broke out, all his men went into the army and the Theological College was first closed and then re-opened as a war hospital. My father took on the work of young priests who had gone to France as army chaplains and was a parish priest again. He was also frequently a night orderly at the hospital. His parish work took him down to the poorer parts of Ely, at the foot of the hill and near the river. There was poverty there then, bad housing conditions and the sicknesses and distresses of old age. My father loved people, especially if they were ill or old, and in visiting he was happy and relaxed and able to bring great comfort and help.

Occasionally he took me with him and it horrified me to find that many old and dying people had no light and airy bedroom of their own, such as we had at home, but had their bed in the downstairs front room into which the front door frequently opened from the noisy street. With the one window filled with geraniums or an aspidistra it could be dark inside, overcrowded with heavy furniture and with a smell of cooking coming in from the kitchen beyond. I was distressed for the old people but I think now that they were perhaps happier in the front room, with their own people near them, than they are now in the bright hygienic geriatric wards of today. But if my father was a good parish priest in caring for sick and old people he failed utterly when it came to hordes of Sunday-school children. Accustomed as he was to lecturing to Oxford and Cambridge graduates he could not get his mind down to the children's level. Nor could he keep them in order. To his chagrin, and also intense amusement, the children defeated him.

The poverty and bad housing were the dark patch upon the beauty of Ely. It was that creeping evil that invades all lovely things, as dirt seeps into the corners of rooms and worms wriggle into fine-wrought furniture and perfect moulded fruit. For years I was pursued by a recurring nightmare. I would be taking part in some happy festivity when a sudden silence would fall and a stillness of horror. Then someone would point and we would see it, sometimes in the middle of the floor where perhaps we had just been dancing, or up in the corner of the ceiling. It was always

quite small and in different nightmares it would change
its shape. Sometimes it was some foul black creature, very
much alive but quite still as it bided its time, but at other
times it was merely some queer shape lying there on the
floor without movement, a sort of box. Whatever it was the
feeling of horror and terror was the same because either
symbol spoke of the same thing; the snake that crept into
Eden. We know what happens when the worm creeps in.
Some work of mercy inspired by love of God and man comes
into flower and for a while all is as God wanted it to be.
Then there is quarrelling and jealousy and the flower
sickens at the root. A war starts as a crusade of liberation and
at first a nation can be enriched by it, but somewhere along
the way there falls the retribution that waits for those who do
evil that good may come and they become as evil as the
thing they fight. The examples are legion and can cause a
despair that may destroy all faith in God.

The mysterious doctrine of the Fall has rescued many
from the misery of their atheism, and they have progressed
from this to the even more mysterious doctrine of redemption. At the end of it all, in the midst of the horror of a
collapsing and disappearing universe, perhaps men may
humble themselves to hand over the last dregs of their evil
to God and he will destroy it. When the first Great War had
got beyond the cheering and flag-waving stage and had
plunged into the ghastliness of the trenches and the shells
and the gas we felt very near to that final crash, and the old
Christian belief in the end of the world, a belief which the
scientists are underlying just now, was very much in our
minds. When one reads history it seems that often it is so
in the midst of disaster. The collapse of a civilisation, or of a
nation, can seem like a sort of rehearsal for a final ending.

The outbreak of war and my departure for boarding school
coincided. Personally, since I had no brothers and the young
men I knew had made little impression on my immature

and selfish heart, I am afraid I found the latter event the more distressing. In the tumult of boarding school I found myself no longer the centre of the universe. The knowledge was painfully acquired, and my homesickness, separated from my parents and Ely for the greater part of the year, was terrible, but something important happened to me there; I had my first meeting with the New Forest and the sea marshes of Keyhaven. But I cannot leave Ely for Keyhaven without remembering the Ely ghosts and the deep respect we had for them, and trying to sort out my thoughts upon the subject of extra-sensory perception.

CHAPTER VII

E.S.P.

I

I AM NOT REALLY QUALIFIED TO WRITE ABOUT WHAT WE call extra-sensory perception since I have not studied it enough, and have little to go upon but my own slight experience and what I have learnt from my astonishing mother, but nevertheless I am having a go. What was astonishing about my mother was not that she had remarkable psychic powers but that she resolutely refused to use them. The only explanation she would give me was that once in her youth she had terrified someone by what she did and had decided to turn her back on the whole business. She had also been repulsed by the behaviour of her naughty old grandfather, an amateur mesmerist, who had delighted to enliven a solemn dinner party by forcing the elderly members of it to do the cake-walk round the room against their will, to their shame and distress.

My mother thought it outrageous that one human being could have such power over another. At the very worst point of her illness in Wells, when no doctor could help her and it seemed she was dying, my father took her up to London to see a well-known spiritual healer. They travelled in one of those wonderful invalid coaches which were tacked on to trains in those days, complete with bed. As she was too ill to go to him the healer came to the hotel where they were staying to see her. She stood up to receive him, he took her hands and looked into her eyes and was transfixed. They stood so for a moment, then she pulled her hands away and said, "I am sorry, but I cannot have treatment from you,

I am going home again." He was greatly distressed, and so was my father who had had all the anguish of bringing a very sick woman all the way from Somerset to London, and now had to take her back with nothing accomplished. They both argued with her but she would not give way. Alone again with my father she said, "It was his eyes. They went right through me. He would have had great power over me. No human being must have that sort of power over another." Privately to my father the healer said, "I am so sorry, for I believe I could have helped her. Your wife has great powers and had she wished she could have been a very fine medium."

I could understand my mother's fear of domination, both in herself and others, and I could understand her dislike of the cultivation of psychic states simply for the sake of experiencing them, with no helpful purpose in view, for that way danger lies. But I could never understand why she turned away from the prayer of silence and of contemplation. When she was praying, as soon as the prayer of silence began gently to take her, she would break off. The thing which so many of us, myself for instance, so desperately long for, and are too self-centred to receive, she could have had, and she refused it. I have no explanation. Nevertheless in the prayer she allowed herself she found peace and strength to endure, and often a very sure knowledge of what she ought to be doing for other people, and though she abhorred any sort of prying into the future she would sometimes in times of tribulation feel a wave of warmth and joy breaking over her and she would say, "It will be all right," and it always was. One power my mother had which could be uncomfortable to live with. She often knew what people were thinking. They did not need to speak. And when one's thoughts were not what they should be, well, one wished her less gifted.

I have inherited very little of my mother's e.s.p., only enough to be a worry to myself and not much help to other people. Only twice in my life has telepathy enabled me to to know that someone I loved was in trouble and come up with the help needed. Sometimes I know when a friend is suffering or has died, at other times I do not. Often I am convinced that someone is in trouble and I write to find out what it is and nothing is the matter. I cannot trust my intuitions. My dogs have always known far more than I do; but then the powers of animals are so exquisite that ours dwindle to nothing beside them.

But meagre though my small shoots of perception were my mother discouraged them whenever they appeared. When I tried to tell her about my encounters with our Ely ghost, whom I disliked intensely, she made no comment. That she also had her meetings with him I have no doubt, but she would not say that she did, and when I asked if I might change my haunted bedroom for another she referred the matter to my father, who from first to last of our time in that house remained untroubled by our ghost. He was not a man to see things, hear things or imagine things. He belittled himself when he said he had nothing of the mystic in him, and no imagination whatever, but he was a hardworking intellectual who prayed and toiled from six in the morning till twelve o'clock at night, when he fell into bed and was instantly unconscious, and so had no interstices in his life through which bogles and their like could insert a clammy finger. Appealed to about my bedroom he had no intention of yielding to teenage bletherings but being a just man he said he would look into the matter of my ghost. We should exchange bedrooms for the night and he would sleep in my room, and hope to have a personal experience of the phenomenon. To my disappointment he reported in the morning that he had seen nothing, but nevertheless what with the howling of the wind round my high attic and the scuttling of the mice he had scarcely slept all night. Never had he experienced a noisier bedroom and I might change it for another.

So keeping the old schoolroom as a sitting room only I moved into a smaller and more sheltered room that looked out on the next-door garden; a peaceful green view, but I missed the sight of the sun rising over the fen. However, the ghost came there just the same, and when later I moved to yet another room he followed. But it was not as bad as it sounds for as these were my boarding school and college days, I was only at home in the holidays and he was not a very frequent visitor. Nor is he now. For I was not alone in seeing that ghost. Subsequent dwellers in the house have seen him too. I do not know how he appeared to them but to me he appeared as a grey-cowled monk with no face. Where his face should have been there was only darkness. The experience was always the same. I would wake suddenly from sleep as though woken up and alerted, and would find him standing beside me. I would feel fear and revulsion, a sense of struggle as though I fought against something, and then he was gone. He was not a pleasant person, not like the angel figure who haunted the next-door house but one.

This apparition was so unusual that Canon and Mrs Glazebrook, who lived in the house at that time, came to the conclusion that it was not a ghost at all. For what ghost stands still to have its portrait painted? And Mrs Glazebrook being a painter, that is what this ghost obligingly did. Yet it could inspire fear for it appeared in the spare room, and guests from the outside world were not acclimatised to the unexplainable as we were who lived always in the shadow of history and legend. One of the guests went to bed early in the Glazebrooks' spare room and was later heard frantically tugging at the bell-rope that hung beside her bed. It was answered by the old, serene and saintly housemaid who had been with her master and mistress for some years in that house and did not leave it until she died.

"What is the matter, miss?" she asked mildly.

"I cannot stay in the room with that!" cried the terrified

guest, and pointed to the beautiful figure who stood in the moonlight against a blank wall.

"Why, that's nothing to be afraid of," said the old maid soothingly. "I can see it in my room too and I call it my angel. When the moonlight leaves the wall it will go."

She fetched her mistress to comfort the girl and when the moon moved on so did the ghost. That was the extraordinary thing about this ghost. It appeared only when the moon shone upon a particular patch of wall, and upon the wall of the old maid's room above it. It was so to speak a double ghost, slightly smaller in the upper room. The portrait that Mrs Glazebrook painted and then showed to my mother portrayed a figure in a long robe, resembling a saint in a stained-glass window. It was as though the reflection of some window was cast upon the wall by the moonlight. But the window that could have cast such a reflection was just not there. Another theory advanced by someone was that the bright moonlight brought out the outlines of some hidden fresco. But that did not seem feasible either. The mystery was not solved while I lived at Ely, and whether that angelic figure can still be seen I do not know.

The house next to our own, on my left as I went out by our back door for evensong on dark nights, had something rather nasty. I never discovered what it was, I only knew that some guest, a male one this time, was reputed to have rushed headlong from the house in terror. The house on the right, also joined to ours, had been relieved of its haunting some years before our arrival. The family who lived there then had seen nothing but had been weighed down with a sense of misery in a certain part of the house. They endured it for a while and then alterations to the house required the pulling down of an old wall, and the skeleton of a walled-up monk was found behind it. The bones were taken away and buried and the misery went with them, but I could seldom walk down the lane without horrible thoughts of what it must feel like to be walled up. They were walled up in a standing position. The agony must have been hideous.

2

The question, what is a ghost? has bothered me until not long ago. That it is the spirit of a dead person is unthinkable. The punishment of being tied to a certain place, century after century, is one that a God of love would no more impose on a soul he had created than he would condemn it to eternal punishment in hell. There are those who have the faculty of seeing past events, as Miss Wordsworth and Miss Jourdain, visiting Versailles, found themselves in the Versailles of Marie Antoinette, and Miss Edith Olivier, an old friend of my father's, driving home one night in the dark towards Salisbury, and not knowing quite where she was, found herself driving down an avenue of giant megaliths. Then she guessed she was near Avebury. The avenue led her to the earthwork that surrounds the temple area, and here she left her car, and, climbing to the top of the bank, was delighted to see a fair, lit by flames and torches, taking place in the village. Later she discovered that the avenue of megaliths had disappeared years ago and that the Avebury annual fair had been discontinued in 1850.* But in these experiences the onlooker is in much the same position as a member of the audience in a cinema. The thing pictured has already happened and though he sees it as though it were happening still, and may even for a while feel that it is, he sees it only once. But a ghost is seen again and again and the sense of personal involvement is much greater and can be deeply troubling.

But now, in two very different publications, I have found a comforting explanation of the phenomenon we call a ghost.

*An Adventure by Miss Moberley and Miss Jouidain. Without Knowing Mr Walkley by Edith Olivier.

The suggestion is that it is not an earthbound spirit but a cast-off shell. As we go through life we leave old selves behind us as a snake leaves old skins. A man may go through the experience we call conversion and find himself a man re-born; the old faithless self is cast off and he goes on into life a new creature. For another there may be a long period of illness and then healing; the sick self is left behind and forgotten in the joy of renewed health. There may be a great grief, or some other rending or terrible experience, and the person who emerges from it is not the same.

According to the shell theory someone who has passed through great suffering, or perhaps great joy, in a particular place has lived so intensely that something of himself, some fragment of his eternal living, remains in the place and can be seen even though the person who suffered or enjoyed has passed to a new life and severed all connection with his cast-off shells.

It is a comforting theory but it does not quite explain the monk with darkness for a face. For why did he follow me from room to room? Possibly he did not follow me. The first 'seeing' was perhaps a genuine one but the others may have been mere hallucinations caused by my fear and revulsion; for the power of thought is so terrible that there is no doubt we can attract to us what we deeply fear. It does, however, explain another experience that made me unhappy for years.

Just after the last great war, when my mother and I lived in Devon, we had to have some work done on the cottage, and to get my mother away from the noise we rented a bungalow on the coast, a few miles away, and stayed there a month. It was a modern bungalow with a pretty garden looking over the sea, the war was over, the summer weather was perfect and we took with us a friend whom my mother and I loved dearly. It should have been a wonderful holiday but it was one of the longest months of my life. The owner of the bungalow was a widow, young and pretty, and she told me, when I went to see it, that she felt lonely since her husband's death and so she frequently let her home and went to stay with friends. There were three bedrooms and mine had the advantage of french windows opening on the garden and the disadvantage of a large bed with broken springs in the middle. The latter did not bother me since the bed was big enough for me to avoid them, but what did bother me was my sleepless misery. The moment I was in bed and had put the light out it fell on me, black and hopeless. Oddly enough I did not connect it with the man who had died. I explained it by tiredness, and by the fact that depression is the skeleton in the family cupboard. But there was no obvious reason for it to stalk out just now. The war was over and we were having a holiday.

About half-way through our time I went to bed for a day with some minor ailment. My mother had not been in my room until then because though it was next to her own even the short distance was a bit too much for her walking powers. But that day she came, though she got no farther than a few steps inside the door. Then she stopped and there was silence as the room made its impact upon her. "Nothing would induce me to sleep here," she said vehemently and went out and shut the door. A few days later our friend, a practical Scot who was nevertheless not Scottish for nothing, asked me if I would like to change rooms with her. "We should take turns with that mattress," she said. But I said no. She liked her room and I did not mind the broken springs. The look she gave me was penetrating but she did not argue. When we got home again she told me why she had made the offer. She had been in the kitchen looking through the very large hatch which gave her a view of the dining room, its open door opposite the door of my bedroom which was just across the passage. A man in a grey suit was standing in the dining room reading a letter. He finished the letter and still holding it walked across the room and the passage and disappeared into the room I was using.

The day we went home the owner of the bungalow arrived a little while before we were due to leave, and while we waited for the taxi she and I sat in the garden talking. She had told me before that she was lonely but now she told me that she was finding it hard to continue living in her home because she could not forget her husband's long illness. His room had been the one I had used, with the french window. They had chosen that one for him so that he should have easy access to the garden. I understood then, especially after our friend told me of the man reading the letter. There had been a time-switch and she had seen some incident in the past. Had he been reading a specialist's report, sent by his doctor and telling him he was fatally ill? I had picked up something of his misery, and so had my mother when she briefly visited his room. For a long time I hated to think of that experience because it seemed as though the man's spirit must be earthbound still, tied to the place where he had suffered. How could God allow such a thing? Why had he not been allowed to go free? The shell theory, when I finally reached it, was comforting. He had gone free. What the three of us had felt or seen in that bungalow was only the cast-off shell of his misery.

3

Yet sometimes I think the apparitions we see are not shells but real spirits; but they are the happy ones and we should rejoice to see them. Children, I think, see them most often. The story of a little boy whose encounter with a monastic ghost was happier than mine was told me by his mother. It was during the last war and she had accompanied her soldier husband to the training camp where he had been posted as commandant. They rented as a temporary home a very old house which, they were told, had once been a monastery. They themselves found it unpleasantly haunted but their small son was not aware of anything frightening; on the contrary he said the old man who wore a sort of dressing-gown with a rope round his waist, and sat on his bed and talked to him before he went to sleep, was a nice old man and he loved him. "He is teaching me a prayer," he told his mother. Presently he said to her, "I know the prayer now. I can say it." She asked him if he could say it out loud to her and he said yes, and carefully recited the Lord's Prayer in Latin, without hesitation or mistake. She was astonished. He had not yet been to any school and she could think of no living person who could possibly have taught it to him.

Into this category might come the playmates, unseen by the grown-ups, who come to play with lonely children; that is if these playmates are not merely projections of the children's own longing; and also the friendly but inquisitive spirits who keep an eye upon the welfare of a much-loved home. Something of this kind was experienced by Jessie, the friend with whom I live, myself and our dog, when twenty years ago we came to live in our 300-year-old Oxfordshire cottage. Our immediate predecessors had been here only for a short while. They had found the empty cottage, repaired and modernised it with great skill and then, finding it too lonely, they sold it to me. Its owner before them was a gallant old lady who is still remembered as the village washer-woman. She inherited the cottage from her father, the Rector's coachman, and lived in it for fifty years.

We had been here only a short while when we became aware of her presence; or we thought we were, for there is always that 'if'. We humans saw no one, but Tiki the dog most certainly did. In the evenings, when Jessie was out at some meeting or concert and I was alone in the living room

writing, Tiki would be lying on the floor beside me. Our long
raftered room was once two rooms, kitchen and parlour, but
my predecessors made one room of it. Tiki and I would be
at the parlour end facing what had once been the kitchen.
All would be quiet and peaceful and then suddenly Tiki
would leap to her feet and facing the corner of the room,
where perhaps there had once been a rocking-chair beside
the kitchen fire, would bark furiously at someone whom she
could see but I could not see. Finally, though the person
felt friendly, I am ashamed to say that I grew frightened and
on lonely evenings took to writing upstairs with Tiki lying
on my bed. But this ruse was not always successful for Tiki
would occasionly behave in almost the same manner. She
did not bark but she would sit up lift her head high and
growl at someone who apparently came into the room,
then her head would move round slowly as her dark eyes
watched that someone wander round the room and go out
again. Then Tiki would curl up and settle down once more.
Our little spare room, once the old washhouse, opens out of
the sitting room at the parlour end. We said nothing of our
haunting when a friend, a practical Yorkshire woman of
whom one would expect no odd fancies, came to stay with
us. She was aware of something. "I'm not at all afraid,"
she said, "but I cannot go into my room at night without
turning round and facing the far end of the sitting room. I
don't see anything but I have to face it, and then I am all
right. I can go into my room and shut the door."

Then, as we settled down in our new home and began to
love it dearly, Tiki ceased to bark and growl and no longer
even glanced at what I now call the rocking-chair corner. We
concluded that the old lady was satisfied and was no longer
visiting us. And yet only two years ago a friend came to stay
the night. He arrived in the morning very tired and after
lunch went to his bed for a rest. He emerged at tea-time en-

quiring, "Who's the old lady I've just seen in my room?"

I believe hopefully in sight-seeing ghosts, though to my knowledge I have never seen one, and if they exist I hope that after I die I may be allowed days off from purgatory to be one myself. We die with so many places that we long to see still unvisited. I have been luckier than most for many places that I longed to see I have seen, but there are many others that I know I shall not see in this life. But as a ghost, perhaps? I hope so. And better that way for one would travel so light, and miss the turmoil at the airports and not get tired. And there would be the extraordinary blessed loneliness of no one seeing you, though you are there.

I experienced this once in an unforgettáble dream. I was a ghost in my dream, not of the sightseeing sort but of the re-visiting old haunts variety. I was not visiting an old house but Peppard Church, whose spire I can see from my bedroom window and whose bell sounds across the fields to tell us the time. I confess with shame that I have never enjoyed church services; unless taking place in Ely Cathedral, and then it was the Cathedral that worked its alchemy upon the services and not the other way round. But there is an exception, a completely simple early-morning Communion service at any village church. At such a service one is not so much a complicated human being coming to a ritual that can be almost as complicated as oneself, one is that simple creature, the hart, coming to the water springs. And the place where they spring can become as beloved as one's home, and those who are with you there are no longer the congregation but the family. I was one with them in my dream, loving them, and yet because they could not see me I experienced at the same time that happiness which reprehensible solitaries like myself feel when they can slip into an empty church and be alone there. When they went up to the altar I went with them and knelt at the far end of the line, the

last of them. But I woke up just before the priest reached me
and so I cannot tell you what a priest does when confronted
with a ghost at the altar rail.

4

Devon as I knew it when I lived there thirty years ago,
before almost the whole county became a holiday playground and the fairies fled, was an unearthly place. The
round green hills where the sheep grazed, the wooded valleys
and the lanes full of wild flowers, the farms and apple orchards were all full of magic, and the birds sang in that long-
ago Devon as I have never heard them singing anywhere
else in the world; in the spring we used to say it sounded as
though the earth itself was singing.

The villages folded in the hills still had their white witches
with their ancient wisdom, and even black witches were
not unknown. I have never had dealings with a witch either
black or white, though Francis, our village chimney-sweep,
a most gentle and courteous man, was I think half-way to
being a white warlock. He was skilful at protecting his pigs
from being overlooked. He placed pails of water on the
kitchen floor to drown the Evil Eye and nothing ever went
wrong with his pigs before their inevitable and intended end.
And I think he had skill in the healing arts. He and his two
brothers and their old father all lived together in a grim
grey house, scorning female co-operation and wonderfully
happy without it. They were contented too to have no
medical attention; no doctor was allowed within those grey
walls and Francis saw to all their medical and surgical needs.
When the old father's poisoned finger became obviously
very bad indeed his sons took him down to the wood-shed
and chopped it off with a chopper, and with Francis's
skilful care it healed beautifully.

The author's parents when young

E.G. as a little girl—'a very spoilt child'

The Principal's
House, Wells

Wells Cathedral

The author's grandparents about the time of their marriage

Marie and E.G.   Aunts on Sunday

The author's grandmother with her 'Rain Umbrella'

Her father in the Ely garden

Ely Cathedral

The house at Christ Church
Canon Scott Holland in the garden he made

The author's mother at
Providence Cottage

uthor's father at Christ Church

Rose Cottage

Jessie and the author
Rose Cottage, 1953

Tiki when young

Randa

Randa with Jessie

Froda in her bower

The author

Black magic is a thing too vile to speak of but many of the white witches and warlocks were wonderful people, dedicated to their work of healing. I knew the daughter of a Dartmoor white witch and she told me how her mother never failed to answer a call for help. Fortified by prayer and a dram of whisky she would go out on the coldest winter night, carrying her lantern, and tramp for miles across the moor to bring help to someone ill at a lonely farm. And she brought real help. She must have had the true charismatic gift, and perhaps too knowledge of the healing herbs.

The father of one of my friends had a white witch in his parish in the valley of the Dart. She was growing old and she came to him one evening and asked him if she might teach him her spells before she died. They must always, she said, be handed on secretly from woman to man, or from man to woman, never to a member of the witch's or warlock's own sex, "And you, sir," she told him, "are the best man I know. It is to you I want to give my knowledge." Patiently he tried to explain why it is best that a priest should not also be a warlock, but it was hard for her to understand. "But they are *good* spells," she kept telling him. "I know they are," he said, "but I cannot use them." She was convinced at last but she went away weeping.

I think that in my heart I have always believed in fairies; not fairies as seen in the picture books but nature spirits whose life is part of the wind and the flowers and the trees. Born in the West-country, and returning to it in middle life, how could I do anything else? But, alas, I have never seen them. William Blake saw fairies, but he was a unique person, and so was a Dartmoor friend of mine who used to see them, and how I envied her! But if I did not see them I could feel how magic ran in the earth and branched through one's veins when one sat down. The stories that some of my Dartmoor friends told me would be laughed at by most people, but they were sensible persons and they did not laugh.

I think that probably the one among my friends who experienced most was the one who said least about it, Adelaide Phillpotts, Eden Phillpotts' daughter. She lived for years upon the moor and she loved it so deeply that she was not afraid to spend whole nights alone on the tors; but she is a mystic and mystics seem always unafraid. Her book *The Lodestar* is full of the wild spirit of the moor.

The friend who saw fairies, when she first went to live in her cottage on the moor, was visited early in the morning by a little old woman, wearing a bonnet, who walked quietly into the kitchen where she was preparing breakfast. Friendly and smiling the old woman refused breakfast but sat down to chat. She wanted to know exactly what my friend intended to do in the garden. What flowers would she have? What vegetables? She had very bright eyes and nodded her head in approval as they talked. She seemed a happy old woman, very much at home in the kitchen, but when my friend turned away for a moment she found on looking round again that her visitor had left her. She was never seen again and when the neighbours were questioned they denied ever having seen such an old woman in the village.

Another friend was driving back to her home on the moor one summer evening when she found herself in the most beautiful wood. She had no sense of strangeness but drove through it entranced by the loveliness of the evening light shining through the trees. Coming out of the wood she found herself at her home, put the car away and went about the normal business of the evening, and only gradually did she remember that her road home lay through an open stretch of moorland. There was no wood there; not now. The next day she went to see an old man who had lived all his life upon the moor and told him what had happened. He nodded his head. "I know the wood, ma'am," he told her. "I've been in it myself. But only once. You'll not see it again. It's only once in a lifetime."

This experience of a long-vanished wood is the same sort of experience as that of Edith Olivier at Avebury, and that of Miss Wordsworth and Miss Jourdain at Versailles. We can hardly ever have what we think is a unique experience without discovering it has been shared by many others. Only the details differ, not the experience. Two more examples are the moor terror and the singing in the lonely places, but these did not come to me on Dartmoor. Nothing surprising happened to me on Dartmoor; at least nothing more surprising than the sense of being lifted up into another world, enclosed in its own mystery and belonging to itself alone, and that happens to all of us when we climb up to the mountains or the moors. The keen air is like wine and we are not our valley selves as we watch the cloud shadows passing along the flanks of the hills, and listen to the sound of falling streams and the crying of the curlews. The whisper of wind stirring the grasses has a distinct voice, insistent at the door of our hearing, and behind it all the vast silence and stillness of this world of the heights seems like the stillness and silence of eternity itself.

Yet this surprise of entering another world is always new and fresh however often it comes. Spring is always new, and the first blue flower opening on the stringy tangle of a plant of morning glory is always a profound shock however much you were expecting it. Expectation, shock, wonder and worship. And terror too; not in the heart of the morning glory but in the heart of the silence and stillness. It seems to be of God, indeed almost to *be* God, but the moors and the mountains have their dark mysteries as well as their holy ones, and terror can leap out of the heart of what felt like a holy day just as suddenly as out of a dark and frightening storm.

I was in Skye when I had my only (I hope) experience of the moor terror. It was years ago when Skye was wilder than it is now. I was on a walking holiday with a friend, but

she was tired that day and I climbed up alone to the great
stretch of moorland behind the little hotel where we were
staying. It was a long pull and it was good to sit and rest.
There was not a sign of a human habitation or of another
human being. I felt alone in this magic world and gloried
in the loneliness. For once it was not raining in Skye, it was a
blue, still, warm day. I could see the Cuillins in the misty
distance and the blue line of the sea was not far away. The
bees hummed in the wild thyme but there was no other sound.
I sat without moving for I do not know how long, sinking
deeper and deeper into happiness and peace, and then
suddenly there was a loud, shattering, double-rap behind
me. It was like two mighty blows of a door-knocker in quick
succession, but much louder. I have sometimes been wakened
from sleep at night into a state of momentary fear by this
same double rap but this was infinitely more terrifying and
it came from exactly behind me. I jumped to my feet and
turned round but there was nothing to be seen; only the
empty miles of moorland quivering a little in the heat-haze.
But the terror remained. I was not brave enough to stay, and
left the lovely place more precipitately than I have ever
left anywhere. I did not actually run but the pace was good
and steady and did not slacken until I reached the homely
little hotel beside the harbour down below. It was years
before I spoke to anyone about this terrifying experience
and then I was told casually, "That's the moor terror.
Everyone has it at some time or other."

And many people too have heard the singing, though
I had not heard anyone speak of it until I heard it myself.
If I did hear it. . . For again there must always be that 'if'.
The subconscious mind can play queer tricks upon one,
projecting scents and sounds and images that appear to us
completely objective, but nevertheless their origin is within
ourselves. Or there may be a perfectly ordinary explanation

for what seems a very un-ordinary phenomenon; only we do not happen to know what the explanation is. Or, as is pointed out in that wonderful book by Renée Haynes, *The Hidden Springs*, an experience may be both objective and subjective. Some good or evil influence may be present in some particular place, at some particular time, an objective presence outside ourselves, and spiritually we are aware of it; but, if we see or hear anything, this may be merely the response and projection of our own subconscious mind. When we think of the phenomenon we call 'seeing a ghost' this can be an alternative to the shell theory. Well, whatever the explanation of the singing I heard I shall remember it until I die. It happened, of course, in Devon, where these un-explainable things are commonplace.

My mother and I had a cottage in an apple orchard at the edge of a village. Behind our cottage between the orchard and the village, was a steep hill. To the right Dartmoor was visible, but otherwise the place was a little valley in the hills that had a magic of its own. There were a few other small dwellings besides ours, an old house behind a high wall, a farm and some cottages, and so strictly speaking the place was not a lonely one, and yet, because of its particular magic, it was. Especially in the early morning, and especially after a snow-fall. There is something very lonely about a deep snow-fall and Devon snow, because the average rainfall is high, is almost always deep. One is walled in and cut off. The world seems very far away and the heart rejoices.

In spring, in Devon, there is often a sudden late snow-fall taking one entirely by surprise. I remember once seeing irises and tulips with their bright heads lifted above a deep counterpane of snow, and boughs of apple blossom sprinkled with sparkling silver. But the snow-fall that seemed to bring the singing was earlier in the year. There were only the low-growing flowers in bloom in the garden and they were all buried out of sight. There had been no wind in the night, no suggestion that the last snow of the year was falling, and when I drew the curtains early in the morning I was astonished to see the white world. And what a world! I had never seen a snow-fall so beautiful and I was out in the garden at the first possible moment. The snowclouds had dropped their whole treasure in the night and were gone. The huge empty sky was deep blue, the air sparkling and clear. The sun was rising and the tree shadows lay blue across the sparkle of whiteness. The whole world was pure blue and white and it seemed that the sun had lit every crystal to a point of fire. There was a silence so absolute that it seemed a living presence. And then came the singing.

It was a solo voice, ringing out joy and praise. One would have said it was a woman's voice, only could any woman sing like that, with such simplicity and beauty? It lasted for some minutes, and then ceased, and the deep silence came back once more. I stayed where I was, as rooted in the snow as the trees, but there was no return of the singing and so I went back to the cottage and mechanically began the first task of the day, raking out the ashes of the dead fire and lighting a new one. The light of the flames helped me to think. None of us, in the little group of dwellings in the valley had a voice much above a sparrow's chirp. No one in the village that I knew of had a voice like that. It was war-time and visitors from the outside world seldom came. Even if by some extraordinary chance some great singer had descended upon us, what would she be doing struggling down the steep lane from the village in deep snow at this hour of a cold morning? And wouldn't I have seen her? I could see both lanes from the little terrace outside the cottage and had seen no one. There were only two explanations. Either I was mad or I had heard a seraph singing.

Later when I took my mother her breakfast I told her of the singing. She looked at me and, as usual, made no comment whatever.

And so, for some years, I inclined to the former view and I told no one else about the singing. And then, one day after the war had ended, a very sensitive and sympathetic cousin came to visit us and told me about a holiday he had had in the wilds of Argyll. He had always wanted, he said, to talk to someone who had heard the singing and at last he had come upon an old crofter who could tell him about it. The old man had been alone in the hills when he had heard a clear voice, unearthly and very beautiful, singing in the silence. He could see no one, he could distinguish no words in the singing and the song was one he did not know. He tried to hum the air and my cousin tried to write it down, but they neither of them made much of a job of it. "You never heard it again?" my cousin asked and the old man said, like the old country-man who was in the wood only once, "No, never again." My cousin told his tale so beautifully that I was too awed and shy to tell him, then, about my own experience. Besides, the great paean of praise that I had heard in the snow seemed at that moment a little theatrical in comparison with the soft unearthly singing in the hills of Argyll. But, some years later, I did tell him. He was very kind, and he did not doubt my sincerity, but somehow I seemed to see at the back of his mind the figure of a stout lady from Covent Garden who had somehow or other, even in war-time and deep snow, got herself hidden behind the fir trees at the corner of our Devon garden. It does not matter. I remember that singing every morning of my life and I greet every sunrise with the memory. The birds, who had been singing so riotously, had been chilled to silence by that snowstorm. I have decided now that she, whoever she was, sang their dawn-song for them.

5

Dreams have for us all a perennial fascination, and no wonder, for they are so mysterious. Birds are equally mysterious, and they are connected in my mind, perhaps because of a marvellous bird whom I once saw in a dream, but also because one so often passes from a good dream to the sound of the birds singing in the early morning, and the two seem to merge into one. Not that my dreams are always good since all my life I have suffered from nightmares, but I refuse to call nightmares dreams because the word 'dream' for me signifies an experience of mystery and loveliness. Nightmares are not lovely and they are not generally mysterious, merely the result of fear or pain, or a recapitulation of some dreadful thing heard of, or read of, or perhaps experienced. Now and then there does indeed come some strange evil dream that cannot be pigeon-holed, and for that reason is not forgotten, but I think not often. And what I call 'wanderings' are not proper dreams either, just a mere jumble of the impressions and events of the past few days, through which one pushes one's way vaguely as though through the rubbish of a junk shop, and which upon waking one immediately forgets.

Real dreams seem to me to fall into two categories, the dreams of heaven and the magical fairyland dreams. Of the first I would dare to say that though they are symbolically experienced the picture represents the truth. These come to me very rarely but those who are nearer the unseen world than I am are I expect more fortunate. It is hard to share these particular dreams with anyone for they are a nothing when put into words, yet they are never forgotten, and the comfort and strength they give is lasting. They are linked, I think, to the waking-dreams which give glimpses of the future, and in which commands seem to be laid upon us which must be obeyed. They are teaching-dreams.

Yet there is another kind of experience in sleep which

goes deeper and is not remembered upon waking, and we all know it. We simply wake up in a state of unbelievable joy, and upon the rare occasions when this has happened to me I had fallen asleep in a state that was the very reverse of joyous. Where have we been that against all probability we bring back with us this joy? Perhaps it is possible for the soul to leave the body for a while, as the Egyptians believed, and as many believe today; only these modern believers would, I think, speak of the astral body rather than the soul. The golden bowl is not broken but the silver cord is sufficiently loosed to allow us to float out and travel a little way beyond the confines of our normal living. I was told that an anthology had been made of the experiences of those who die but whose hearts were set beating again by one of the terrible mechanisms of modern medical science. A few said they were aware of the silver cord, that they even saw it. But it was not allowed to carry them completely free. They were drawn back again from 'the green peace' to the prison of the painful body.

Even without dying it is possible to find oneself looking at a body from which, or so it appears, one is momentarily parted. In illness people frequently do this, or after some sudden shock. I think I know a little how they feel; though whether my experience was a true one or a dream I cannot know, for there are dreams (and nightmares too) when what is happening to you appears to be happening in your own bed, or your own room, and it is hard to know if you are awake or asleep. I had fallen into deep sleep with a light still burning beside my bed. I awoke and I felt as though years, not hours, had passed. I did not know where I was, only knew I was in pitch darkness but thinking clearly. My mind seemed to be instructing me, "You are between life and death. Wait. In a moment you will be in the life beyond death." I waited, not at all afraid, full of hope. But my mind was mistaken, for what I slowly became aware of was not what

I had hoped for; it was a sense of slipping back once more
into my body on the bed and then seeing the light burning
on the table beside it. Becoming one with my body again
I had a feeling of disgust; it was so heavy, so gross. There was
no joy in that particular awakening.

Then there are the fairytale dreams, all alight with colour
and beauty, experienced sometimes alone, sometimes in the
company of others, but perhaps because I have loved the
beauty of the world too much and people not enough these
companions almost always fade away upon waking while the
landscapes remain with me. . . That is unless the companion
of a dream is someone I love who has left this world. Then
I remember. . . One landscape in particular remains with
me. I had come to it struggling up some steep hill out of mist
and darkness. Reaching it was like bursting open the door of
some dark house and being hit between the eyes by the
sun. The dividing line between the darkness of the hill and
the flooding light was one of those familiar drystone walls of
the West-country. I could lean upon it and look out over the
valley below to the mountains that were the dream's horizon.
The valley contained all the familiar things, meadows and
streams, farmsteads and grazing sheep, shadowed woods and
the open patches of golden gorse. The mountains were distant
but clear and rainbow-coloured. It was a familiar beauty.
Only the light and the peace had a clearness and depth that
were not quite of earth; perhaps because of the knowledge
that they were eternal things that could not be clouded or
broken. There was no sound in this dream, everything was
held in a charmed silence and nothing stirred. But in another
dream a magnificent wind swayed the great trees upon a
vast rolling green hillside, waking voices in them.

My father loved the beauty of the world perhaps even
more than I do but his love for human beings equalled it.
Being both of us great dreamers we sometimes told each
other our dreams, and one of the delights of his were the

people he met. They were none of them people he knew, or had known, in his waking hours but they were his friends nevertheless, and it was a delight to be in their company in dream after dream over a period of years. One of the wisest men I know has described a dream life even richer than my father's. "In one's sleep one may know of things one had no normal means of knowing; can think with a clarity of vision, even speak fluently in other languages in which one is normally halting." This man believes that between the material in which we live now, and the spiritual world to which we shall eventually pass after death but of which in the nature of things we can know so little, there lies an intermediate state, almost a fairyland, built up partly perhaps from our own dreams, longings and memories, into which we pass when we leave our bodies and in which we become progressively more and more aware of the penetrating light of the world beyond. The intermediate state is like a bridge between the so-called dead and those they have left behind. My friend thinks that "it is through some such dream world that they speak to us, still linked to past memories, still carrying the unmistakable imprint of their personality. But they are no longer limited by the confines of a factually constricting world, with its impassable barriers of time and space. They now live in perfect liberation from these."

Those who have lived to a great age and are longing for a release that does not come, or who are imprisoned in pain that will not let them go, say sometimes, "It is so difficult to die." Yet to those whom I have been with in their dying the actual moment of parting from the body has seemed to come so gently, with hardly more trouble than a petal has when a breath of air lifts it away from the flower. They seem gone as easily as that. So is it not possible for us too, in the deep sleep that is so like death, to leave our bodies and drift to them as gently as that and be with them for a short while in that

intermediate world of beauty; and if they have passed beyond
it to the world of light do they not come back and meet us on
the bridge? We feel them with us sometimes even in our
waking moments, as though they had returned for a short
while to comfort us. Why would they too not have the same
delight in finding we have come to them? The deep joy in
which we sometimes wake from sleep could be a shadow of
the joy we have had in each other's company.

Thinking of birds has made me remember the lovely
symbolism of an Irish poem of the tenth century.

Round the Tree of Life the flowers
Are ranged, abundant, even;
Its crest on every side spreads out
On the fields and plains of Heaven.

Glorious flocks of singing birds
Celebrate their truth,
Green abounding branches bear
Choicest leaves and fruit.

The lovely flocks maintain their song
In the changeless weather.
A hundred feathers for every bird,
A hundred tunes for every feather.*

* Adapted from the Irish by Brendan Kennelly.

CHAPTER VIII

Non-Education

I

THE SCHOOL WHERE I SPENT THE YEARS OF THE FIRST WORLD War was an anachronism, for that terrible war ended the era to which it belonged. The famous words of Lord Grey of Fallodon, "The lights are going out all over Europe", were the truth. They were the lights of a way of life that had lasted a long time. Looking back to my childhood I think that our way of life then, and the people who lived it, had more in common with the age of Jane Austen, or even with the life and people of the seventeenth century, than it has with the life and people of today. And the 1914 war, which began for the majority as a chivalrous adventure and ended in bitterness and disillusionment, was the dividing chasm. It is easy to see the way in which that war began, and how it went on, by comparing two poets of that war, Rupert Brooke and Wilfred Owen. The first was the poet of the euphoria of the beginning, the second the poet of the endurance of the whole ghastly progression.

The Second World War, with the concentration camps, and the saturation bombing of cities seemed to produce a few fine poems but no great poet. It was possibly too terrible for poetry. In England it was an airman writing prose, Richard Hilary, who spoke for the young men who suffered with him.

Jane Austen would have felt at home in the boarding school I went to. The only examinations were private ones for our school alone; and a child could escape those if she knew how to make her nose bleed. A few subjects were well

taught, music, divinity, the court curtsey and, wonder of
wonders, English literature. Our English mistress, Miss
Bartlett, a severe elderly lady with grey hair scraped back in
a bun, a dry sense of humour and the sublime faculty of
keeping effortless order, taught us to love poetry; above all
the poetry of Shakespeare... She taught a handful of
thoughtless girls to love Shakespeare. Could such a miracle
have occurred in any other girls' school in the world? She
lived to a great old age, and she felt it her duty to read nearly
all my books. I do not think that one mistake in grammar or
one clumsy sentence escaped her notice. And when it came
to the use of a colloquialism, well, it was not in her essentially
loving nature to be vituperative, but I will never forget the
letter she wrote when I used the phrase 'by and large'. I
have never used it again and I never will.

Miss Lumby, our headmistress, was utterly unlike the
usual conception of a headmistress, her intelligence and
strong will warmed and softened by her charm, and by the
lovely soft clothes she wore. The only subject she taught
was divinity and she taught it well. She also taught us to love
God, though how I do not quite know. Not by the daily
tramp down the hill, the sea wind in our faces, to the parish
church for matins, which was our starting point for the day,
and not by the divinity lessons. More, I think, by the infection
of her own love, which so penetrated and illumined all she
did with us and for us. The way in which the spirit of the one
man or woman at the helm can subtly alter the whole atmosphere of some institution, such as a school or ship or hospital,
is extremely mysterious. I doubt if her raw schoolgirls were
aware of the power of her presence until it was withdrawn.
Towards the end of my schooldays she died, and then we
knew. She died of cancer with great courage. We used to go
in twos and threes and sit with her. She was glad of the
pain, she said, "because if we suffer we shall also reign with
him".

We were taught to love music. A fine musician, Mr Moberley, conducted the school orchestra; how he endured us I do not know but he never lost his temper. A magnificent old lady who had stepped straight out of the eighteenth century visited us several days a week to give us piano lessons. She was tall and stately with masses of white hair piled on top of her head and a large picture hat poised on top of all. When we played badly she wilted but when we improved a little she would rock herself backwards and forwards in ecstasy singing at the top of her voice.

And so it was a good school and we were happy there. Even I was happy at times, deadly homesick as I was all through every term. Nevertheless from an academic point of view we learned almost nothing and were not in any way prepared for any future profession. Such an anachronism was this school, blooming there among the rhododendrons and pines of its high garden, that working for a living was hardly considered. In spite of the war raging on the other side of the English Channel it was assumed that we should all go home and help our mothers do the flowers, be presented at court and get married. Yet telegrams arrived now and then telling of the deaths of fathers and brothers and sorrow and dismay would run through the school; and then we would settle back again into our quiet routine of church-going and lessons, with occasional treats of picnics by the sea and in the New Forest.

2

Today, from Poole to the Solent, the lovely curve of the coast has been almost (though not quite) ruined by what is known as modern development, but then it was unspoilt; wild and lonely in some places, in others touched here and there with little circles of human habitation. But the human touch had been gentle, in some places magical. One such place was Lymington, a favourite place for a school outing. It was a little port always humming with activity about the harbour, but the streets of old houses that climbed above the harbour were, as I remember them, quiet streets. There was life in them but it did not seem to have changed much since the days when aristocratic refugees from the French Revolution made their home there . . . Damerosehay. That was the name I gave to the house where the Eliots lived in the three novels I wrote about them; but in reality it was the name of a field near the saltmarshes that separate Lymington from Keyhaven. It is only my fancy that it was named after some lovely French lady who wore powdered hair in the evening and patches on her face. Madame . . . ? What French name could have sounded to English ears like Rosehay?

Once a year on Ascension Day the whole school went to the New Forest but there were also Saturday outings for small groups of older girls, I think as a reward for good marks. It was on one of those expeditions that I discovered the seamarshes; Keyhaven itself I did not discover until many years later.

It was a still, misty day in late autumn, verging on winter. Tired and hungry, three or four girls and a young member of the staff, we had tea in a cottage belonging to an old sailor and his wife. They welcomed us lovingly and there was a fire burning. I do not know quite where it could have been. It seemed at the world's end, a small human habitation that had grown up out of the earth, as trees do, almost on the sea strand and raised only slightly above it. As we ate the old man told us the story of the Great Storm, experienced in his own lifetime. The sea had raged over the marshes, nearly but not quite carrying away the strong old cottage where we were sitting, flooding the ground floors of the houses at Keyhaven and rising to just below the ceilings of the rooms. He was not exaggerating. Years later I sat in the lofty drawing room of Harewood House (that I called Damerose-hay) and looked at the ineradicable mark of salt water just below the cornice of the room and remembered the old man in the cottage at the world's end. Not that I had ever for-gotten him, for the experience of that afternoon was un-forgettable; though, in the telling of it, there seems nothing in it whatever.

Somehow I was by myself at the edge of the sea, the others as non-existent as though the sea mist had swallowed them for ever. I do not know how I had managed to escape them but escaping was one of my few skills in those days. It was so still that the half-moons of water from the incoming tide moved as silently as shadows on the sand. The thinning mist half hid, half revealed the sea-marshes to my left. I was so awed that I could not move. I kept listening and watching but I could not hear anything, or see anything clearly. It was all hidden in the mist . . . Keyhaven. The harbour and the old houses, the yachts at anchor and the circling gulls, the rough road through the marshes and the old cornfield that had sprung up by itself after a grain-ship had been wrecked there, Damerosehay and its garden, the oak trees and the ilex tree. It was all there with me in that moment that seemed out of time and all I knew about it was my sense of awe. I do not remember how I found the others or how they found me. For all I can remember I might be standing there still.

3

I do not remember the last Ely years in such detail as I remember the early ones, but two events stand out very clearly, one was the arrival of Hélène and the other was my grandfather's last visit to us. Hélène was the only child of my mother's brother. Her parents lived in Java and, as was

the custom in those days, as soon as she began to wilt in the
heat she had to be brought home to England for good.
Nowadays, either by sending the children to school in the
hills, or if they are sent to an English school having the
motherly BOAC fly them out for holidays with their parents,
this traumatic experience is a thing of the past. Two children
together could perhaps weather it but how one child alone
battled through I do not know. Hélène when she arrived
had been kept too long in the heat and was a thin delicate
child, with great dark eyes in a white face. Between her and
her father there was one of those father-and-daughter loves
that are strong as a steel hawser. The parting was dreadful
for them but they were both tough Channel Islanders and
they survived. Hélène was perhaps luckier than some
children. She went to the school where Marie was Vice-
Principal and Marie loved her greatly. And when she came
for the holidays to Ely, and later to Oxford, my parents equally loved her. She was thirteen years younger than I was, a
gap difficult to bridge for a child and a much older girl
who had hitherto been cock of the walk, reigning with a
supremacy that must now be shared, but if our love was
a delicate plant to begin with it became with the years a
very strong one.

Hélène was a true Channel Islander, brave, vivacious
and fascinating. She was very like my mother in temperament and they understood each other completely. My
father delighted in her. She was a passionate child with very
deep feelings. When she learned at school of Socrates drinking the hemlock she fell into a storm of grief and fury, "They
killed him for telling the truth?" she demanded of her startled
teacher. "Beasts! Beasts! Beasts!" When Marie told my
father this story he was utterly delighted, but when he discovered that his own daughter, at her school, had never been
told a single word about one of the greatest civilisations the
world has ever known, and hardly even knew who Socrates

was, he suffered from severe shock. Later, when we were on a short holiday together, we sat in two chairs one on each side of the fire, and I heard the whole story of Socrates. "There," he said when he had finished, "now you know how Hélène felt."

Our Guernsey grandfather would have loved Hélène as much as my father did but he never saw her after her first visit to Guernsey when she was a baby. During the First World War, though there was not the tragedy of enemy occupation as in the second war, no one might visit the Channel Islands unless they had an urgent reason to do so. Marie and Emily could go but I could not, and so I was separated from my grandfather for some years. At the end of the war my grandmother died, leaving her husband totally broken by his loss. Emily gave up her work to be with him and they both came to stay with us at Ely for a while. My grandfather was now over eighty and almost blind. He faced the journey to see my mother again, but Hélène was not then with us. Emily took him up to London to see a famous eye-surgeon, hoping something could be done to save the remnants of his sight. Nothing could be done and despair took hold of him.

I could hardly reconcile this old, broken man sunk in darkness with the laughing grandfather I had known. With Marie-Louise dead there was no one who could comfort him, not even my mother. Without faith he could not pray and believed that Marie-Louise had passed into oblivion. He was not musical and could find no joy in listening to music. The only thing that anyone could do to help him was to read aloud, for his mind was still active and for the period of the reading he would emerge a little from his darkness and a shadow of his old alert expression would come back to his face. I was usually exempt from the duty of reading aloud to him for when immersed in the first torture of boarding school I had developed a shocking stammer, which I did not

conquer until late middle life, and the experience of listening
to my reading aloud was another sort of torture for the
unfortunate hearer. However, if no one else was available,
my grandfather considered my reading aloud better than
none, and a little real interest flickered up in him as he tried
to help me with my speech troubles. For he still loved us all.
If despair had killed all hope he still had love.

But one grey dismal afternoon when we were sitting
together neither the book I was trying to read to him nor the
peculiarities of my stammer could interest him. A wretched
silence fell between us. My mother was lying down and
my father and Emily were out. There was no one I could
fetch to comfort him and I did not know how to do it myself.
Then he began to speak, not fumbling for words, voicing his
despair quite clearly. "I must die soon," he said, "and go
into nothingness. What I have cared for all my life has been
knowledge, scientific knowledge. I have read and studied in
every free moment I have had. I have now great knowledge
and could be useful, yet I must die and all that I know will
die with me. All that I have and am must die. It is all totally
wasted."

He sank back into silence and I sat frozen with dismay. I
could not speak. But why did I not do as I would have done
as a small child, run to him and hug him? Why did I not *do*
something? I cannot remember how it ended. I only hope
that my father or Emily came back quickly. The visit ended,
my grandfather and Emily went back to Guernsey and she
wisely moved them from the house where Marie-Louise
had died to a little flat at St Peter Port, looking down on the
harbour. Here my grandfather sat at the window all day
long. He could see little or nothing of the busy life of the
harbour but he could hear it; the varying voices of the ships,
men shouting to each other, the gulls crying and the sound
of the sea when the wind blew, and Emily thought it com-

forted him. But he did not survive the move for long and quietly died.

I totally failed my grandfather but he did not fail me, though it was years before I realised what it was he had done for me in rooting my faith, that I believe grew up out of his despair. Children lucky enough to grow up in a Christian home are given a good start, since small children are copycats and believe what their parents believe and do as their parents do, and later they sail out from a harbour that has a lighthouse on the rocks and however far they travel it is difficult to forget the harbour with the green fields of childhood behind it, and the light always haunts them; it is a finger of light feeling for them.

But neither a copy-cat religion nor a haunting is faith. Somewhere, if one is lucky enough to have faith, however wobbly and constantly tested it may be, there must have been a moment of conviction that fell like a seed to the earth and struck root. When my grandfather said that all that he was, all that he knew, was going into nothingness I felt at first furious, and then incredulous. What he said was a lie. It was impossible. His knowledge was a closed book to me but I knew what he was in himself, what sort of a man his chosen life of selfless love and struggle had made him. Among living creatures man alone, it appears, is capable of making this deliberate choice, and my grandfather was only one among a great multitude of selfless lovers and seekers. If all this love and struggle and knowledge was to go to waste then not only must God be so crazy that he could not exist but the universe also was crazy and pointless. Yet it did not seem to be. It seemed to bear witness to a marvellous provenance and order. It seemed to bear witness to a God who is not crazy. This is what I worked out later. At the time I simply knew the thing was impossible, and I think faith roots more easily in these sudden convictions, coming like blinks of light from the lighthouse, than by any muddled reasoning of a thing as limited as the normal human mind.

4

After the war ended my father faced and carried through the difficult task of re-starting the Theological College. When it had been fully restored his vice-principal took his place as principal and he went to King's College, London, to teach theology under Dr Matthews, who later became Dean of St Paul's. He loved and admired Dr Matthews and his short time there was one of his happiest. He kept his canonry at Ely Cathedral and we still lived there; indeed I think we hardly contemplated having our home anywhere else. My father lived in his rooms at King's College during the week and came home to Ely at the weekends. He loved London and he loved Ely and the swing between them was something he enjoyed.

Someone who lived at Ely at the time wrote to me not long ago and told me one of her memories of my father in those days. She was walking along the Gallery, the street that led from the Porta to the Cathedral green, when she saw my father coming slowly towards her. He was a fast, light walker but he had slowed his steps to match those of the old tramp walking beside him. They were deep in conversation and my father was carrying the tramp's bundle. They were on their way to our house so that my father might get the old man a meal.

The little incident is typical of the many things of this kind that he was constantly doing. That was an Ely incident, remarked because he was so well known in Ely, but what did he do in London on those walks he took on his free afternoons, exploring the city's nooks and crannies? What strange characters did he meet in the places to which he penetrated?

What did he say to them? What did they do? What would I
not give now to know more about those London adventures,
of which he spoke once with a light on his face, but he was a
reticent man and with the awful self-centredness of youth (at
least my youth) I never asked a single question, for my own
affairs at this period were too absorbing.

I was in love for the first time and for a while the world
shone with the same sort of beauty that had lighted the
garden at Wells in my childhood. It ended in tears, of course.
Does not every first love end in tears? That is if it does end,
but sometimes I think that first love is one of the hidden
beauties that are a part of us forever. In my case how glad
I am that that particular magic was a part of Ely as well as of
myself.

What to do with me when I left school was a problem for
my poor parents, once they had grasped the fact that their
daughter knew next to nothing. That girls as well as men
could now go to an Oxford or Cambridge college was still
like a dream come true, but very few of us who went to that
old-fashioned happy school achieved it, and they only the
brightest after a long period of intensive coaching. Acade-
mically speaking there was no hope for me. Many of
my school friends had wealthy parents but whatever my
father earned it always seemed drained away by the upkeep
of some large ecclesiastical house; his lazy ignorant daughter
would have to earn her own living.

Parents of that era realised that unless their daughters had
exceptional beauty and charm they would not marry. The
First World War left few young men alive. The phrase used
at that time, 'the lost generation', sounds poetical but it was
the truth. The few who came home when it was all over were
so exhausted that they succumbed easily to the influenza that
devastated Europe as soon as the fighting ceased. At least it
was called influenza for politeness sake. It was more like some
form of plague; so many thousands of dead men and horses

all over Europe were not buried deep enough. There was
hardly a household that did not have its dead through this
illness. I remember the winter as being one of still, dark cold
like a pall over the land. No sun, no rain, just a heavy mantle
of grey. . . . But probably memory is playing tricks with me
and I have spread a few grey days over the whole period.
And so at that time there were millions more women than
men in England.

But for the unmarried women their fate was mitigated, if
not transmuted altogether, by the wonderful fact that they
were needed as a labour force. They had proved their worth
in the war and now they had the vote and a large and varied
field of work was open to them. Women today consider themselves not yet sufficiently free but old women of my age
cannot get over the conviction that we were liberated fifty
years ago. I am one of many who have found great joy in work
and in building up a career. I have even lived to 'thank God
fasting' for the single state. Though you have to be fairly old
before you can recognise and deeply prize the blessings of a
single life, for up to that point the deprivation of childlessness
is hard to bear. Yet for the childless woman there is no lack
of children in the world to love, even if they are not her own,
and nothing to prevent a single woman experiencing the
richness of falling in love now and again all her life. And
indeed it *is* richness, for to every human being the pain of
perhaps not having love returned is less important than the
blessed fact of loving.

5

But at our prehistoric school we were unaware of all the
opportunities that would soon open before us and still
considered that a girl who must earn her own living had
only two choices, to be an actress or a nurse according to

temperament, and so I went through a stage-struck period and had I not been a stammerer I might have opted for that, and if by some miracle I had got there and my father had not liked it, that would have been his own fault.

The magic thing happened one winter's day when I was going home for the Christmas holidays, towards the end of my time at school. It was a cold dreary day, the war was going badly and school had been shadowed by Miss Lumby's death, but I was in high spirits as the train pounded towards Waterloo because my father would meet me there. He always had to meet me on every return from school, and convey me across London to Liverpool Street and the train to Ely, because not only was it not de rigueur then for girls to travel alone but my mother was perpetually haunted by a thing called The White Slave Traffic; a menace which I never fully understood but to which I was favourably disposed because it was largely responsible for my father meeting me in his top hat. He hated his top hat but I insisted that he should wear it when meeting me. I was immensely proud of him (no other girl at school had a father as good-looking as mine) and I considered that his charm was increased by his top hat. Looking back now I think I was wrong about this for he was not a top hat man. He looked his best in the cassock with a leather belt that for warmth's sake he always wore at home in our cold house, for that expressed something of what he was in himself.

No one could have suspected that the scrubby schoolgirl falling joyously from the railway carriage was this good-looking man's daughter. Our school uniform must have been designed to discourage vanity in even the prettiest girl, and I had no beauty except the long hair hidden from sight in a tight pigtail. In summer and winter alike we wore dark blue serge coats and skirts, and the skirt was long for it had to "cover the fat part of the leg", which was as well, for our thick black woollen stockings were not things of beauty.

Tucked into the waist of the skirt was a high-necked white shirt blouse and somehow this always parted company with the skirt at the back, hanging down like a white tail, so the two were generally tethered together by a large black safety-pin. The school tie was thick and cumbersome and when knotted under the collar of the blouse it would maintain its position only for a short while; sooner or later it slipped sideways. The school hat was a hard sailor, tipped forward over the nose and secured with elastic. The elastic used to stretch and we tied knots in it, and somehow the knots always looked black and dirty. And the sailor hats, I don't know how, used to develop a chewed appearance round the edges. In this condition I fell into my father's arms and heard his voice saying above my head, "I am going to take you to your first theatre."

What those words meant to a schoolgirl of my generation cannot possibly be understood today. There was no cinema at Wells in those days, there was no T.V. At the age of six or seven I had seen *Peter Pan* and been captivated by the crocodile with a ticking clock in his stomach but not, I am ashamed to say, by anything else, and once at the seaside Nanny and I had seen an amateur performance of *Little Lord Fauntleroy*. Hard-hearted little beast that I was I remained unmoved but Nanny cried enough for both of us. And I had attended performances of *Merrie England* and *The Pirates of Penzance* presented by the Wells Operatic Society amidst potted plants on the platform of the Town Hall, and there had been our own excruciating performances of scenes from Shakespeare at school, but that was the extent of my dramatic experience.

"What," I gasped.

"*Twelfth Night*, a matinée at the Court Theatre," said my father. "Come along quickly. There's not much time."

Shakespeare! And Miss Bartlett had taught me to love him. Could it be true? A porter was grabbed (there were always plenty of kind and friendly porters in those days) and my big battered black trunk was trundled along to a taxi. My father strode after him carrying my violin in its case and I ran behind clasping my big black umbrella. The taxi carried us to Liverpool Street where we put the impedimenta into 'the left luggage', swallowed buns and coffee in the refreshment room and raced for a bus. We reached the theatre just in time and sat palpitating in the good seats my father had already booked. *Peter Pan* was dim in my mind (apart from the crocodile) and this for me was truly what my father had called it, 'your first theatre'. The auditorium was full and there was a hushed expectancy before the long rose-red curtains, the light stealing up them from the hidden footlights. Then the curtains parted and the opening words of the play came across to us, "If music be the food of love, play on."

I do not now remember the names of any of the actors except Mary Grey and that great actor Miles Malleson and in any case I was hardly aware that they were actors because they were the people. The play flowed on, funny and lovely and touching, another country, another world. I think I have forgotten hardly anything of it, but the clearest of all to me in Antonio's voice asking for a song of the old days:

> That old and antique song we heard last night:
> Me thought it did relieve my passion much,
> More than light airs and recollected terms
> Of these most brisk and giddy-paced times . . .
> Mark it, Cesario; it is old and plain;
> The spinsters and the knitters in the sun
> And the free maids that weave their thread with bones
> Do use to chant it: it is silly sooth,
> And dallies with the innocence of love,
> Like the old age.

And then Feste the jester singing, "Come away, come away, death . . ."

It was over, a supreme experience, but I do not remember any desolation because it had ended. Because of course it had not ended, but was a part of me forever. I was now stage-struck. I could never be an actress but from then on, scribbling in my odd moments, I struggled to write plays as well as fairy stories.

6

My school reports were mostly bad but one did make the suggestion that a gift for writing should be encouraged. Well, that was a crumb of comfort for my parents for at least their child was not completely a dolt, but the ability to write a passable essay was no help towards earning a living. What did I want to do? "I would like to be a nurse," I said, I was merely passing to the second of the two choices but I had always been obsessed with the thought of suffering, especially the suffering of children. It might have come to pass but mercifully for the patients (for I have discovered myself to be the world's worst nurse) providence rescued them by sending me a heart complaint. Could I train at Great Ormond Street? we asked our doctor. "Dead in a week," he replied briefly. So we had to think again.

My mother had an idea. I loved making things with my hands and I loved children. Why not take a training in handicrafts and then, if my stammer subsided with time, teach in a school for crippled children? My father's old friend Professor de Burgh was Vice-Chancellor of Reading College (not yet a university) and a family of dear cousins lived at Reading and had students to live with them. The Art School at the College was a good one. And so I went there a little rebelliously. I lived with my cousins and walking to college every morning I had to pass the hospital. I would look at it longingly and pass on scowling. Then with a flood of other students I would be sucked into the College portal and borne along on the noisy morning tide of hurry and confusion to the haven of the Art School.

At that time, just after the war, there was what amounted to almost a passion for handicrafts. Metal work, leather work, basket making, spinning, weaving, tapestry, embroidery, designing for textiles, we did the lot in the handicraft department. We mingled at times with the art students, working with them in the life-class, joining their flower study and composition classes; for we were never allowed to use any patterns in embroidery or tapestry or leather work that we had not designed ourselves and we had to learn to wield a pencil and paintbrush sufficiently well for the purpose. The art students considered us beneath contempt but tolerated our presence with them. In the same manner the rest of the College, engaged in such great matters as agriculture, science and mathematics, considered the entire Art School beneath contempt. "Work," they said scathingly, "is playing around with paint work?" I was as indignant as the rest of us and as time went on I ceased to look longingly at the hospital as I passed it. The work of creation is hard work however desperately badly one creates, but it is also a joy that gets hold of one more and more.

I was never so happy as in the greenhouse making studies of flowers that would later be used for embroidery and leather-work designs. Perhaps because I loved them so much I could paint flowers passably well but I could draw nothing else. When we were taken out sketching my efforts to capture something of the wider world of nature that I loved also were pitiable. I was mad with frustration. All this beauty and I could not portray it. It was the same with the composition class, where with the future illustrating of books in mind the art students would be told to illustrate a scene from some particular fairy tale or romance. This was done at home, then brought to the class for criticism. The pictures would be

pinned up all round the wall and Professor Seaby, the head
of the Art School, would pass judgment. My contributions
were always hilariously bad. Professor Seaby, a kindly man,
generally refrained from comment. Yet there was one occasion when he stopped in front of my atrocity and considered
it, and it was obvious that he was about to speak. My heart
beat hard as the silence lengthened. "The worst drawing of
the lot," he said, "but the best evocation of the atmosphere
of a fairytale." Then he passed on and again I felt crazy with
frustration. What was the use of my having lived in the story,
having seen it all so clearly, the rippling stream, the wind in
the trees, and the knight in armour on his white horse riding
over the grass where the flowers were close set like jewels in
green enamel (I admired the pre-Raphaelites in those days)
if I could not say what I had seen? It was the same with my
struggle to play the violin and piano. The music was glorious
in my head but I had a faulty ear and clumsy fingers.

Yet I was now a little comforted. Professor Seaby was a
comforting sort of man, probably because he was a humble
one. He was also a splendid teacher. If I remember rightly
he taught largely by patient encouragement and by his own
enthusiasm. Looking back at him, grey-bearded, handsome
and gentle, the one outstanding figure of those days, I think
he was a great man. He was certainly a great artist. His
passion was for birds and they figured largely in his exquisite
woodcuts and colour prints. When he retired he went to live
in the New Forest that he might be permanently among the
birds. It was from his studio there that he wrote to me
twenty years later, after reading one of my books. "Now you
have found how to do it," he said. "Now you will be happy."
We had not met in twenty years. Hundreds of students must
have passed through his hands. Surely it is the mark of a very
great teacher to remember a potentiality in a pupil who must
have been the worst of the lot.

I used my handicraft training for such a short while that

from the point of view of earning a living it appeared sheer waste. Yet looking back I see what an excellent thing it was for a writer. It taught me to observe things in minute detail; the shape of a petal, the sheen on a bird's wing. It taught me the balance of pattern. Above all it stimulated imagination. I think now that every writer should have a period of work at an Art School as part of his training.

At college I had been almost as homesick for Ely and my parents as I had been at school (how I could even have imagined I could have been a nurse with only a fortnight's holiday a year I do not know) and home again I vowed I would stay there for the present. I turned what had been the schoolroom into what I grandly called a studio and established a big loom there, a spinning wheel and embroidery frames and a large table for leather work. And here, incredibly, I had pupils. They must have come for the fun of the thing or for the pleasure of being in that high airy room with its view of the fens, for I can't think I taught them much. I was hopeless as a teacher, and when in later years at Oxford I tried to teach handicrafts in a school on Boars Hill they had the wisdom to give me the sack with remarkable speed. I was far better at making things than at teaching others how to make them and was remarkably happy working at my loom and finding that you must always sing as you weave. I fashioned terrible sack-like garments from the woven materials and embroidered them. Church embroidery with lots of gold thread was as absorbing as illuminating manuscripts must have been to the monks who once lived at Ely, and my mother and I learned to make lace. But this halcyon period lasted only for a year or so and then the blow fell. Ely, the home of homes, was to be abandoned. My father was offered the appointment of Regius Professor of Divinity at Oxford. It was considered a great honour.

He did not want the honour and was tormented as to whether or not it was his duty to accept it. He loved the work

he was doing at King's College and he was afraid of what
Oxford might do to my mother. She liked wide spaces and
clean air. How would she fare in a city in the Thames valley?
And whether we wanted to or not we should have to live in
an old house in Tom Quad at Christ Church, with the river
mists just beyond Christ Church Meadows. On the other
hand he regarded himself as a soldier does, as a man under
orders. The Archbishop wanted him to accept and pressure
came on him from all sides. My mother was too good a wife to
refuse to budge but for a short space she was unusually silent.
Then she gradually came round to the knowledge that what
she wanted was what was best for her husband. Oxford, she
thought, was best. The two Regius Professors of Divinity, at
Oxford and Cambridge respectively, filled the highest
teaching posts the Church of England had to offer. They
ranked with bishops, she had been told, and that to her was a
pleasing idea. She was told by someone else that my father
would now be able to don a court suit and present himself at
Buckingham Palace, and during the period when my father
refrained from telling her that he intended to do no such, to
him, useless and silly thing, the thought of the court suit was,
to her, very comforting.

But better still was the thought that her three beloved
maids, Phyllis, Muriel and Florence, all of them born in the
Fen country, showed the courage of the Fens and vowed they
would not desert her. They would come too. Suddenly she
swept us all up into a fever of preparation; turning out and
sorting the accumulation of years in a home so loved that we
had come to think it was ours eternally, and where we had
hoarded possessions, as though it were that eternal home in
the heavens from whose treasure one is never parted. But it
was not and the hell in which I do not believe appeared at
the bottom of the garden in the shape of an abominable
bonfire, consuming the oddments that moth and rust had
already corrupted here on earth.

On a spring day we left Ely. I cannot recall a single thing about it. The bonfire seems to have burned up my memory. But very vivid, at the other end of a tunnel of forgetfulness, is the memory of my mother's despairing breakdown when we finally landed in our new home, the old beautiful dark house that we could never learn to love.

CHAPTER IX

Oxford

I

THE OXFORD OF FIFTY YEARS AGO WHEN MY FATHER, AN absent-minded man, could bicycle down the High Street on the wrong side of the road and come to no harm, was not yet the Oxford of today. Essentially Oxford never changes. Old shops and dwelling houses may be swept away and when they are lovely one may grieve to see them go, but the essential Oxford is what it always was, a power house of the knowledge for which men are always searching. The search does not seem to change much through the centuries and the buildings that house the search do not change much either. What they hold has seemed to communicate its own changelessness to them.

Our new home in Tom Quad, with windows looking down on green lawns about the central fountain, Tom Tower and its great bell to the right and the Cathedral to the left, was a small integral part of the changelessness, It was a strange house, long and narrow. At one end my father's study with the drawing room above it, and at the other the big old-fashioned kitchen with the spare-room and its powdering closet over it, spanned the width of the house, but all the other rooms looked north upon the walled garden behind the house and only the long passages enjoyed the sun. In the rather dismal dining room large oil paintings of the previous divines who had died in this house through the centuries (they never looked to me as though they had lived in the house, only died in it), gazed down upon us with disapproval. There was a large and ancient cellar under the

house where the gentlemen in the oil paintings must have
kept their wine and brandy, but in our day it only contained,
in wet winters, several feet of water. The house had a flat
roof through which melting snow would seep, encouraging
fungus growths in the rooms below. There was a large population of mice, and a smaller one of rats.

But the house had its glories. The oak-panelled study and
the high sunny drawing room above it were beautiful rooms,
and in my mother's bedroom a carved Adam mantelpiece
framed a strange dark oil painting that we loved for its
mysteriousness. But best of all was the wide curving oak
staircase that seemed made for the ascending and descending
of kings and queens, and upon which one would suddenly
feel a sense of joy and a lifting of the heart. But apart from
these things it was a house without atmosphere. There was
not even a ghost in it. There were plenty of haunted houses
in Oxford but ours was ghostless. Not one of the old gentlemen in the portraits appeared to have left a trace of himself.
Never, returning after an absence, did I feel any sense of
welcome when I came in at the front door. What was the
matter with the house? Or with us that we could not love it?

Our immediate predecessors, Dr and Mrs Headlam, had
not loved it either, but I believe the Regius Professor
before Dr Headlam, Canon Scott Holland, had loved it. But
then he was a saint and as saints glow with the love of God
no doubt their surroundings reflect their own warmth back
to them. I have a photo of him sitting in the walled garden,
that we were told was a dreary place before he came and saw
what could be done with it, and he looks happy and serene
as he surveys what he accomplished. It was difficult to make
flowers grow in the garden because the soil was so poor and
stony and the house cut off the south sun, but Canon Scott
Holland planted roses in beds filled with imported earth, and
as irises like stony soil he made a long bed filled with all the
different species of iris that he could find. But to my mother.

it was a draughty, stuffy town garden and she could love only
its one supreme glory, a wonderful acacia tree in the north-
east corner. Its perfect shape and white flowers against a blue
summer sky was one of the sights of Oxford. Over the garden
wall, just beyond the archway that leads from Tom Quad to
Peckwater, one would often find a painter sitting sketching
the tree, for it towered up like an archangel and all the light
in the sky seemed to flow towards it.

There is more light and warmth in that house now for
after we left it was thoroughly renovated. Windows were
enlarged and central heating was installed. Perhaps now it
feels like a home and the acacia tree rejoices.

Phyllis, Muriel and Florence had been seized with a despair
almost equal to my mother's when they saw the house, but
as the chaos of removal began to give way to some sort of
order we began to revive. The lift we had installed for my
mother at Ely, a comic thing like a large wardrobe worked by
a mechanism of ropes and weights, had come with us and it
enabled her to go from just outside her bedroom door to the
garden door in a matter of minutes. She left her bed and sat
in her wheelchair in the garden and tried to concentrate upon
the acacia tree, but the air that came to her was the air of a
city and she said she could not breathe. And I, when I tried
to make a workroom out of a drak north room near the
kitchen, found when I had set up my loom that there was
scarcely enough light to work by, and who, in a city like
Oxford with a fine art school, would even wish to be taught
handicrafts by a nobody like myself in a room like this? My
father was back in Oxford, his adored city where he had
once been so happy and neither of his females appreciated
it . . . I remember that we did have the grace to be ashamed
of ourselves.

Driven by my shame, I began to discover Oxford's glories.
I was not, like my mother, a sick woman, I was young and I
had a strong pair of legs. Anyone who loves Oxford knows

what I discovered, sometimes with my father, sometimes alone. Kingfishers in Christ Church Meadows and bluebells in Bagley Wood. The Library at Merton and the great fan-roofed stone staircase that ascended to the hall at Christ Church, and which echoed at the end of every summer term to the music of Byrd when the Cathedral choir stood there singing in the evening. New College garden and the cloisters at Magdalen.

Those cloisters were for me the heart of Oxford; why I cannot explain. For me it just was so. Through all the years at Oxford, however unhappy I was, however restless and distracted, as soon as I had opened the door in the wall, gone in and shut it behind me, I was at peace. And nearly always alone. It seemed almost as though I was the only person who knew about the door in the wall. Or if there was anyone else there, sitting or strolling quietly, and if one met their eyes, there was the ghost of a smile there, as though they recognised another of a fraternity . . . Here is our peace . . . The noise of the city could not, in those days, be heard in that enclosed place and there was one of those living trees there; a still, dark tree.

All trees are alive, I know, as miraculously alive as any other living creature, but some trees seem to have an added depth in their living, just as saints have. I have loved and remembered many such trees. The cedar tree at Wells into whose arms I climbed so often. The ilex tree at Damerosehay. The acacia tree. The wild cherry in the garden here in Oxfordshire, nearly as tall as a church steeple and, in a good spring, snow white, from top to toe, and so many more. Perhaps their added quality is that they have been very much loved. With the saints it is the other way round; they love very much. In both cases what Tolstoy said is true, "Where love is, God is." Which makes me suddenly remember the limerick Ronald Knox wrote about a tree in a college quad.

There was a young man who said 'God
Must think it remarkably odd,
To find that this tree
Continues to be
When there's no one about in the Quad.'

'Dear sir, your astonishment's odd,
I am always about in the Quad
And that's why the tree
Continues to be
While observed by, yours faithfully, God.'

2

The tall, thin, black figure of Monsignor Ronald Knox
strolling round Oxford, his rather wide clerical hat unusually
bent about the brim, his head bent a little forward, a half-
smile on his face and a distant look in his eyes, apparently
as blissfully indifferent to traffic as though his long loping
legs carried him over the empty spaces of the moors instead
of along busy streets, was a heart-warming sight. Even before
I knew who he was I was fascinated by the sight of him,
linking him in my mind with my father. Was he also a
theologian? My father did not lope and stroll, he walked
rapidly through the Oxford streets, wasting no time, his
hands behind his back, but he often had that same half-smile
on his face, and the distant look in the eyes. Since they were
unaware of obstacles in their way it appeared as though the
obstacles melted away, for they were not halted upon the
path as were lesser men. I tried a trick on my father to see if
he could be halted. Frequently, I leaving home and he returning to it, he would hurry past me without a sign of recognition.
One day I side-stepped and confronted him. He stopped but
there was quite a pause before his eyes could focus upon me
or his mind remember that he had a daughter. Then he
smiled. It was a moment of triumph for me. Yes, these men

could be halted. Great though their intellectual power was it could not actually reduce material objects to vapour.

How remarkable they were, those Oxford Characters. They were themselves to such a degree that they had a sort of validity that made them unforgettable. Though today it may seem to us in our black moments that human beings are becoming automatons, that we grow more and more like the machines that govern us, indifferent and insensitive to God and the world and each other, it is mercifully not yet the truth. I still know many Characters upon whom I could bestow the accolade of a capital C. But there are not so many of them as there used to be and they are not as noticeable as they were. They were very noticeable indeed in that faraway Oxford, and so many of them come flocking into my mind now that it is hard to know which to take as a prototype. Perhaps I should describe as well as I can the one who was the prince of them all.

Dr Clive Jenkins was not in Oxford when we first went there, but after a few years had gone by he was our near neighbour in Tom Quad. He was a notable scholar and bibliophile, he was good and he was lovable, he did not like women but never failed in Christian patience and courtesy towards them. They are, after all, one of the ills of life that cannot be avoided and he himself was personally encumbered by them when he moved from Canterbury to Oxford, his mother and two maids coming with him. Indeed, it was said that he deeply loved his mother, a gentle old lady who was already over ninety when she was taken from her old home. Like my mother, her spirit was willing but her body did not take kindly to transplantation. She was too old and frail to leave the house and so the beauty of Oxford could give her no comfort; and her house was much like ours; it was visited by more sunshine than ours was, but also by more rats. She had not been in it long before she died.

Her maids remained to look after her son, a task which cannot have been easy for he had a very independent spirit and women do not find that easy in the men they care for. He would not have his daily newspaper delivered at the house, like the rest of us, he liked to fetch it himself, and each morning (one could have set one's watch by his punctuality) he could be seen issuing from his front door and crossing the quad on his way to fetch it. He was a slender, white-haired man and I think he had a jaunty, trotting sort of walk; no Character walks like anyone else, his walk is his own. I cannot remember that he ever wore an overcoat for this outing but if it was cold he would wind one end of a woolly scarf round his neck. This scarf was of a great age and with much washing had lengthened considerably; the other end of it trailed on the ground behind him. In the centre of Tom Quad is a pool with a fountain, as almost the whole world knows as it is photographed so often, and in the centre of the pool is a beautiful airy statue of Mercury. Upon one bitter cold day when the ice on the pool was thick enough to bear a man's weight, it was seen that persons unknown had draped a long woollen scarf round Mercury's neck.

Dr Jenkins's morning punctuality did not extend to his meal-times. When he was working in his study he did not like to be disturbed by a summons to a meal. He was partial to mutton chops but did not wish his luncheon chop to be brought to him until he had got to a good stopping place, when he rang for it. He rang one day, the parlourmaid came and he said, "My chop," and it was brought. An hour later he summoned his parlourmaid again and said, "My chop." She protested that she had brought it an hour ago. "I can't see it," he said. Nor could she, at first, but after a period of excavation she found it, stone-cold with congealing fat, under a pile of books.

After God, his deepest love was for his books. They proliferated. My father's books proliferated too but he had a plan by which when he bought six new books he sold six old ones, thus keeping the tide down and slightly salving his conscience over the expense of the new books. But Dr Jenkins could not have parted with a book to save his life. A multitude flowed into his house but none flowed out. When every bookcase in the study was full they stood in piles of varying heights all over the floor so that the room looked like a wood where the trees had all been cut down. "And when I go to see him," said the Bishop of Oxford, "there is a cup of tea he has forgotten to drink on the top of each tree stump." When the books had overflowed the library Dr Jenkins began piling them up on each side of the staircase, and there was barely room for his slender figure to go up and down between them. It was said that he only possessed two suits of clothes and that the best suit mysteriously disappeared and was found eventually well-pressed beneath the books on the stairs.

In the course of time his two maids either left or died of heartbreak, I do not remember which, and for a while Dr Jenkins managed with a daily helper who came in. Then he decided that a woman in the house, any woman, was intolerable. Outside the blessed harbour of his home they must be courteously endured, but inside, why bother with them? He was perfectly capable of looking after himself by himself. During his last years we were no longer living in Oxford and so we did not see him with his clothes growing green with age and his gown becoming more and more tattered, but always courteously refusing female assistance. Just once, I was told, his courtesy failed him. Christ Church is a royal foundation and royalty was to pay one of its periodic visits. One of the dons' wives pleaded with Dr Jenkins that she might be allowed to mend his torn gown. He courteously refused the kind offer. In despair she actually stole the gown from him and accomplished the necessary repairs. It was an insult to his independence, an unsufferable liberty, and just that once he was angry.

He was amazingly kind to me after my father died. The widows of clergy, living in official houses, are given only a short while to pack up and go. This cannot be helped, for a successor must come as quickly as possible to carry on the work of the man who has died. But a clergy-widow's pension is small and unless she has private means she must move into a house as small as her pension. In those days clerical houses were almost always on the too-large-white-elephant scale and so the problem was how to deal with the surplus possessions when you were moving from a house containing thirteen rooms to one containing four. It can seem an insuperable problem; especially if the books have proliferated. Dr Jenkins said he was going to help me sort my father's books, since I had to know which were valuable and which were not, to whom they could be given or where they would be sold, and we set aside a whole morning for the task. He arrived very early in cap and torn gown and we went into the study, and I can see now how his eyes lit up and his face kindled as the book-lined walls enfolded him. He had been in the study many times before of course, but only talking to my father, not let loose among the books.

He took a quick happy trot around the walls and gave a sudden cry of delight. He had found a particular treasure. He took it out, caressed it and opened it, then holding it in his left hand he raised his right to command my attention and began a loving, and long, dissertation upon it. He replaced it tenderly, went a little further and cried out again. Another treasure. He took it from the shelf and the process was repeated. It went on like that all the morning. I remember that I got tired and sat down. The lunch-hour struck in one boom from Tom Tower and we still had not sorted the books. But Dr Jenkins thought we had. He put the book he was holding back in its place, came to me and took my hand and held it. He spoke no word of sympathy, he knew better, merely filled the room with it for a moment or two. I never

saw him again. He was a wonderful Character and so great
was his individuality that I think he came near to being a
saint.

Dr Spooner, Warden of New College, was another small
white-haired gentleman of great charm and learning. Spoon-
erisms have now disappeared from the social scene but they
were a great delight to the Oxford, and indeed to the England,
of those days. Actually Dr Spooner said (or it was said that
he said, for legends tend to grow about a genuine Character
and the truth is hard to come by) that he only perpetrated
one and that afterwards Oxford delighted in making them
up for him. His one, he said, was when he gave out the first
lines of a hymn. "We will now sing hymn number 175

> 'Kinquering kongs their titles take
> From the foes they captive make.' "

But this is not strictly speaking a Spoonerism. It is a nonsense.
A true Spoonerism, though dotty, must make sense of a sort.
A good example is the criticism Dr Spooner is said to have
addressed to one of his laziest pupils when saying good-bye
at the end of term. "Sir, you have hissed all my mystery
lectures and tasted the whole worm."

Dr Spooner had a sense of humour and he did sometimes
deliberately make up a Spoonerism for himself. Travelling
up to London in the train with other members of the
University for an important luncheon he was unusually
silent. He seemed wrapped in meditation and they forbore to
disturb him. Later, at the luncheon, he made a speech
including the most exquisite Latin Spoonerism.

I said that I thought Dr Jenkins, the prince of Characters,
came near to being a saint. I think many Characters do, even
if they don't actually arrive, but there is no doubt that all
saints are Characters. It is hard to say what a saint *is*. I think
that the nearest one can come to a definition is to say that a

saint is a man or woman who has attained to the highest
degree of selflessness that is possible in this world. This is a
very limiting definition, making a saint a very rare bird
indeed. He is individual to a degree, and so a Character.
Someone asked me not long ago, out of the blue, "Have you
known any saints?" And I heard myself answering, "Bishop
Gore, and Mrs Rogers our Oxford charwoman." Only two?
Sometimes I think my father was a saint but then my father
could at rare intervals, to use a modern phrase, 'blow his top',
and I remember that Jacapone da Todi and Father Damian
were never 'raised to the altars' by their church because of
their shocking tempers. So that leaves only two in a long life.

Bishop Gore was a friend of my father's, and what my
father felt about him was so compounded of reverence and
love that the very thought of him filled me with awe even
before I saw him for the first time in my college days. He
came to preach at St Giles, Reading, and I went to hear him.
His reputation had filled the large church and his sermon on
the great crowd of witnesses made them practically visible.
The children of the clergy are not generally fond of sermons,
for they have had to sit through too many, but this was a
sermon to rank with the great discourses that John Donne
used to preach at St Paul's and I listened as though it was the
first sermon I had ever heard. Then, when we moved to
Oxford, Bishop Gore came to stay with us for a few days. I
expected to be terrified but even though he resembled the
Isaiah of my youthful imaginings I was not afraid; and I had
always thought Isaiah would have been as terrifying to meet
as Beethoven. "Truly great men and women are never
terrifying," someone told me lately. "Their humility puts
you at your ease. If a very important person frightens you he
is not great; he only thinks he is."

Nor can one dog-lover easily be frightened by another
and Bishop Gore was a dog-lover; or at least upon this visit
he lost his heart to our dog. We had at the time a very great

dog. It has been said that the dog is the saint among the animals, so great are his powers of love and forgiveness, and if that is so then Brownie was a pre-eminent saint among very many. He was a large dog, possessed of quietness and dignity, and I will say no more of him at the moment, returning to him with what I fear may be great length later. Suffice it to say here that he and Bishop Gore greeted each other with what appeared to be a kind of recognition. It was very odd. There was only one person who ever willingly sat in our dismal dining room under the eyes of those humourless men in the portraits, and that person was Brownie. He liked the place. Stretched out on the wide comfortable sofa he could feel himself separated from the ceaseless comings and goings of a busy house. He liked to meditate and here he could do so in peace. One day during his visit to us Bishop Gore could not be found. He was discovered with Brownie in the dining room, sharing the sofa, caressing the big dog's wise domed forehead and long silky ears and murmuring over and over again, "I like you, Brownie, Brownie, I like you."

Mrs Rogers our charwoman had given her heart to cats rather than dogs. At one time she had fifteen cats in the dark little house off St Aldates where she lived with her sister. When I went to see her there I thought it was a wretched house but I doubt if she did. I don't think she ever envied the good fortune of others because I think she never realised that her own life was a hard one. When she compared herself with other people it was always with compassion for them. She said to me one day, with absolute sincerity and much love, "I'm so sorry for ladies. Poor dears, they're so helpless." How ashamed I was! At this period of my life I hardly knew how to peel a potato.

Thinking of her, and of the greatness of her example, I think one of the saintly qualities is this unconscious refusal to envy the lot of others. For the unselfish, envy is an impossible exercise anyway since it is destructive; a symptom of a hidden

urge to smash and destroy, while love is bound up with the
urge to create and give; even if there is nothing to give
except compassion. She was a small, bent woman, worn with
hard work. She looked old but to judge by the amount of
hard work she could do she was perhaps only in her fifties.
Her sister was older, and delicate, and did not go out to work.
Mrs Rogers supported her and the cats, who were all strays.
Supporting the stray cats of St Aldates was one of the ways in
which Mrs Rogers and her sister served God and I know that
if anyone went hungry it was not the cats. "Who sweeps a
room, as for the Lord, makes that and the action fine." Mrs
Rogers not only swept but scrubbed floors and passages on
hands and knees, with thoroughness and devotion, and when
she was resting and drinking a cup of tea she gave good advice
to the young maids. "Never deceive your mistress," she
would say. "Serve your mistress well and God will never
desert you." I know they exploded with mirth as soon as she
had returned to work, but I am quite sure they were silent in
her presence for she had a dignity that commanded respect
and when she smiled it was as though a light shone from her
face.

3

  I am sure that my father visited Mrs Rogers and the cats,
contributing to the upkeep of the latter. The slum districts
of the Oxford of those days, some of them existing not far
from Cardinal Wolsey's great wealthy College, made him
angry and miserable and started him off asking his habitual
awkward questions. He was a much-loved man but he was
disliked too; he could never leave well alone if in his opinion
it was not well. After all these years I am not sure of my facts
here. I am not sure whether Christ Church actually owned
some of the slum property or whether my father had been

told so and was determined to find out. And if his College was not guilty then who was? And so he had a rather bad start at Oxford. Theologians are expected to stick to theology and not stir up hornets' nests in their odd moments, but my father was hornet-minded and could not help himself. London-born, the contrasts of social existence had bothered him from the beginning. At Ely we had lived in a big house that we had loved, quietly and simply. In the University life of those days it was very difficult to be either quiet or simple and life seemed to us a whirl of social gaiety. My mother had all the social graces and had she been well she would have enjoyed it all. My father and I, not being so gifted, knew we ought to be enjoying it more than we did and felt guilty because other people, less fortunate than we, would have thought our life paradise.

That first summer term passed like a pageant; dances and parties, pealing bells and concerts, gardens full of flowers and sunshine on water. I see it now as a kaleidoscope of colour and because I was young enjoyment did break through, even through the distress of my mother's increasing illness. Oxford in the summer might be beautiful but it was airless and even in those days sometimes noisy. After the sinus operations she had had (and she had several more after the original one) she could not stand noise of any kind. Bells at a distance are a joy but peals pealing out almost over your head are not, and on Saturdays bell-ringers from other parts of England would come and peal the Christ Church bells hour after hour.

And night after night there were explosions of what now would be called 'student unrest'. But those students were not protesting against anything for they accepted the authority that in those days was taken for granted and they had no grievances. They were merely ridding themselves of a surplus of energy. At that time no undergraduates lived in Tom Quad, their rooms were in Peckwater and Meadow buildings, but Tom Quad, cool and quiet and immensely beautiful under the moon, was the vacuum into which they exploded, and unfortunately it was a college tradition that they should blow hunting horns and crack whips as they came tearing through the dark arches into the moonlight. Sheer noise, and dipping each other in Mercury, kept them happy for some while. Later they might shatter the lamps and break a few windows. Next day, having found out whose windows they had broken, they would come and apologise; polite, seemingly penitent, charming young men with whom it seemed impossible to equate the fiendish row of the night before.

Other of their activities were exquisitely silent. The Alpine Club explored all the ways of leaving and entering the college after Tom had tolled the curfew and the gates were shut. Walls were scaled and roofs climbed over with great skill and no sound at all. Equally silent were the nocturnal enterings of professors' houses (old windows open easily; it only needs a knife to push the catch back) and the performing there of harmless, inventive actions that were often so comic that coming down in the morning no one in his senses could mind at all. Furniture would have been noiselessly moved from one room to another, and in our house one night the great beam with its ancient hooks that stretched across the kitchen ceiling was by morning ornamented with dustpans, brushes and mops suspended from each hook. If wine was in the house, it might of course be sampled. In our house, on another night, it could not be found and in protest the wine glasses were set out in neat array on the hall table and filled with the contents of a bottle of Parrish's Food—a claret-coloured tonic much in vogue at that time. Unfortunately the college authorities discovered what was happening and put a stop to this cheerful affair. All the ground-floor windows in our houses were made burglar-proof and we were sorry; it had been such a quiet way of getting rid of energy.

Looking back on the young men and women of that time I wonder if it is true that the young of today have to a large extent lost their tolerance and humour. Is that because privilege is a thing that makes them bitterly and intensely angry? Too angry for tolerance? To look well-born and well-endowed is a separating thing and they have no wish to be separated from the vast majority of suffering humanity. And here, how right they are and how much they have gained. I believe they are more concerned about injustice and exploitation than their grandparents were at their age. Not that their parents and grandparents did not care, many of them cared intensely and most creatively, but social barriers were tight and information about what was happening in the world harder to come by than it is now. But it seems as though the tragedy of the young today, and so the tragedy of the whole world, is that in their compassionate anger they care more about pulling down than about building up, and without the discipline which they refuse they are like men trying to cross an abyss on a narrow plank which has no handrail.

It is a terrible thing to have to think, but is the destructiveness of so many of them, and the lassitude and inaction of so many others, because they have no hope? Perhaps basically we are all in the same state, old and young together, whether we know it or not, for the future is so dark and problematical. But where there is creative compassion there should be hope, and when there is hope there is always inspiration. Perhaps what the world needs is more compassion, more and more of it, not for human beings only but for every single living creature whose small span of life and enjoyment can be shattered by the lack of it.

CHAPTER X

Barton

I

TOWARDS THE END OF THAT FIRST TERM WE REALISED THAT my mother could not stay in Oxford any longer, and my father consulted the map and railway timetable. The easiest seaside place to get to from Oxford was New Milton in Hampshire. He went there, found a bungalow he liked and rented it for the rest of the summer. The one of our maids who was nearest and dearest to my mother, and I, took her down there and in a short time she was reviving. Term ended and Hélène came from boarding school and my father from Oxford to join us and the pendulum once more swung towards well-being. For my mother was so much the Queen Bee of our hive that we all revolved round her. She was our life. We wilted when she did, revived when she did.

I have often wondered what it was that gave my mother her power of capturing everyone around her. I think it was because her strong will and her powers of penetration were veiled by such gentle and outstanding charm, and this charm was not assumed, it was a perfectly natural grace arising from her loving nature. A dominant woman is generally obviously so, but not so my mother. She was also complex. Living with her was like being on a journey of discovery that never ended. But until the attainment of the last years of her life I think that she would have been the first to say that spiritually my father was the greater of the two. She would also have said that the possession of psychic' powers does not necessarily make a man or woman more spiritually advanced than someone less gifted. Their powers are born with them. My mother was a very small child when she found she had the power of levitation and could, as she expressed it, 'fly downstairs'. Real spiritual greatness is, I believe, largely a matter of slow, hard, slogging discipline.

My father knew how to slog. He worked harder than anyone I have ever known. A fine mind, with a good brain for its tool, had not made him complex. He had a delightful simplicity and was only able to enjoy things that were simple. It was this I think that made him so uneasy when trapped in elaborate social life. Once, in total exasperation, he cried out, "I wish I possessed nothing but a cell and a crucifix." My mother took this as a personal insult and he had hastily to assure her that after God she was the glory of his life ; which indeed she was. But I think he spoke the truth about himself. He would have made a happy monk. He so hated the least breath of ostentation, refusing either to employ a secretary or own a car. He would never, for himself alone, take a taxi. In his seventies, if he had to go away, he was still lugging a heavy suitcase to Carfax and catching the bus to the station. Through such economies he had more money to give away.

And so he appreciated the simplicity of our life in the small country bungalow we now acquired ; for in our restored state of well-being we had a look at the new pattern of our life and knew that my mother could not live always in Oxford, and we bought this tiny home, which my mother called Innisfree after Yeats's poem, at Barton-on-Sea, two miles from New Milton. I am quite sure we got into debt to do it for if I remember rightly it cost the whole of five hundred pounds and that was a great deal of money in those days ; the whole of my father's total annual income when we lived at Wells. From then on my mother spent only the winter months in Oxford and these she could manage, for she lived only in the two adjoining rooms of her bedroom and the drawing room, with warm fires and closed windows keeping the damp out, and for the rest of the year she and Brownie

lived at Innisfree with her special maid to look after her, and
my father and Hélène and I joined her for the Easter and
summer holidays. I had to be my father's so-called hostess
and housekeeper at Oxford, and how sorry I was for him!
Not only was he separated from his adored wife but she was
an accomplished hostess and I was the reverse. He and I
barely survived; living for the holidays.

Innisfree was in a country lane that wound through green
fields to the sea. Barton (the name means a hill) was then a
flat green plateau that is now a vast bungalow town, but
then it was open country. It faced west across the fields,
sheltered from the sea winds that swept across them behind
a bank crowned by a rampart of hawthorn trees. The
bank, separated from the bungalow by a small lawn, was
covered with wild primroses in the spring and the trees, a
mass of blossom in the spring and jewelled with red berries
in autumn, had been twisted by the gales into fantastic and
living shapes. I will always remember a sentence of a speech
made by a man who was pleading for the trees, that their
lives might be spared as much as possible in this age of
wholesale destruction. He said, "They pay no taxes. They
have no voice but the wind." I will never forget either the
voices or the shapes of those trees. They seemed to fascinate
Brownie too, for every evening he would lie at the top of the
steps that led to the verandah and the little front door, and
watch motionless as the setting sun spread its gold over the
sky behind the trees.

> And now the trembling light
> Glimmers behind the little hills, and corn,
> Ling'ring as loth to part

wrote Samuel Palmer. And that was the way the parting
sun glimmered behind our trees. When it had nearly gone
Brownie and I would walk up the lane to the cliff-top and
watch the last lights fade from sea and sky.

2

Brownie was happy at Oxford but I think he liked Barton even more. It was his place. He came to us there, a brown ball of fluff the size of a rolled-up hedgehog, and it was at Barton, years later, that he died and was buried in the garden. He was a great gentleman, and in this he was a complete contrast to the Ely dog, Max, who was the reverse of a gentleman. I had bought Max in the Wells days with some birthday money, a darling snow-white puppy with black ears whom I had seen in the window of a pet shop at Bath. It was not my intention to offer good advice in this book (I should not presume) but if I did, I would say, never buy puppies from a pet-shop window. The information given you as to their ancestry and breeding, and probable size when full grown, is seldom correct.

My little white ball grew into one of those large, rangy, smooth-haired fox-terrier types who are seldom seen now; and it is as well. It was an agony to take him out for walks for he was a bloody fighter. He was also a killer; five pounds' worth of turkeys killed in twenty minutes was a mere nothing to him, and cats were not safe in his presence. The even tenor of life in a clerical household bored him stiff and every now and then, like the prodigal son, he would leave to follow his own evil courses in a far country. At the end of a week or ten days he might be heard of incarcerated in some police station, and I would have to go and bail him out at great expense. He lived long and pleasurably, as the Psalmist laments that the wicked so often do, but at the last he met a violent end in the far country. We heard of his death with sorrow, for he had an affectionate, though not a loving heart, and enormous courage in war, and we were fond of him. Believing as I do (and I have no less a person than C. S. Lewis to back me up) that the love we have for our animals insures their immortality for as long as the love lasts, I nevertheless cánnot see Max in Paradise. For one thing our mutual affection was not deep enough to be called love, and for another thing Paradise would bore him so dreadfully. You can't have dog-fights going on all over Paradise, and it was in war that Max was best able to express his personality and, to use a modern phrase, 'do his own thing'.

Brownie was never involved in dog-fights, and to my knowledge he never killed another living creature. Not that he lacked courage; one only had to look in his great golden eyes, and to observe the fortitude with which he bore the illnesses and rheumatic pains of his last years, to know that; it was just that he had a tolerant mind and a loving heart. He hated no one except our doctor. This one hatred was because he could not for a long while make up his mind whether illness brought the doctor, or the doctor brought illness, and coming unfortunately to the latter conclusion he acted accordingly in defence of his family.

He was the scion of two noble houses. His mother was Marie's beautiful golden pedigree chow, Swankie, and it was Marie who gave Brownie to us. Swankie made a love-match on her own, thought at the time to be unfortunate but as all the offspring proved totally delightful, afterwards considered fortunate. Swankie's chosen beloved was a pedigree liver and white Norfolk spaniel. I was introduced to him at one time and apart from Brownie himself I have never seen a more dignified dog, and Brownie was richly endowed with the best beauties and qualities of both parents.

In appearance he was a large woolly dog, the colour of a ripe horse-chestnut. He had the noble forehead and long, drooping ears of a spaniel but the superb plumey tail that curved over his back was a chow's. He had a chow's frown (an intellectual frown, not a bad-tempered one) and a purple-black tongue. When we were out together, Brownie pacing beside me with incomparable dignity, head well up, imperial and unfussed, dog-lovers would stop me in the street and say,

"What a wonderful dog!" and then, after a puzzled pause, "But what *is* he?" I would explain the love-match of aristocratic parents, pointing out how the mingling of two noble breeds had produced a dog more beautiful than either. They would agree, saying he was indeed unique. He would look up at them, his golden eyes full of love, and they would leave him with a sad reluctance, and feeling the better, I am sure, for this brief encounter with so perfect a being.

Truly, he had no faults; for attacking our doctor was a misapprehension on his part, not a fault. He had avoided the arrogance of a chow, retaining only the dignity, and in his loving he was never effusive or sentimental as spaniels sometimes are. He loved deeply but was not in favour of too many endearments.

In this he was like my mother for whom his devotion was that of a medieval knight for his lady. He was with her as much as possible. If she was ill he lay beside her sofa or under her bed and it was difficult to persuade him to leave her. If she went out in her bathchair he went too, as a round ball of a puppy on her lap or as a grown dog pacing beside her. When once she was obliged to leave him behind he came to meet her with his furry face seamed with the dark runnels of tears. I have had a dog who learned to smile like a human being but Brownie was the only dog I have known who could weep as humans do. When my mother was once suddenly taken away from the Barton bungalow for an emergency operation Brownie spent the weeks of her absence huddled in the corner of the sitting room. But he did not weep then for his anguish was too great for the relief of tears. However he was always a dog of common sense and he would come out of his corner for food and exercise. He knew he must keep in health for his family's sake. And at night he would lie beside my bed and take the necessary sleep.

He was devoted to my father too and took him for long walks in the winter country round Oxford. When he grew old, with a grey muzzle, he still struggled on with these walks until one day, half-way across Tom Quad, he sank to the ground and laid his head down on his paws. My father came back and brought him home and tried to comfort him, but he would not be comforted and wept a little. After that he showed his usual common sense and accepted the infirmity of old age with dignity and patience, strolling round the Christ Church Meadows with me instead of climbing the hills and exploring the woods with my father, but never failing to keep my father company in his study late at night, after all the females had gone to bed. If there was some good music my father would sometimes switch on his wireless set. Brownie enjoyed classical music, especially Beethoven, as much as his master, but modern music insulted his ears and made him howl dismally. My father was only too pleased to switch it off. Their musical tastes were identical.

Brownie died not long before my father. He was walking slowly and with dignity up the side of the lane that led to the sea at Barton when he suddenly swerved out just as a horse and cart were coming up behind him. He was not run over but something, the wheel or the horse's hoof, hit him. He swerved back again into the hedge and died instantly. He and my mother had been inseparable and after his death she was sure his still living spirit was often with her, until he had her a little comforted. So why did he, apparently, choose to die? Was his deepest love really for his master and he thought that for once he would go on ahead instead of following behind? Who knows what goes on in a dog's mind? We may read into their thoughts more than is actually there, and yet on the other hand, since they seem to have so little sense of the passing of time, perhaps for them the future runs into the present and they know far more of it than we do.

Brownie was too great a dog, and too greatly loved, for it to be possible to think of having another. It was not until the last war was over that The Hobbits came. Three of them in succession, Tiki, Randa and Froda. Not great dogs, but magical.

3

I owe more than I can say to Barton. Here I really discovered the Keyhaven saltmarshes that had caught hold of me in my schooldays, and it was from Barton that I first went to stay with Mrs Adams at the house that I have called Damerosehay. It was her husband's family home but after his death she could neither afford to live there nor bear to leave it, so she ran it as a hotel for her friends and their friends. Only those with this introduction of friendship could go there, and this insured that only quiet folk in search of peace came to this domain of peace and did not disturb its special atmosphere; and Mrs Adams could leave her ancestral treasures, the old pictures and furniture and china, in the places where they had been for years and be sure no harm would come to them. There was no feeling of a hotel about the lovely place, one was simply staying with Mrs Adams in her home.

It was also at Barton that my private hobby of writing got more and more of a hold on me. If it had not been such a happy thing I could have likened it to an octopus, for the stranglehold was growing tighter and tighter. Getting up early in the morning and going to bed late at night I had already written my first long and atrocious novel, but not even the partiality of a parent for her first-born could make me think that there was anywhere to put it except the fire and so I put it there and told myself that I was no novelist. But my handicraft training was not now providing me with what I wanted, a home-based career so that I could be with my mother as much as possible, and so my love of the theatre flared up afresh and I started on a long slog of writing plays. Like so many beginners I thought they would be easier than

novels, being shorter, and only experience could teach me
that they are more difficult than any other form of writing;
especially for women, who tend to suffer from the organic
female disease of using a hundred words where one would do.
Men are more concise in their writing and therefore more
dramatic.

It was not surprising that I was once more stage-struck,
for the Oxford Playhouse was producing the plays of Ibsen
and Shaw and Galsworthy week after week in the dingy little
ex-museum in North Oxford that housed its young, great
days. I saved up my pin-money to go there, and occasionally
I got to a London matinée to see even greater things. I lay
awake all night after seeing the young John Gielgud's
Hamlet; it was impossible to sleep after such an experience.
I saw Edith Evans and Peggy Ashcroft in all their glory. I
would come home to my mother in a state of trance and tell
her about these experiences. She was sympathetic but always
ended by saying, "You should have seen Irving and Ellen
Terry." I would be annoyed, not knowing yet that we are
faithful always to the artists who spin their spells about us
when we are young.

With woe I discovered that I could no more write a good
play than I could write a good novel. Because my plays read
well, and deceived those who read them, I achieved a few
Sunday-night try-outs and one repertory performance, but
if the plays read well (and perhaps for that reason) they
did not act well; they did not 'come over'. But all the work
and disappointment were well worth it because they brought
me, for a short while and to a minute degree, inside the
theatre world, and because I was presented with a candid
criticism. "Why waste your time writing bad plays when you
could write a good novel?" Remembering the bonfire that
had raged about my first book I doubted that, but I tried
again, inspired this time by two loves more intimate than
love of the theatre, love of my mother and of the Island, and I

wrote *Island Magic* in a corner of my mother's bedroom at Barton.

It is largely about her childhood and has in it many of the stories she told me. Peronelle is my mother as I pictured her at that age. The portrait of André is not worthy of my grandfather but I think that Rachel is a true picture of my grandmother. I had no idea to whom to send the manuscript. I wrote out a list of publishers taken at random from *The Writers' and Artists' Year Book*, which I found at the Free Library at Oxford, and sent it out on its rounds. Finally I was lucky for it was accepted by Gerald Duckworth. Of the three publishers who for so many years have helped and advised me, and to whom I owe more than I can express, the deepest love and gratitude go to Duckworth. If writers find it depressing to look with a critical eye at their past books they find it the opposite to look back and see the stepping stones that one by one begin to lift them above failure. Duckworth gave me my first stepping stone and Nancy Pearn gave me my second, the beloved old *Strand* magazine.

Nancy Pearn, when I first knew her, was one third of a new literary agency that had just removed itself from the parent tree of Curtis Brown to start on its own as Pearn, Pollinger and Higham, and Nancy, believing in me on the strength of one insignificant book, took me out to lunch and suggested that I should join their slowly growing family of writers. The sun shone that day; it did so literally, for I remember its warmth as Nancy and I walked down the street to her club; and I remember the love I felt for her that day and always until she died. I trusted her entirely and did all she ever advised me to do. I owe as much to her and to David Higham as I do to my publishers. I think Nancy truly regarded her writers as her children. "Kate O'Brien and Stella Gibbons and you, I've had you from the cradle," she said to me one day, and certainly she brooded over us with real affection. The first thing she did for me was to get me a commission to write short stories for the *Strand* and David Higham settled that stone in place with a piece of good advice. "Write short stories for a living while you build up a reputation with your books. Don't, yet, look to books for a living." That was good advice at that date, when there was a large public for magazines and I followed it. Now, I don't know what they do in the cradle, apart from journalism. I am afraid they must often go hungry.

4

My good luck delighted my astonished family and opened for me many new doors. Until now my microscopic earnings had not enabled me to go off on my own for holidays; now that I could do that my mother encouraged me and was glad to have Nanny or one of her sisters to look after her while I was away. Barton was my point of departure for what, for me, was high adventure, for apart from one short visit to France I had never been anywhere except to the Island, to the seaside places nearest to Wells and Ely and to the cottage in the Cotswolds that was the aunts' home after they finally left the Island. Both Hélène and I loved this cottage, high up in the backwoods above Stroud. That had been the extent of my travelling.

If my mother always longed for the sea I longed even more for high hills and the first of my adventures was a walking holiday with a friend who lived in the Lake District. The Westmorland and Cumberland hills were the highest I had ever seen and being with them was utter joy. Those were the days when you could walk all day with a pack on you back and meet only a few people doing the same thing. And no itinerary need be planned. When evening came and you were tired any farm that you happened to find in a fold of the hills would welcome you and give you supper and a bed, and in the morning breakfast and a packet of sandwiches for the next day's tramp over the fells. On fine days we would stop walking and sit in the sun listening to the music of the streams as they came down from the heights, and the bleating of the sheep, looking down with wonder on a valley floor far below and seeing the microscopic farms and the patchwork fields held in a trance of stillness and silence. My friend always had a book in her pack and I had a paintbox. But how could anyone except Turner paint such landscapes and skyscapes as we saw from the high eyries where we rested? Each day I gave up in despair yet each day, in spite of my friend's laughter, I tried again, for something has to be done to ease the pressure of certain types of joy.

This kind of holiday was repeated again in the highlands of Scotland and in Skye, and later I discovered the mountains of North Wales and of Norway. But of all the holidays of my life the most glorious was a Hellenic Travellers' cruise which took my father, Marie and myself through the Mediterranean to Greece, and on to Constantinople, and home by way of Crete, Sicily and Corsica. It would be foolish to try and say much about it for what we saw, and what we felt in seeing it, is well known to most people today. But we had the advantage that forty years ago the world was quieter and less populated than it is today. We were alone when we stood by the Lion Gate at Mycenae and saw the hills where the beacons were lit when Troy fell, and looked out over the plain of Argos shimmering in the heat.

We were blest with perfect weather all the way. We saw the Acropolis honey-coloured against a cloudless blue sky and at Olympia the anemones were red as fire in the green grass. We approached Constantinople in a golden dawn and left it in a flaming sunset, with a school of dolphins playing and leaping around the ship as they escorted us out to sea. San Sophia was still in use as a mosque then and was not the echoing museum which I am told it is today. Holy old men sat there reading the Koran and it was warm with the atmosphere of prayer and gleaming with soft pale gold in the sunlight. Crete was flaming with marigolds and in Corsica I climbed a hill blue with wild lupins, and outside Syracuse there was a hill where wild mignonette smelt like paradise in the sun.

The holiday went by like a dream and we came home to my mother and Hélène. I think now how shocking it was that I went to Greece and Hélène did not. Child though she was then she had loved Socrates before I did. She died when she was still only in her fifties and never saw his country while I, undeservedly, saw Greece.

CHAPTER XI

Pain and the Love of God

I

IT SEEMED TO MY FATHER AND TO ME THAT SOME DOOM HUNG over my mother because she could not stop being ill. Barton made life possible for her but never easy. During the last years at Oxford and Barton she had one severe illness and two bad operations and from all three she nearly died. The last operation was on her spine, for at last the injury to her back had been discovered, not by a doctor but by our district nurse at Barton, and an Oxford surgeon operated and removed the coccyx. But the years of neglect had done such damage, and she suffered so much for so long after the operation, that it was only just worth while. She was reviving at last when my father was for a time devastated by an operation, and then the same thing happened to me.

In this world where we live now no single man or woman can come to the end of their life without suffering, some not more than can reasonably be borne, some more that that, some intolerably and hideously. If we all suffered equally there would be no problem, but we do not suffer equally, and it is the inequality that creates the heart-searching for those among us who believe in the love of God. My father would say austerely, "It does not matter what we suffer as long as we suffer enough." He believed whole-heartedly in the cleansing and redemptive power of pain and its value when offered as intercession, but he acknowledged the problem and staggered under it because of the fact that unbearable suffering can corrupt as well as redeem.

"I am tormented by the suffering of so many good and

innocent people," someone said to Archbishop Temple
during the last war. "Yes," he replied, "but what bothers
me even more is the suffering of the wicked."

That would suggest that how an individual takes his pain,
what he allows it to do in him and through him, is much
more important than the pain itself. The scene of suffering
in each person seems to be a battleground where a thing evil
in its origin comes up against the battling love of God that
would transform it into an instrument of victory; not victory
for the individual alone but also for God himself in the
cosmic battle between good and evil.

My mother's illness had troubled me all my life, and I felt
guilty as well as unhappy, so bound together are we all by
the guilt and sorrow of the world that we all share. But I
confess with shame that I do not believe my faith in the love
of God was badly shaken until the evil touched me myself.
"It is when it touches your *own* flesh," my mother said once,
"it is then that you know." It did not touch my flesh so badly
as it touched my mind for after the little succession of family
disasters I fell headlong into what is called a nervous breakdown, a state which as all its victims know can be terrifying.
We all feel frightened because we feel that the division
between nervous and mental illness is so thin that the thing
we all dread more than anything else seems only just round
the next corner of the mind. Fanny Burney in her Diary tells
us how Dr Johnson, fearing in his old age that he might be
heading for insanity, got up early in the morning and wrote
out a heartfelt prayer to God that whatever evil might come
upon him now might strike his body alone and not his mind.
And King Lear prays,

O, let me not be mad, not mad, sweet heaven!
Keep me in temper: I would not be mad!

We all feel the same.

And I think we all feel the same about the temptation to suicide, that is a perfectly normal part of any nervous breakdown. We are frightened of it. If it has been conquered for the time being we dread its return in some time of strain, and it possibly will return, like any other temptation, though probably getting weaker every time we get the better of it. I am sure we should try not to be frightened and that the right attitude towards it should be just that—a temptation like any other. Not a dreadful thing at all, perfectly ordinary, and a surprising number of people suffer from it, for we are never alone in what we suffer.

I know I am digressing from what was supposed to be the subject of this chapter, and I want to digress even more because there is something that I badly want to say, and that is that what we are accustomed to call 'the world' (meaning by this, I think, in this context, all the idiots among the human race who love to sit on the judgment-seat of total ignorance) continues to judge suicide too harshly, as though it were a clear-headed, deliberate action. It may be so as when Captain Oates went out to die in the blizzard for the sake of his companions. Many men and women, I believe, do as he did, and take their lives for love's sake, and when a thing is done for the sake of love no one should dare to criticise.

But others who take their lives are not in a clear-headed state. They are either overwhelmed by anxiety, shock, depression or grief, or taken unaware by the suddenness of the temptation (and it can be as sudden as losing one's temper) or they are in great pain. I am lucky enough to be able to say that I have never experienced great pain, but I do know from the minor pain of migraine headaches how confused one can be. It wakes you in the middle of the night and you hunt for the appropriate pills. An hour later, when the pain has reached its height, you are so confused that you cannot remember if you took them or not. A quarter of an hour later you are quite sure you did not. If one can be so muddle-headed with a migraine what can the mental confusion be like when a person is in fearful pain?

To come back to the question of harsh judgment—do those who judge harshly never yield to their own temptations? Temptation is a matter of temperament and you are no more responsible for your particular temptations than you are responsible for your own temperament. All we can any of us do is to try and muster the will-power to deal courageously with both, and the love to try not to be too great a burden on other people.

How difficult some temperaments (mine, for instance) are to live with and how dependent we all are on the love and understanding of those who are with us. Especially the introverts. I think I only realise now how much both my parents always helped me. At the time I took them far too much for granted. If you grow up with wonderful people about you always you do tend to take them for granted. It needs emergence into the world, and contact with the other sort, to know your luck.

2

I come back again to where I started, pain and the love of God. When my mother suffered I was miserable and my faith in God's love was sorely tried. When I suffered myself it was nearly shattered. Blind as a bat I could not see that what I had to put up with myself was not only a microscopic burden but also an extremely common one, and I scarcely considered the example of my father, carrying his recurrent darkness so selflessly that it damaged neither mind nor body. I had hardly considered anyone but myself until the day I went to the oculist.

A thread of comedy seems to be twisted into everything which happens to us but the ability to find it requires a corresponding ability not to take oneself too seriously, and as I had generally done that I saw nothing funny in the fact that the beginning of a return to faith should come in an oculist's waiting-room. I sat in it mounded up with self-pity and glooming over my fate, until I found myself looking across at the stranger opposite me, an elderly woman sitting upright and completely still. Her face had the glazed look of someone who has suffered much, something that I did not recognise then, but I do now. She was very near me and I could look directly into her eyes. She did not look as though she were blind but her eyes did not see me. It is a strange experience to look straight into the eyes of someone who is not even aware that you are there. I began to feel shivery. What she feared, what she had already endured, I could not know, but I did know that anything I had suffered myself faded into nothingness in comparison. For a few moments I seemed to fall into a cold misery that I cannot describe. It was not her alone, it was all the people whom until now, apart from my mother, I had refused to think about; battering them down under hatches so that I should not have to feel too miserable. Quite suddenly, if only for a short while, she had let me through into their company.

Speaking of those who suffer I am not forgetting the birds and animals. It is impossible to forget them, but with them the problem is different because their suffering is largely laid upon them by human cruelty. It is ourselves we have to question, not God. If we question God at all it is to wonder why he allows man to continue to fester upon the face of the earth when all he seems to do there is to pollute, torture and destroy all the loveliness God has created? Here our rage is turned upon ourselves, and not one of us is innocent. We all know by what processes we are provided with certain foods, clothes, drugs and cosmetics.

I am sure Teilhard de Chardin was thinking of all living creatures when he wrote,

> The problem of evil . . . will always remain one of the most disturbing mysteries of the universe for both our hearts and our minds. A full understanding of the suffering of God's creatures . . . presupposes in us an appreciation of the nature and value of 'participated being' which, for lack of any point of comparison, we cannot have.*

We cannot understand—not yet—but we can see how the more we lose our sense of separateness in the knowledge of the one-ness of all living creatures, millions of small leaves on the one single tree of life, the more we shall lose our sense of self-importance, and so be liberated from our self-pity; a bondage so horrible that I believe it can bring us at last to a state not unlike that of Gollum, the dreadful creature Tolkien created, living alone in the dark, talking to himself, murmuring, "My preciouss. My preciouss."

But if that "my preciouss" were to be the song of the leaves on the tree, each leaf delighting in all the others there could be no love of self, no hatred and no sin, and none of the suffering that springs from sin. And since a tree has no voice but the wind, and the leaves know it, they would soon know who it was who was singing their song with them and through them, and lifting and swinging them in the dance. If we can find a little of our one-ness with all other creatures, and love for them, then I believe we are half-way towards finding God.

3

But at this time I had not yet tried to read Teilhard de Chardin, tried desperately to understand him, failed com-

---

* *Le Milieu Divin*, Pierre Teilhard de Chardin.

pletely, yet found my life immeasurably enriched by the
mere failure. My brief awareness in the waiting-room did
not make my problem much easier, but it did drive me to try
and work something out for myself. I had a little earlier than
this fallen in love with the doctrine of reincarnation, since
to believe that nothing happens to us that is not the result of
our previous actions absolves God from the charge of injustice.
But this my father had dismissed with two withering words,
"Utter nonsense." I think now that he may have been wrong
but at that time I could not believe that my father could be
wrong, and I was withered.

So now I had to think again. I could not totally disbelieve
in God because during my worst and most despairing nights
there had seemed to be something there; some rock down at
the bottom . . . And always my parents' love and faith, the
world's beauty and the sound of great music, seemed un-
explainable without God . . . Therefore I had to find a God
I could love. I could not love a God who did not stop this
suffering therefore I had to have a God who could not, a God
who was not Almighty. I was aware of the cosmic struggle
since I had experienced the faint echo of it in myself, the
spiritual powers of good and evil in conflict. I worked it out
that one was not stronger than the other, and at the end of it
all evil might win. God might again die and this time have no
resurrection. But if he was finally defeated it would be our
fault, not his, for he would have withstood evil to the utmost
limit, as he did on Calvary, and would die only because we
are afraid to do the same. Our wounds are in his flesh, always,
our griefs in his heart, but he is powerless to stop the evil of
sin and pain by himself. He is a God who needs us and cannot
do without us. I could love that weak God.

I was happy with this for a while, and then I told my
father of my conclusions. The result was disastrous. How
unoriginal human beings are! Our great ideas are seldom new.
I had thought up the heresy of Manicheism, a faith for which

men and women had been willing to be martyred, and which had tempted even Augustine. It was hard to let go of my lovely heresy, but my father had no mercy on it. A God who is not Almighty is not God, and to believe in his possible defeat is not conforting; that way lies despair.

I do not remember all he said of his own faith, possibly I did not understand it, but I remember my own conclusions. If our own small intuition, upheld by the experience of the saints and mystics of all religions through all the centuries, persists in murmuring that God exists then there is nothing left for us except the humble acceptance of paradox and mystery. If it is true that God is Almighty, it is also true that he needs us, since he chose that his son should be true man as well as true God, by this choice making Christ and man inseparable. Apart from Christ we have no life; we are merely a dead leaf fallen from the tree. Apart from us he has no body in the world, no hands and feet and heart and voice to bring God's mercy to a suffering world.

But the deepest mystery of all, for me, is this one. Suffering, we believe, stems from evil, and evil has no part in the will of God. Yet God allowed the cruelty, jealousy and cowardice of man to put his son upon the cross and when he was there made no move to end his torture; God himself in man had to stick it out until the end. And so God and the suffering caused by sin are inseparably united, and will be so until sin ends. The mind boggles but there is enormous comfort here. For one thing it is hard to doubt the love of a God who is ready to suffer and die for us. For another thing, when we suffer we must be as close to God as we are to the pain. At the worst of it we may feel, as Christ did, that God forsakes when unbearable pain takes over. But the truth must be the reverse. Devout people used to say of pain or grief, "God touched me." Gerard Manley Hopkins says, "And dost thou touch me afresh? Over again I feel thy finger and find thee."

Then comes the trembling, wondering thought—if, as St Paul thought, Christ "bore our sins in his own body on the tree," took our vileness into his body as a sponge sucks up water, that it might die with him on the cross, is it possible that our wretched little pain, united with his huge suffering, can also redeem? The answer surely is—to the measure of our loving, yes.

Everything seems to boil down to the measure of our loving. Faith is a gift that we cannot compel, and it seems to be given more to the measure of our loving than to the struggling of our minds. It can strike suddenly, or come as slowly as the greening of spring.

> Whether at once, as once at a crash Paul,
> Or as Austin, a lingering-out sweet skill,

and the skill is Christ's, and cannot be described, only worshipped and adored. There are those who can believe in the love of God without believing that Christ on the cross is God. In the face of human misery that is a leap of faith that I should find it hard to take. The love of God is too mighty and dreadful for our contemplation but in accepting the life and death of Christ as the utmost revelation we can have of it now, in this world and this time, I can feel at rest. Does it seem impossible, too startling to be true, that a man on the gallows should be God? Yet in this amazing universe where every new discovery shocks us afresh, is it not just what we should expect of this startling Creator? As the years go on we fall in love with him more and more, we cannot help it. The mind may reel and protest but we cannot help it. His immense love is too strong. Our frail loving is too strong. Finally we fight against neither. I do not know certainly who it was, though I think it was Charles Williams, who when he was finally captured said, "There is nothing possible for me now except to believe the impossible."

4

(Here I have to stop for a moment, for I am so ashamed to
write of the facts, and the people, in the next paragraphs, I
who as a practising Christian am such a failure. But those who
have failed sometimes see things more clearly than those who
have succeeded. Failure has, at least, the advantage of clear
sight.)

It is his skill, not ours, that yields faith to our loving, but
what of those many loving people who do not find God? Are
they in this world deprived of Christ? I think the answer is
again in the cross. Wherever there is suffering, there they find
him, and with or without recognition that is always where
the greatest men and women do find him. Francis of Assisi,
Father Damian, Elizabeth Fry, Albert Schweitzer, these and
many other Christians knew that they found Christ in those
whom they served and acknowledged that the love they
felt was God's love in them, but those who do not know do the
same work for the same God and have a richness and fulfilment in their lives unknown to many so-called Christians.
I know of one, a man who has suffered the impossible things,
war, grief, torture and inprisonment, and come through
uncorrupted, with a compassion so strong that wherever he
may be in the world he must find his way to those who suffer
most, no matter how terrible their suffering or how dreadful
the place where they are, and keep them company and serve
them as far as he is able.

Conversion is sterile one can face and implement the
paradox of Christ. He is God and a man on the gallows. His
voice is the beauty of the world and the crying of a hungry
child. He is peace in our hearts and conviction of sin. He
draws us to him with tenderness and then says the most
uncomfortable things to us. To go through the gospels and
note them all is a frightening experience.

Hypocrites that are like whitewashed tombs, which make a fine show from without, but are full inside of dead men's bones and every kind of filth . . . Harlots have the lead of *you* on the road to the Kingdom of God . . . I was hungry and you did not feed me; I was thristy but you did not give me drink; I was homeless and you did not bring me in; naked and you did not clothe me; sick and in prison and you did not visit me . . . Hear the truth . . . In so far as you did not do these things to one of these little ones, you did not do them to me.

I believe that the converted can face a great danger. It is that when the skill of Christ has brought us to him we forget about his children in concentration about himself. It seems impossible, but we can almost forget the very suffering the thought of which was at one time driving us nearly mad. But Christ won't be concentrated upon in this one-sided manner. He won't have us on these terms. He is completely identified with all suffering creatures and we have him with them, or not at all. It can come about that some man or woman finds God not by way of a sense of unity with his children but through a journey lonely as that of the Prodigal Son, but I believe that if we go home like the Prodigal Son we must go out again as the Good Samaritan.

I feel myself that I have come really to know this too late and I understand what my father felt when towards the end of his life he said (and it was the only time when I ever saw him close to weeping), "When I come to the end I shall be saying to God 'Let me go back and try again.'" Was it simply a cry of penitence or did he feel at last as I do now, that one life on this earth is not enough to satisfy the hunger that we have to serve him in all the ways that are open to us under earthly conditions? One earthly life may have been enough for Christ, so perfectly balanced was he, so entirely concentrated on the matter in hand, yet able to turn from one thing to another as though there were no difficult transitions between storm and calm, teaching and healing, praying and going to a party, suffering and dying, but all were the one smooth flow of the music of the will of God.

But we are torn and exhausted by the trivialities and conflicts of self, by stress and strain and busyness. Those who are devotedly serving their fellow men are often too tired to pray, creative artists are so absorbed in the world of their own creativity that the tiny place assumes enormous proportions and they are in danger of forgetting the suffering world outside; and in proportion as they forget their own world darkens. Only the contemplatives seem in better shape, for their prayer has no walls. It embraces all the world and all the people in it and all their pain. They tell us that their deep prayer actually shares the pain and so to those of us to whom prayer goes no deeper than "the conscious occupation of the praying mind, or the sound of the voice praying", such prayer seems a frightening thing. Nevertheless it has the music and if in old age we feel heartbroken because we know that we have failed Christ in his suffering children it is not too late to try and reach out to them in that life of selfless prayer. Death may come upon us before we have done more than merely try to reach out, but it will not matter too much. I believe that death interrupts nothing of importance if the goal is Christ.

CHAPTER XII

The Ark

I

IN THE SPRING OF 1939 MY FATHER DIED AT BARTON. HE
had a bad fall, a fortnight of pain and bewilderment, and
then he became unconscious and died in his sleep. The nurses
at the nursing home where he died told me I was wasting
my time, sitting so many hours by the bed of a dying man
who would never regain consciousness. But he did. He appeared to come back from some great distance and said
slowly and distinctly, "Dear one, it is loving that matters,"
and then drifted away again upon the great, peaceful
journey. So that is the end of it for these great men. All their
accumulated knowledge, all the argument and controversy,
seem of little importance. Only love remains important and
is immortal. Baron von Hugel was much like my father in
his dying for his last words to his niece were, "It is caring
that matters. It is caring."

I had come very near to my father at the end of his life
for he had been so marvellously good to me in my miseries
and problems. For most of my life it had been between us as
in my first memory of him, he had always been far on ahead
of me, disappearing into countries of the mind and spirit
where I could not follow him. But in the last year of his
life it was as though he turned back upon his path to find
and be with me on mine. We were close to each other as
never before, and part of my sorrow when he died was that
our closeness was given no time to mature and grow greater.
But between my father and my mother the closeness had
been lifelong. They had been almost one person. What the

parting meant to her she allowed no one to know. Her eyes lost all their brightness but no one saw her cry.

All times of devastation, whether they are the normal personal losses that visit every life, or the devastation of great wars, famines and earthquakes, leave the survivors with a feeling of amazement. Is it possible that such weak creatures as we know ourselves to be have coped with this? Done what had to be done, borne what had to be borne, picked up the pieces and become ready to begin again and go on living. It took more than a year, moves to three different houses, and the outbreak of a war to bring my mother and myself to this condition of amazement, followed by humble gratitude.

For no one supposes that this competence and survival has much to do with their everyday selves. Christians acknowledge the power and grace of God and marvel at it. Non-believers marvel at the discovery of a toughness within them that they did not know they had, a source of strength that seems not available in everyday living and opens up only when disaster strikes. The believer acknowledges this too but gives the name of God to the well of power within him, and believes also that he has a prepared path under his feet and moves along it step by step to a prepared end. Much later, looking back, he realises how many stars there were showing the way at the cross-roads, stars which can be called either coincidence or Providence according to personal belief.

My mother and I called the cottage in Devon in which we finally began again Providence Cottage. It was of course considered a sentimental name by a number of friends ("*What* have you called the place? Tranquillity Lodge? Serenity Mansion? Peace Villa?") but our feelings were not hurt for we knew what we knew. Above all we knew that my father still lived and still loved us. So great was his spiritual power that he was able to make that unmistakably clear to both of us after his death, and so we came to believe that human love at its best is so great a thing that only a God of love could possibly have created it.

2

Once she had mastered her first shock and grief my mother behaved like a phoenix, drove herself back into life and then flamed up into activity and optimism, even into a spurious state of health and strength that amazed Nanny and myself. For Nanny of course had now come to us. Her own parents had died, she was living with her sisters and was free to help us until we had settled into a new home. Hélène was no longer living with us as her parents had come back to England for good and she was with them, and so my mother now only had Nanny and me to galvanise into activity.

We packed up the family treasures to go into store, sold the rest of the contents of the big Oxford house to help pay the large sum that was owing to the Inland Revenue (that detested bogey) when my father died, and our first move was back to Barton, where Innisfree was now home. And we knew how lucky we were. Not many clergy widows, turning out in a hurry, have anywhere to go and we had our bungalow already furnished with the little we needed. Indeed we were lucky for unless I could manage to work much harder and write much better than I was doing at the moment we were going to be very badly off. That the position and the frailty of the bungalow would make it desperately cold for my mother in the stormy Barton winters was at the back of our minds, but we firmly kept it there. The turmoil of leaving Oxford over, exhausted by it and with nothing more to do we sank into black misery until my mother was suddenly aware of the first star, the first pointer. "We need a holiday," she said. "We are going to Devon for a month."

Devon? Why Devon? Nanny and I were dumbfounded.
She and I had never been there and my mother only for a
short while when she and my father were on their honeymoon. We knew no one there and where could we stay?
But my mother had seen an advertisement in the paper. A
small wooden bungalow could be cheaply rented for a summer holiday at a village called Marldon, four miles from
Paignton, and she was quite certain that that was where we
must go. So Nanny and I dragged ourselves out of the ooze
of our exhaustion and we set off, driven by a Barton friend
who had a large comfortable car and said he knew the way.
More or less he did and very late in the afternoon we found
the wooden bungalow and inside it our unknown landlady,
who kept a guest-house next door, had lit a glowing fire.

For it was what those who do not love Devon call 'a typical
Devon day'; that is to say it was raining, that steady relent-
less rain that lifted the Ark above the primeval flood, and
at the same time, since the day was windless, a thick mist
covered the face of the earth. We could know nothing of our
surroundings except that the bungalow seemed poised upon
the summit of a hill and that its wooden walls did not look
very weather-proof. It was felt that food would be reassuring
and Nanny and I began quickly getting some sort of a meal
together, but the friend who had brought us down took me
away from the preparations for a few moments to the western-
facing window. "Look," he said. "What do you think is
out there?" The downpour was slackening at last and no
longer drummed on the roof. A small wet green lawn sloped
from the window and appeared to fall into the mist as though
it was green water sliding over the edge of a precipice. We
could see nothing through the mist yet we were aware that
behind it was the westering sun, and also that it seemed to
fill a deep valley and that rising beyond the valley was—
what? "Something grand," said our friend. "You'll know
in the morning."

A tremor went through me, and I think through him too, for we seemed to be sharing one of those inexplicable moments of expectation and intimation that come some-times when a small earthly mystery seems to be speaking of a mystery beyond itself. It was a deeper thing than the thrill I had felt standing on the beach near Keyhaven as a schoolgirl. That kind of thrill seems to promise something to one's own small life, the other seems to foretell some future greatness for life itself. It is perhaps almost a pagan thrill, since one is as ready as the so-called pagans were to worship the small mystery itself; the rising sun, a certain grove of trees, a bush burning with scarlet flowers, a great lion, a bird who sings in the dark.

I was woken up in the morning by a sound I had not heard for a long time, a cock crowing in the garden, across the lane, eastward where the sun would soon be rising. I remembered the hidden mystery in the west. "You'll see in the morning," our friend had said. Had the mist lifted? When later I pulled back my curtains it was still there, but the morning sun was shining through it and turning it to gold, and every bush and tree that lined the lane was glistening with diamond drops.

It was a morning of settling in but always I was slipping back to the two eastward-facing rooms, the sitting room and my mother's bedroom, because the sun was gradually drawing up the mist. Finally in mercy, and because she was losing patience, Nanny put a deckchair at the edge of the small green lawn and said, "You'd better stay there." And so leaving her to work alone I stayed.

It was what the lovers of Devon call 'a typical Devon day', that is to say, a morning of clear shining after rain. The sun was drawing up the mist and building with it galleons and cities in the air. They drifted across a sky so deeply blue that it was hard to believe it had been dark with rain the day before, and the vastness of the skyscape was almost worthy

of the Fen country. Because of the slope of the land the hill
seemed higher than it actually was; it seemed high as
Ararat, with the wooden bungalow perched like the Ark
on its summit. The valley below was even wider and deeper
than I had realised the night before and it seemed to hold
every beauty that a pastoral Devon valley knows, woods
and farms and orchards, green slopes where sheep were
grazing, fields of black and white cows, and where there were
fields of tilled earth it was the crimson of the earth of South
Devon and looked like a field of flowers. And along the
eastern horizon lay the range of blue hills called Dartmoor.

I felt I had come home. Certainly Ely was the home of
homes, holding as it did the great Cathedral and so much
happiness, and yet I have never felt so deeply rooted anywhere
as I was in the earth of Devon. Or rather I did not so much
put roots down as find roots that were already there. And
yet I had not been born in Devon, I had been born over the
border in Somerset. I could not understand it then, and I do
not understand it now. I was ashamed that I should not feel
one tremor of homesickness for Oxford, or even for Barton.
The only tremor was the realisation that in a few weeks' time
we should have to leave this earthly paradise and go back
to Barton where my father had died. There seemed no death
here, only life.

3

In difficult times in life a certain poet so often seems to
travel with one. At this time I had just discovered Humbert
Wolfe.

> But, slowly
> making more holy what is holy
> from the guarded pool

of the spirit, swift, cold and beautiful,
in mists diaphanous his rain
a God draws back again;
and, as the sun builds with the clouds, of these
he builds his city of peace—

That describes the lifting of the mist that day, and also what happened to my mother during the Devon years. She said to me suddenly, a short while after our arrival at the Ark, "It is never too late to be a saint." She had a strange dread that her husband, in his new life, would develop spiritually so far beyond her that when she also died she would not be with him. It was not like her to entertain dreads and she set her strong will to work at once on this one in the only possible way; with God's help she must grow. And slowly, steadily and deliberately, during the Devon years, she grew. She was always something of a grande dame and the change in her was rather as though Queen Elizabeth the First should grow into Saint Teresa of Avila.

Suddenly the war broke out. We could not know then that all through the winter it would be only what we called 'the phoney war'. At the time we expected that bombs would fall instantly on London and parents fell into a state of panic about their children. We had an S.O.S. from a friend of my mother's brother, Hélène's father, who lived in London and had four small children. Would we let him buy our Barton bungalow exactly as it was, with its contents, that he might send his family to live there immediately? My mother never hesitated. Indeed I think she sent a telegram of acceptance, and then said to me, "We are going to live here—in Devon." I think she made the decision chiefly because I loved the place so much, but she too loved it. The lanes with the streams running down them, the wet ferns and the steep banks and the seagulls flying inland, reminded her of the Island. Our landlady said we might stay in the Ark through the winter if necessary, and we set to work to find a permanent home.

We made no headway since anything we could afford to pay for, my mother could not ever contemplate as her future home. And she was quite right. It would have been like trying to grow a Guernsey lily in a tin can and she would have wilted and died. And then there occurred one of those apparent coincidences that are not what they appear. We had hired a car and were on one of our invariably hopeless house-hunting expeditions when we found ourselves, apparently by accident, facing some new houses that were being built on the edge of a wooded valley not far from Cockington. They were lovely houses with steep, sloping, large gardens and were quite obviously more expensive than we could afford; but my mother insisted that Nanny and I must look at them. We protested but she took no notice of our protests, so leaving her in the car we looked at the impossible houses.

We were in one of them when we heard a step behind us. "You want to buy one of my houses?" asked a genial voice. We turned round and found ourselves confronting a tall stout man with white hair and moustache and a rosy trustworthy Westcountry face. With a sense of guilt (since what were we doing inside a house we couldn't afford when we wanted a cheap bungalow?) I asked the price. It was of course impossible, and I must have been looking crestfallen as well as guilty for with a direct, kindly look he asked, "What is it exactly that you *do* want?" I told him. A bungalow suitable for an invalid, half the price of this house, with a small flat garden convenient for a bathchair. He looked at the large steep gardens of the houses he had built and flung back his head and laughed.

All the while Nanny had been silent but staring rather intently at the builder. When he laughed she half-smiled, as though in recognition, but she remained puzzled. Then with twinkling blue eyes he asked where we came from. Were we Devon folk? Oxford and Ely both seemed to vanish from my mind and I replied, "No, but from the West-country. Somerset."

"Where?" he demanded.

"I was born in Wells," I told him.

"What?" he almost shouted. "My name is Clare. My brother kept the draper's shop in the market place at Wells."

All the puzzlement vanished from Nanny's face and it shone with sudden joy. "Mr Clare!" she exclaimed. "There is a family resemblance."

I could understand her joy. Hadn't Mr Clare of the market place been one of our best friends? Hadn't she and I been visiting his drapery establishment ever since I could walk? We had bought the materials for my mother's teagowns there, and the muslin for my Sunday dress and ribbons for my dolls. The shop had been one of the marvels of my life. There had been an overhead railway there, that fetched the change. A fascinating thing. Having bought a yard of pink ribbon at twopence-three-farthings the yard, and given the girl behind the counter a sixpence, she put the sixpence and the bill inside a round wooden ball that came in half in the middle and was then screwed up again, and placed it upon the railway above her head. Then with bated breath and wondering eyes we watched it travel all round the shop and come to rest in the cashier's desk, when the cashier (quite casually as though this marvellous occurrence were nothing of importance) unscrewed the ball, took out the sixpence, put back the receipted bill and three-pence-farthing, and sent the lovely ball all the way round the shop and back to us again.

It was in Mr Clare's shop that Nanny allowed me, for the first time, to choose a material for myself. I might choose what I liked for my summer dressing-gown. I chose a materi-

al which I think was called delaine. It was white, patterned
with little roses of a blinding shade of pink. I thought it
beautiful and I could not wait to show it to my father. Perhaps I remember this incident so vividly because it was the
only time in my life that I ever approached him in his study
without a sense of awe. I did not wait for his intimidating
"Come in." I burst the door open, ran to him, shook out the
delaine and dropped the appalling pink roses on top of the
sermon he was writing. "My dressing-gown," I gasped. "I
chose it." He did not fail me. He half-closed his eyes and his
face took on the expression of the Bisto kids in the advertisement. "Beautiful," he murmured in apparent ecstasy.
"Beautiful." Then disentagling himself and his sermon from
the roses he handed them back to me, returned to his work
and forgot me. But I was quite satisfied. We had been at one
in our admiration of perfect beauty.

So, with these memories, no wonder Nanny and I were
overcome with joy as we gazed at our Mr Clare's brother.
We took him straight back to my mother in the car and the
four of us were instantly held by that bond which unites all
who have ever lived in Wells, and those also who at any time
have merely loved the place. Though I loved Ely so much I
have not found that love of Ely creates quite this bond, for it
was a homely sort of bond, and there is nothing homely about
the great Cathedral at Ely, nor about the city and the fen
winds sweeping over it. One cannot call Wells Cathedral
homely, it is far too beautiful, but it does not terrify or domi-
nate, and the town had great homeliness in the days of my
childhood. It nestled cosily and promised safety. And so Mr
Clare also seemed to promise safety.

For the fact was that at this time I was more than a little
scared, and even my brave mother was not without anxiety.
My father had been too generous a man to be any good at
what the Edwardians called 'putting by' and he had had to

live in large ecclesiastical houses that took a lot of upkeep, so he had been able to leave my mother very little. She herself, in reaction from the poverty of her childhood, had always veered slightly towards a queenly extravagance. All my father's pupils, from Wells to Oxford days, with wonderful generosity, had joined together to make a gift to my mother in his memory and so she now had a little annuity, but my work remained necessary to us, and since the shock of my father's death I had not been able to write. Neither of us was blest with physical strength and the outlook had seemed a bit bleak before the advent of Mr Clare. But he changed everything. He gave us the confidence to believe that even if at the moment we could not pay for the bungalow he said he would put up for us at Marldon, the village we already loved so much and where land was still cheap, we would be able to do so when the time came.

And so almost at once as it seemed Mr Clare's architect son had drawn out the plans for a small bungalow, Mr Clare had found an ideal plot of land not far from the Ark and his men were digging the foundations, and we hoped we would be in by Christmas. I think we hardly realised his goodness to the full at that time. He was a well-known Torquay builder with a reputation for excellent houses, and the putting up of a small bungalow in an obscure village was hardly the kind of thing he was accustomed to do. He promised he would build it at prewar prices and even though the building was delayed by bad weather, and the price of building materials had soared meanwhile, he kept his promise.

He built a compact little cottage which had about it an air of charm and originality that suited my mother. And the site was one of the loveliest that could be imagined. The Ark was at the southern edge of the village and the lane that led past it dropped steeply downhill under arching trees to a small valley that had the lovely name of Westerland; a

perfect name for a West-country valley. Here were a farm
and orchards and a few houses, and then the lane wound
steeply uphill again towards Totnes. In one of the orchards,
a small cider-apple orchard separated from the lane by a
hedge of nut trees and a steep bank where primroses grew,
Mr Clare built Providence Cottage on a gentle southern
slope, the hill behind to protect it from north winds. In the
southwest corner of the orchard, in strange contrast to the
old gnarled apple trees, was a group of three giant pines,
old and tough and strong. Just where they stood the valley
opened out to a view of Dartmoor, and they caught the
westerly gales. Their voice in the wind was one of the two
great voices of the place. The other, when the wind was in the
east, was the voice of the sea after an easterly gale had blown
itself out. There were many other voices, the bleating of the
sheep and lambs in the fields, the crying of the gulls, the
owls at night and the cuckoos in the spring.

Nevertheless our neighbours thought that only those who
had taken leave of their senses would contemplate the building of a home in that old orchard, for it was completely
tangled over with briars, nettles and docks so lush and large
that they entirely hid the assortment of tin cans and rusty
buckets that had accumulated in the orchard over the years.
"You'll never get it cleared," they said. "And you'll never
get rid of those dock roots. Never." The latter statement was
sadly true, the former was not. My mother and Mr Clare
were not discouraged for they shared the same sort of san-
guine temperament; plus charm and strength of will. If
possessed of these three glorious attributes a person does not,
I have come to believe, need to do much personally, he or she
need only hope and smile and will and other people will
do most of it for them. By the following spring the jungle
had been partially cleared, the garden was emerging and we
were installed in the cottage, eased into it by the kindness of
the people of Marldon. It was partly my mother's and Mr
Clare's magic, and the rest was their own friendly help.

4

There are those who say that a Devon village does not readily accept strangers into the community. Like Cornish folk they regard people from another county as 'foreigners'. I can only say, using a biblical phrase, that they 'lie in their teeth'. After a year in Marldon my mother and I felt we might have been there all our lives.

But during that preceding winter in the Ark, the winter of the phoney war, I was hardly aware of the village for there was little room in my anxious mind for anything except the necessity for hard work, and I shut myself inside my tiny bedroom and found among my papers the first pages of a novel I had begun to write before my father died, a book called *The Bird in the Tree*. I did not imagine I could do anything with it for how, now, could I recapture Damerose-hay and Keyhaven? I felt I was living in another age and another time and that Keyhaven belonged to a lost century. But no memories are ever lost and as I struggled to pick up the threads of the story they came thronging back; the marshes and the cornfield, the cool lofty rooms of Damerose-hay and the blackbird singing in the ilex tree; and presently I was continuing the story. But I have seldom had to struggle so hard over a book and at one point I reached deadlock. Usually my characters manipulate me, not I them, but now they suddenly went dead as dormice. I could see no way through, and nothing that could possibly happen next.

So many people say that mental problems are solved in sleep, but that had never yet happened to me. But why shouldn't it? In desperation I prayed that I might dream the rest of the book, and I did. In a dream full of lovely light the story unrolled smoothly and afterwards I only had to write down what I had dreamed. By the time spring came the book was finished and in sheer relief I wrote a light-hearted little children's book, *Smoky House*, for Nanny who had been toiling in the Ark's kitchen while I toiled in my bedroom.

Now, using part of my mother's wonderful gift from my father's pupils, my own savings, and with two books written, there would be enough in the kitty to pay for the cottage.

The Ark had been a refuge indeed. During the autumn gales it groaned and creaked and shuddered but stood firm, and during the intense cold of that January, when every twig of every tree was encased in tinkling ice and the poor frozen birds fell dead from the branches, it kept us alive. When the bad weather passed there were still, grey days, balmy and damp in true Devonshire fashion, and I would leave my work for a while and go a little way down the hill to where I could climb to the top of a bank and see our orchard down below me in Westerland. The twisted bare twigs and branches of the apple trees made a haze of pale colour, amethyst and blue and grey, and through them I could see the skeleton of the growing cottage, its roof timbers still without tiles and its windows unglazed. Sometimes a blue column of smoke would rise up through the trees, where the workmen were burning some of the undergrowth they had cleared away, and their cheery voices would come faintly up to me through the still air. I was one of them, I felt, for I had worked hard too to build that twiggy thing down there, looking at the moment more like a nest than a house, and I felt awed as I looked down, as though the building of a home was something entirely new in the world.

Having lived always in old houses that were only on loan for as long as the temporary owner could do the job of work they represented, I had no conception of what it feels like to make a home that is yours for as long as you wish it to be. Having no knowledge of the future I believed I would live in Westerland for the rest of my life. I think I even believed that Marldon would wear forever the beauty it had already worn for centuries. Tidal waves come in very quickly and no one realised then how soon a flood of bungalows and holiday camps, caravans and petrol pumps, shops and motor roads and roaring traffic would wash away most of the beauty that looked so eternal. And of course it never occurred to me that I myself was a criminal, for here, as at Barton, our bungalow was one of the first of the flood that was held back now only by the approach of a dreadful war. The war did do that; it isolated and preserved much country beauty for at least another ten years.

CHAPTER XIII

Westerland

I

THE COTTAGE WAS FINISHED BY THE TIME THE APPLE BLOSSOM was in bud. We moved in and almost at once, her task accomplished, my mother broke down and was very ill. But she had willed herself to her feet again by the time Holland was invaded and the war began in earnest. The news burst upon us on a day so perfect that the horror could hardly be believed. No one who lived through that summer will ever forget it. It was halcyon weather almost from beginning to end. The sun shone down from a clear sky and the days were scented and balmy but never too hot. Expecting invasion day by day we had the feeling that England had clothed herself in all possible beauty to confront her doom. She was like the Israelite Queen who "painted her face and tired her head and looked out of the window" when she heard the sound of her murderer's chariot wheels.

But nature herself was quite indifferent to our danger. The cuckoos and the air-raid sirens shouted together and once, just after the sound of a distant bomb explosion had died away, I remember that I heard a hen in the next-door garden cackling with satisfaction because she had just laid an egg. I found that extremely comforting. Whatever happened nest-building and egg-laying would go on and the earth would continue to pass through all the seasonal changes of her beauty. "While the earth remaineth, seed time and harvest, and cold and heat, and summer and winter and day and night shall not cease." The interweaving joy and woe of that summer were typical of all the years that my mother and I spent in Devon. The loveliness lightened the sorrow and the sorrow shadowed the loveliness and the mind was in a state of perpetual confusion.

The first air-raids struck all round the south coast of England, where the children were taking refuge from the bombs that did not yet fall on London. My mother and I were anxious about the children now living in the Barton bungalow, but they remained safe through the raids there, while near us in Devon there was a direct hit on a church packed full of children for a children's service. That I think was Devon's first big tragedy. I suppose that my mother and I suffered less in the war than most people did, and we often felt ashamed of our comparative immunity. We suffered two bereavements that hit us hard. The death in the early days of the war of a cousin to whom we were both devoted, to me more a brother than a cousin, and later on Nanny's death during a raid on Bath. Upon her and her two sisters, and the lovely young daughter of a friend of mine who was staying with them, their house fell, burying them beneath the ruins.

It seemed strange that Nanny was no longer in the world to come and be with us in this grief, but Irene came with her strong common sense. "Never think *how* they died," she said. "In war that must be a thing you do not think about." Easier said than done. For some while neither my mother nor I could go to bed at night without feeling the weight of the house falling on us, and wondering, for how long did they live in the suffocating dark before they died? But two bereavements were not many. Parents would lose every one of their sons. Men would come home on leave to find their wives and children dead after a raid. Though I often went to Torquay and Paignton I never actually saw the immediate aftermath of an air-raid. I did not have to carry through the rest of my life the memory of sights almost too terrible to bear.

Actual physical danger came near us only twice, at the beginning and the end of the war. The first two bombs to fall on our parish were the two that fell on the sloping green field opposite our cottage, jettisoned early in the morning by a German plane flying home. They exploded almost together with shattering noise and the cottage seemed to shake and buckle and totter as though nothing could save it. But Mr Clare had built it well and it righted itself, with only superficial damage done. That was not the case with my mother. I had been up and on my feet but she had been in bed, lying flat on her back. The very worst position, our doctor told us, in which the human body can suffer earthquake, and she had a severe concussion.

The noise of the bombs brought our gardener, Bob Patey, instantly to the rescue. He lived in a cottage at the bottom of a steep hill on the other side of Marldon, a good mile and a half from Westerland. "Where did them bombs fall?" he asked, running out of his cottage and accosting the passers-by. "Westerland," he was told.

"Them's my ladies," he said, and waiting only to place in his pocket a roll of bandage and two small safety pins he ran all the way up the steep hill, through the village, and down the other hill to Westerland; and he was an old man, over six feet and possessed of a Falstaffian figure. When he had recovered his breath he showed me the bandage and the two safety pins but was much relieved that he had not had to use them. Then he settled down serenely to a morning's gardening.

Bob Patey was a character. Marldon was full of them and the village itself was one. The part of it that had been there for centuries consisted of grey cottages, all different, climbing haphazardly up a steep little hill dominated by the superb old church. It had a tall bell-tower whose bells were pulled Sunday by Sunday by the men of the village. The word Marldon means 'the blue hill', and the hill, we believed, was the steep field behind the church were gentians used to grow in the days when they were a familiar wild flower of the English countryside.

I have written already in Chapter VII of the old man and his three sons, who were our next-door neighbours at the Ark. There was also the village postmistress. The post office was the front room of her cottage and was filled to the brim with crockery of every sort and kind, china ornaments and great pots of dead flowers. She loved flowers too greatly to throw them away, even when they died, and her room was a mausoleum of flowers. There was a small counter but otherwise little sign that this was a P.O., but when you came in to the jangling of a little bell the postmistress would enquire in her lovely voice, "What would you be wanting, Maid?" (Is an unmarried female whose hair is not yet grey still addressed as "Maid" in Devon? I hope so.) When you asked for twelve stamps she would look round vaguely, rummage hopelessly among the flowerpots under the counter, and then her face would suddenly brighten and lifting the lid of a teapot she would produce three of the required number. If you wanted to send a telegram (a thing she thought no one in their senses should wish to do) it might be ten minutes before the forms could be found in the recesses of a soup tureen in the fireplace, and then there would be fifteen minutes of struggling with the intricacies of composition and mathematics.

But Bob Patey was the prince of the Marldon Characters, and in spite of his choleric temper he was a revered and beloved figure at Smoky House, the village pub. He could drink deeply and gloriously, and in spite of his size he was agile. During his final evening at Smoky House he flung every glass in the place out of doors with such speed and vigour that no one could stop him. But after that his wife told him that he was never to enter the portals of Smoky House again.

Incredibly, he obeyed her, and was sober from that day on. It was a miracle, but between Mrs Patey and her husband was a love so great that it could literally work miracles. She was a dainty little woman with a sweet and merry face, and the whitest apron and the cleanest cottage I have ever seen. She was childless and her husband was her life. In their younger days, she told me, when he was in the navy and away at sea, her life was just waiting for him to come home again, and when she heard that he was coming she would fill the house with flowers. I suspect that in his seagoing days Patey had a sweetheart at every port but I am also sure that the only women he ever deeply loved were Mrs Patey and my mother. I hasten to add that Mrs Patey was not jealous. My mother was Beatrice to Mr Patey's Dante but it was Mrs Patey who utterly and eternally possessed him. After he died her smile was as merry as ever and she refused to despair, though her erect little figure gradually became bent almost double. She only had to wait a short time, she said, before seeing him again. She was quite right.

It was Patey who gave my mother the greatest joy of her Devon days. He took her in her bathchair through the unfrequented loveliness of the lanes. The pageant of flowers that first spring and summer of the war was unbelievable. When the primroses and violets had faded from the hedgerows the bluebells and pink campion took their place, and then came the tall foxgloves, the wild roses and the honeysuckle. Sometimes Patey would bring my mother home intoxicated with beauty, the war and its sorrows momentarily forgotten, in ecstasy yet frantic with frustration. "If only I could fling myself into the beauty and be lost in it," she cried out one day. "But I can't. Not yet."

Patey, being a sailor, walked with a slow, steady, rolling gait and the bathchair rolled too. My mother, accustomed to boats in her youth, was perfectly comfortable but anyone walking behind the bathchair was consumed with mirth; but of this my mother and Patey remained unaware. As a gardener Patey did not share my mother's love of flowers, since vegetables were his passion, but he delighted in bringing her little gifts of plants for her flower garden. But he did not like anyone else to do so. If they did, and we asked him to plant the new gentian or the new primula, he would plant it in silent fury, his face crimson, his teeth clenched upon the flood of fire and brimstone (he never swore in front of my mother) that was nearly choking him. Then he bided his time. Later, when he thought we had forgotten about the plant, he dug it up and threw it away. When he died he left an empty, aching space in our lives, but in time it was filled by a new gardener equally beloved, a man who combined the gentleness and courtesy of the West-countrymen with a courage in misfortune that I have never seen equalled by anyone, not even by my mother.

At Westerland I was not robbed of the great view that had come through the mist on our first morning at the Ark for I could see it from the field above the periwinkle bank. That field was to me, in Devon, what the Magdalen Cloisters had been at Oxford. Near our cottage the high, steep bank that bordered our lane upon the other side was entirely covered with periwinkles. When they were in bloom it was as though a blue tapestry were hung upon a wall. The country name for periwinkle is 'joy of the ground' and certainly those periwinkles seemed to sing for joy, and though they were not as large as the periwinkles in the Wells garden they were as deeply blue. A steep flight of steps had been cut in the bank, each step formed by a stone that looked 'half as old as time', and at the top of the bank was a stone stile that must have been there for centuries, and beyond the stile the field, steep as the slope of a roof, lifted one step by step to the view. Peace is hard to come by but it was forever in that field, and though I went there so often I never found another human being seeking it there. Yet the centre of each of the old stepping stones was so deeply worn that Devon folk must have been coming and going up and down the periwinkle bank for centuries. They must have sat where I sat so often, looking across the blue distance to Dartmoor, dreaming their dreams and seeing their visions and leaving them alive in the field though they themselves were dead.

There were so many wonderful places all around us, two castles, one a haunted place hidden in the woods, a certain deep well beside a green tunnel of a lane, a particular tree where a great white barn-owl used to sit at twilight, all with their own distinctive quality, never to be forgotten, as alive now in memory as human friends.

2

A happier period came to our village. The coastal raids came to an end and no more children were killed. At night we no longer lay awake listening to the German planes streaming over us to Plymouth, and then to the dull distant boom that meant death and agony in the city only a few miles from us, while we lay safe in the shame of our security. The return of the planes meant jettisoned bombs and then some slight shadow of danger did lie over us for a short time as my mother and I shared her bed, determined to be together whatever happened. My mother was never afraid but she liked to have her jewel-case passed to her, for she loved her few pieces of lovely old jewellery and wanted to keep them safe herself. Animated by the same feminine desire to sit upon the eggs I never got into bed beside her without putting the manuscript of the book I was writing, *Green Dolphin Country*, on the bedside table. Women are not very logical creatures at the best of times but in times of crisis their reasoning powers tend to fade out altogether. What, if anything, were we thinking? A bomb falling on a little house like ours would have totally destroyed everything in it. Perhaps, like the Egyptians of old, we subconsciously thought that what was close to our bodies in death would accompany our spirits as they entered a new life.

I do not remember what we thought, but eventually Plymouth was left in ruins and peace, Marldon was once more a safe place for children and joy raised its golden head, for Hélène came to live with us for a while with her small son.

At the outbreak of war Hélène, with the sea in her blood, became a Wren; but only for as long as it took her to decide which man of them all in the navy she wished to marry. Sometimes a very attractive girl gets so confused by sheer scope that she falls in love less wisely than a less attractive girl will do. But Hélène never suffered from confusions. Her marriage was so happy that she could say at the end of her life, "It has been idyllic." I said earlier in this book that only happy marriages were about me in childhood, but I have just realised that on both sides of my family the tradition has been carried on into the younger, and now the youngest, generation. There has never been one broken marriage and I wonder—why? Is it their religion, which compels them to hold on through the stormy periods, and endure and pass through, because that is what they promised before God that they would do? I think so. To love God subtly alters a human being. If the simile is not too homely the lover of God has glue in his veins and tends to be more adherent than other men. The more he loves God the more, for God's sake, he sticks to his woman, his job or his faith. Christians should be judged, I think, by their stickableness, since by that alone can God get anything done in this world; that appears to be disintegrating now before our horrified eyes from sheer lack of glue.

Hélène had at this time one over-riding purpose; to keep her son safe for a father who had been sent to fight on the other side of the world only a short while before the birth of his son and so had never seen him. As soon as the war threatened the safety of one place she snatched up the baby and fled to another; for herself she was fearless as my mother but for her son she was terrified.

The American army, that was later to turn much of Devon into a training ground, had not yet appeared and Westerland was as peaceful as it was beautiful. My mother and Hélène, who so greatly loved each other, were overjoyed to be together again, and Hélène's two-year-old son laughed all day and sang for much of the night; and if his gift of song was less appreciated than his gift of laughter it was none the less joyous. My mother's outings in her bathchair, with Bob Patey's tall figure looming above the cavalcade, looked funnier than ever when Hélène pushed her small son in his minute conveyance alongside the swaying ship. We laughed a great deal, but I am afraid I laughed less than the others because I was caught in the terrible coils of the most marvellous piece of material good fortune. Overnight I had become a best-seller.

3

For years, in between the many other things that had to be done, I had been writing *Green Dolphin Country*, a book about a Guernsey great-uncle, my grandfather's brother. It was a story I had always wanted to tell because it was so extraordinary, and the writing of it took my mind off the war. Though much of the book is imaginary the basic facts are true. My great-uncle went into the British navy but while he was still only a midshipman he fell into trouble. On shore leave at an eastern port he got into a scrape, did not return to his ship at the appointed time and found it had sailed without him. He was now a deserter and was afraid to face the music. He found a ship bound for Australia (in my book

I made it New Zealand because my ignorance of Australia was even more total than my ignorance of New Zealand) and sailed in her to try his luck in a new world. His early struggles over he did well, but he longed for the Island to which he could not now return without being court-martialled. But he had a living link with the Island. He had been in love with a Guernsey girl and he wrote to her father and asked if she would brave the long voyage in a sailing ship and come out and marry him.

But, poor William, he suffered from the family impediment of never being able to remember names correctly. My mother suffered from the same thing and good hostess though she was she could scarcely ever introduce her guests to each other by their right names, frequently unconsciously using the name of the place from which they came; she would introduce Colonel Birmingham to Mrs Winchester. William, writing his letter to his future father-in-law, confused the name of the girl he loved with that of her elder sister, who was less attractive and considerably older than himself. The reply was in the affirmative; yes, she would come. Palpitating with joyous excitement he was at the harbour to meet the ship; but it was the wrong girl. He never told her. How could he? She had come quite alone on the long, stormy voyage, a woman who had never left her safe island home before, and he was a compassionate man. He married her and he made her happy. But he wrote to my grandfather and told him what an agony it was to meet the unwanted bride with a smiling face. I wrote a note at the beginning of the book to say that this mistaking of the names was true, but as no one ever reads a writer's notes I was reprimanded by several reviewers for cooking up such a fantastic story.

As so often happens to a book when it is written over a long period of time, put aside and then picked up again, *Green Dolphin Country* grew longer and longer. In the end finishing it nearly killed me and when my literary agent warned me

that under wartime conditions, with paper so short, it was
more than likely it could not be published I tried to forget
about my poor old Dolphin. I thought he might have to sink
without trace. And then came a cable from America telling
me that my American publisher had sent the book in as a
candidate for a Metro Goldwyn Mayer film prize of £30,000,
and the old Dolphin had won it.

It was hilarious news for everyone. I was not the type of
woman to have this sort of thing happen to me and my unsuit-
ability for the rôle struck everyone as extremely funny. For
the village it was a happy nine-days'-wonder in the midst of
a horrible war. I remember the laughing faces and the
kindness of people who were themselves badly off and yet
could rejoice whole-heartedly at the success of someone else.
And then came a damper in the person of a Jewish gentleman
who with his family had taken refuge in the village from air-
raids. He had considerable knowledge of finance, and
travelling in the bus from Paignton, our shopping town, in
the company of half the village, he told the bus that he
doubted if taxation would leave much out of the £30,000.
A second financier in the village agreed with him. According
to his calculations the American aliens tax, English super
tax, agency fees, lawyers' fees and the share in the prize that
would go to the publishers of the book, would leave me £3000.
I was so relieved that it was like waking up from a nightmare.
£3000 was a large sum but I felt I could cope with that; the
load of £30,000 was enough to crush any poor woman to
death. In the end our village financiers were wrong; it was
£4000.

Nevertheless, I now became a successful writer, because a
book that without the publicity of the film prize might not
have been published for some years, and would perhaps have
failed when it did appear, eventually sold all over the world.
And the good fortune worked backwards as well as forwards
because a successful book re-animates past books as well as

casting a rosy glow over future ones. They are read and in the
course of time one becomes a habit with one's readers. I had to
learn to cope. I did not want to be a rich woman, and hoped
I would succeed in never living as one. But the resolve meant
that I had to learn how to administer what came to me and
the mistakes I made in learning were at times catastrophic. . .
and to think that I had at one time, at our leanest period,
actually prayed for money! Desiring, of course, only a modest
competence.

"The prayer I must pray for you," a great friend told me,
when she had finished laughing at my complaints over my
good fortune, "is the collect for the twelfth Sunday after
Trinity—'Almighty and everlasting God, who art always
more ready to hear than we to pray, and art wont to give
more than either we desire or deserve: Pour down upon us
the abundance of they mercy. . .'"

Apart from my understanding mother they all laughed,
and Hélène laughed more than anyone when she arrived at
the tail end of the tempest of publicity. "I wouldn't have
missed this for anything," she chuckled, as she dumped her
son in his miniature conveyance and hurried out after my
mother and Bob Patey, and the swaying bathchair; all of
them heartlessly escaping and leaving me to cope unaided
with yet another invasion. It was the reporters who invaded,
and those who came to plead for financial help. Also the
postman, who arrived daily with an avalanche of letters.

Reporters and interviewers, mortal men and women who
are persecutors only because they must earn a living like the
rest of us, appeared to me at that time in the guise of vultures.
On one desperate day I cast myself on my bed and vowed that
anyone attacking the front-door bell that afternoon should
go unanswered. But reporters are enterprising people,
especially if female; that particular girl, that afternoon, came
in through the window.

Of the letters, the begging letters were the worst because

the machinations of lawyers in both countries delayed the arrival of the filthy lucre for a long time, there was little in the bank and therefore little I could do immediately to help. One night, trying to cope with the letters of every sort and kind, I reached despair, picked up the whole bundle and dumped it in the fire. That is something that will haunt me till my dying day, for although among the writers of begging letters are many who are only "trying it on" there are also some who are in genuine need. As a tribute to human endurance I recall with undying gratitude that although Providence Cottage had no telephone at this time, the house next-door had, and not once did the poor girl next-door, a busy mother with two young children, outwardly lose her temper.

Many delightful things happened. Opening the door to a knock I found an American sailor on the doorstep. He was the largest young man I have ever seen, with a face like the rising sun and beaming ear-to-ear smile. He had walked all the way from Dartmouth to express his pleasure that an English woman had won an American prize. We had a delightful conversation over coffee, but he was reluctant to eat too much, being convinced that the British rations scarcely supported life in a human being. Indeed he dived into a pocket and produced a slab of chocolate to augment my ration, and having ascertained through kindly enquiry that I had an invalid mother in bed in the house, he dived into another pocket and produced an orange for my mother. Then he said good-bye and left to walk back to Dartmouth, leaving me with an experience of American kindness and generosity that I shall never forget.

4

That small explosion of private excitement died away, a

storm in a teacup. Hélène and her son also went away and once more the war was in the forefront of our living. The American army was now everywhere and gradually all of us in the village began to realise that some hidden undertaking was going on around us. Lanes where we had been accustomed to walk were sealed off, certain orchards and woods could not be entered and the heavy traffic of lorries was heard at night. My mother and I were slow to realise what was happening until one day a neighbour, a man with a mind more enquiring than ours ejaculated, "It only needs an air-raid and a few bombs on this village to blow us all sky-high." Then we realised that all our leafy and shady country places were filling up with stored ammunition.

Our neighbour proved a pessimist. We had the air-raid all along our coastal area, with seven bombs in or near the village, and not one hit the ammunition. In the village, where everyone was cowering under their kitchen tables, a few houses were damaged but no one was hurt.

And then there came an unforgettable night and day. The night was a still, windless night, filled through all its hours by a low, ceaseless rumble, sounding like a lot of grumbling dragons in ceaseless and tireless motion. But no bombs dropped that night, not one. And the morning brought a clear, cool, windless day filled with the most extraordinary silence. When I opened the door in the morning there was not a soul in sight. The world looked as empty as it must have looked to Adam on the first morning of his life.

The silence continued in some measure all day for people were too awed to talk much. Torbay, that had been crowded with shipping, was empty and flat as a pond. All the closed lanes and woods and orchards were once more open, empty, silent and a little haunted, Anxiety gradually took the place of awe. Here was the great quietness but what was happening over there? It was the invasion of Europe, so long planned, hoped for, expected and yet never coming. It was here at last.

If it succeeded the end would be in sight; the end of the
concentration camps, the end of all the agony and horror.
But what if it failed? The queer, unaccustomed, lasting
silence made it easier to pray, but individual prayer seemed
a feeble, fleeting thing in the face of what was happening over
there.

There was still much more to come, the doodle-bugs and
the shattering horror of the dropping of the atomic bombs.
People have grown used to the thought of atomic warfare
now, the present generation have grown up with the bomb,
and so it is hard for them to realise how appalled we were
then. And the dropping of the bombs seemed to tarnish
victory. When it came at last most of us felt almost more
shame than joy.

CHAPTER XIV

To Make An End Is
To Make A Beginning

I

THERE MUST HAVE BEEN A LITTLE SPACE BETWEEN THE
ending of the war and the beginning of my mother's last
illness but I do not remember it. The one thing seems to
merge into the other in my memory. Through all my life
until then, among many doubts there had always been one
thing that I had been quite sure of, and that was that because
my mother had suffered so much in her life she would be
spared a long and painful illness at the end of it. The very
reverse was the case. The last illness was long and hard and
through the last year there was the humiliation of mental
illness added to the physical suffering. When I started this
book I told myself that in writing it I wanted to think only
of the happy memories; unless a dark period should lead out
into some new and happy knowledge. This one did and so I
can write of it.

Anyone who has looked after someone they love through
mental illness knows the particular misery of it. If a patient
remains mentally himself however bad the physical distress
may be the person you know is still there with you, but in
mental illness the beloved personality seems lost and you
appear to be living with a stranger; at times a frightening
stranger, talking (and perhaps with truth) of the nearness of
the powers of darkness. Death seems in some way to have
already taken place for you feel you have lost the person you
love. Physical suffering can ennoble and purify but mental

confusion seems pointless and useless, and it is this which
causes the particular misery of it.

But this illness taught me that it is only a case of 'seems'.
The truth may be otherwise. A few days before her death my
mother returned, weak and dying but entirely herself. And
much more than herself. It was not my imagination but the
truth. She came back peaceful and spiritualised. I do not
know how else to describe it because there are no words for
these things. She had wanted, before she died, to become fit to
be with her husband again, and all through the years that she
had had to live without him she had been growing. In some
hidden way that literally only God knows about, the mental
illness had been the last stage of the purification. On the
morning of the day she died (and our doctor had told me that
her death was not imminent, and so I was not expecting it)
she said she must put on her prettiest nightdress and have the
best counterpane on the bed, "because They are coming
today". Irene, who was with us that day, was aware of the
scent of flowers drifting about the rooms, though there were
no flowers in the cottage and the garden was held in a dead
grey spring cold. In the evening the mysterious 'They', of
whom the dying so often speak, came, and my mother drifted
away into as peaceful a death as it is possible to have.

I only write this because of the possibility that it may a
a little comfort someone who is experiencing the same sense
of useless, pointless suffering when someone they care for is
mentally ill. It may not be useless. My experience is not
unique. I had a friend who for years had been nursing a
war-injured husband. When he became mentally ill, and
was finally taken away from her, she was in despair. Believing
it would be so I told her, "At the end he will come back to
you." After he had died she said, "It happened as you had
thought it would. He came back at the end entirely and
peacefully himself."

My friend had her husband taken from her but my mother

and I were never parted, and I owe that to the goodness of a nurse who lived in the village. Our doctor had said it was too difficult a case to nurse at home but she pleaded with him. She promised him she would help me through and would never let me down. Nor did she, though she had a husband and small son to look after at home, and was often making her way through storm and snow between one home and the other. And those in the village who loved my mother would take turns in giving extra help by day or night when it was needed. This is typical West-country kindness. Such goodness exists all over the world, I know, but the West-country brand of goodness has a particular gentleness and warmth. I was so buoyed up by it, so exalted by the loveliness of my mother's passing, that I could hardly feel any grief at all. With Irene weeping I was ashamed of my dry-eyed calm and happy state. But perhaps that is the way we ought to feel when a soul goes free, and we should hold to our joy for the short time that it is with us. For sinners, it cannot last, and the remorse that follows it as we remember all the failures of inadequate love, all the selfish things done and the sharp words said, all the unthinking cruelties of children (some children) to their parents is one of the hardest, if not *the* hardest, things that we must endure in this life.

But we have to learn to forgive ourselves. After the cross, I think that what most convinces us of the love of God is the forgiveness of the greatest of his sons and daughters. I do not think that love and forgiveness can be separated, since real love by its very nature must forgive. To know oneself forgiven by God and by those we love, is a most humbling and lovely experience and teaches us the necessity for forgiveness. The power to receive some hurt done to you, great or small, with the forgiveness that lets it come to an end in you, puts an end to retaliation, that horrible eye for an eye, tooth for a tooth business that can keep some impulse of cruelty circling round the world for ever. Forgiving others should not be difficult, knowing as we do how great is our own need of it, but forgiving oneself is another matter. There is no one harder to forgive than oneself; it can take years. Nevertheless we know inside ourselves that it must be done, for remorse is a sin that rots away the very vitals of the soul. And we know well the price of a soul to God. If God and his saints in their divine foolishness put such a price upon our soul we should not let it rot.

2

I went to Damerosehay. It was a lovely summer and the old house and the garden, the sea and the marshes were shining in the sun and there was healing in the air of the place. One day, I remember, I was sitting under one of the trees in the garden and the wind from the sea was blowing through the leaves. A moment of joy seized me, so sudden and so startling that I could hardly believe it. Yet it was true. Into the middle of my wretchedness at this time dropped this sudden joy. Joy is what life is about, I believed at that moment. It lies, somehow, at the root of every pain.

There was a shadow of sadness over Damerosehay and I was aware of it. The house had, I think, been used for refugees during the war but Mrs Adams had brought it back to its former use as a quiet hotel for her friends and their friends. But she looked very tired and she was finding it hard to get the staff she needed. The house was shabby and the garden overgrown. It made no difference to the peace of the place but there was sadness now as well as peace, an intuition of what was to come. We who were staying there had no idea at all that in a few years time Damerosehay would have vanished as though it had never been.

For that was what happened. Mrs Adams had eventually to give up the struggle to keep going and leave the house where she had lived for so many years. She took her treasures with her to her new home, the Dresden china figures, the books and pictures, and the house was sold and became an ordinary hotel. But it did not flourish. Perhaps the spirit of it died when Mrs Adams left and it was stripped of its treasures; and of the nine cats, clothed in the furriness of each individual personality, who had been an integral part of its being. For whatever reason, the shell of Damerosehay failed to attract holiday-makers and the hotel failed. For a while the house stood empty, fading into pitiful ruin, while the garden turned back to wilderness. Then bungalows and caravans began to eat their way over the beauty of the marshes and it was decided that the old house must go.

The village postmistress at Keyhaven told me what happened. The house was so filled with old wood that the destroyers thought that burning would get rid of it more quickly than any other method. But even though its spirit had departed the body of the house still had a will to live. It refused to burn down. The wooden bones would not ignite and the flames could not take hold. The destroyers gave up in despair and fetched the bulldozers. The house and garden of Damerosehay could not stand up against those and now I believe (I will never go to see) that no one can find the place where they once had their life. Well, they had it, and one of the things in my working life about which I am most thankful is that someone or something prompted me to write three books about an imaginary family living at Damerosehay, and that those three seem to be my readers' favourites. As long as the three books are read Damerosehay has not quite vanished from the world and I have not lived in vain.

3

I came back to Providence Cottage to find it an empty shell. It had been repainted and looked fresh and pretty.

People came in and out, talking and laughing, but their voices echoed as voices do in a house that is unfurnished and deserted. Without my mother's vivid presence the place was dead. But I had to stay there since she had made me promise not to leave in a hurry but to stick it out for a year. She was quite right. Few things hold one up better than familiar surroundings and the routine of a life that goes with them. Both the surroundings and the routine may have gone dead on you, but at least they are there, like a pair of crutches. You may hate them but they keep you upright. With their help I could get back to work again, and tried to recapture the peace of Damerosehay by starting the third and last book about the Eliot family, *The Heart of the Family*. There is something of my mother in Lucilla Eliot and the company of Lucilla was comforting. But the book was such a struggle that I wondered if my writing days were perhaps ended.

That there is nothing so therapeutic as work I have proved over and over again but for many years I had another reason for always fighting to get back to work. I had a perhaps laughable conviction that I had a visiting demon (I saw him once and he was horrible) who brought darkness and was determined that I should not write books. So when I had once more disentangled myself from him and the sun showed signs of coming out again I would write as hard as I could, determined that I would write books and that they should be happy ones. And I think they were, for a dark background to one's life tends to make the happier times happier still. I had been living in my present home for some years when standing in the garden one day, looking across the fields to the woods in the distance and thinking of nothing except their beauty, I had a sudden conviction that my demon had left me for good; torn off me finally by my father. I left the garden and went back into the house full of grateful thanks to my father. All sheer fantasy, probably. The mind is capable of playing any number of tricks upon one; especially a horrifically imaginative mind. Fantasy or not, from that day my demon seemed to retreat.

The weeks dragged by in Devon and kind friends came to visit me, but I lived in a dusty desert. Everything, I felt, had come to a dead end. There seemed no way out or through. Then the autumn came bringing with it what I suppose is the greatest miracle of every human life, the miracle of renewal. It taught me that no apparently dead end is ever a dead end, but a new beginning. Also that perhaps no true new beginning is possible until you seem to be standing with a shut door facing you. Also that when you have passed through the door you cannot expect to be quite yet out of the shadows. New beginnings grow slowly.

I had intended to live alone that first winter without my mother. Having had no experience of living alone I had not yet discovered that that is a thing I cannot do. At the time I thought it was what I needed. My wisest, closest friend at Marldon disagreed with me so heartily that she gave me the name and address of a friend of her own who she thought would spend at least that winter with me. When I showed signs of resistance she answered, "Go home and write to Jessie Monroe tonight." I went home and turned the idea over in my mind with growing alarm, but felt compelled to make a start on a letter. That evening my friend rang up and asked, "Have you written?" I said I had partly written the letter. "Finish it," she said, and immediately put the receiver down.

And so I wrote to a total stranger at the address given and at first received no answer. My spirits rose. Then I had an answer from Jessie on holiday in Italy. I felt that my own doubt and dismay were echoed in her letter, and in that at least we were united, but she went so far as to say that when she was back in England again she would come, and would

see me through the winter. Thankful that she was not
contemplating anything longer I wrote a welcoming letter
and awaited her arrival with growing alarm.

The appointed day brought her, but not the appointed
hour, and my old friend and bogey, anxiety, reared its ugly
head. It is one of the silliest of mental impediments to think
that those you love (had I already begun to love Jessie?) are
perfectly safe if you are with them but beset with danger on
every side if your powerful protection is absent. Yet I believe
the majority of people do suffer from this silly thing. Possibly
common sense is not the hall mark of the majority. At last I
heard the sound of a car door being slammed with great
determination, went out into the garden and heard a very
clear voice saying the words that are now so delightfully
familiar. "I'm sorry I'm late." We looked at each other. I
saw an upright, capable-looking young woman with a head
of hair like a horse-chestnut on fire, and the white magnolia
skin that goes with such hair. Her eyes were very direct. She
looked young enough to be my daughter and I doubted if she
would stand me for long, yet when I went to bed that night
to my astonishment I found myself flooded with happiness,
and slept deeply.

Jessie has stood me for twenty-one years and has been the
most wonderful event that ever happened to me. Not that
the first months were easy for either of us, for we had to
search for points of contact. I was a firmly embedded member of the Church of England, she was a fiery Celtic Presby-
terian. Her passion was gardening and I am no gardener,
mine was books, and "I've not read any of your books," she
warned me. Well, I thanked God for that. No friendships do
I value more than those not founded on my books. To be
loved as the faulty person you actually are, rather than as
the pleasing personality that people think you are, is an
unspeakable relief. Our religious differences were not so easy.
"Anyone would think you had been brought up on *Foxe's*

Book of Martyrs," I said at the end of a heated argument. "I was," she replied briefly.

We have both mellowed since then and learned that friends who are at one in the basic beliefs of their lives have the one unity that really matters, but at that time our first real point of contact was dogs . . . We got one . . . A Dandie-Dinmont puppy, the first of the Hobbits, the never-to-be-forgotten Tiki, who was with us when we moved from Devon to Oxfordshire.

4

I would never have believed that I could have got myself out of Devon. I thought I was there for the rest of my life. For Jessie it was otherwise. Many passionate gardeners have little affection for places where the rainfall is above average, and so she was glad to have her gum-boots pulled out of the wet, heavy Devon earth and transplanted to a soil possessing potentialities which she had not yet experienced, and more-over to a part of that soil where the rainfall was well below average. I say "pulled out" for that is how it felt to us, since so many things combined to show us what we had to do. It seemed we had to go, and the obvious place was Oxfordshire within easy reach of old friends and relatives who had been urging me to move nearer to them ever since my mother had died. We packed up. Jessie was to stay with her mother for a while and I was to be with a nobly hospitable cousin near Henley who had asked me to stay with her until I could find a new home; the dearest of the cousins with whom I had lived in Reading. It should have been a happy prospect but I will never forget my misery as the train pulled out of the station and I watched Devon slipping away. It was only then that the full force of my mother's loss came over me. She had loved Devon and had seemed a part of it. Now, as it passed away from me I felt her totally lost.

It seemed an interminable journey but I had Tiki on my lap, a solid young dog by this time, honey-coloured, furry and warm, and at the end was my cousin waiting for me at Reading Station, that I knew so well from my college days. Life was becoming repetitive, turning around towards the last half-circle that brings us back to our beginnings.

Once more it was difficult to find the right home, and again I took shelter in the Ark while I searched. But my cousin's house was a different sort of Ark from the wooden cabin perched on the hill-top at Marldon; it was the warmest, most sheltered, comfortable house imaginable, and my cousin's love was as sheltering as her house. We went together on house-hunting expeditions and I was as difficult to please as my mother had been, not liking what I could afford and losing my heart to what I could not afford. I had reached despair one morning when I opened the paper at random and found myself looking not at the leading article but at an advertisement of a seventeenth-century cottage for sale not far from us, and my whole dark mind was suddenly full of light. . . . This was no coincidence. . . . This was it, I believed, and out at the other end of all the legal and financial and structural and human difficulties that surround the buying of a house, it was. Jessie was alerted and travelled down to us at once, arriving late one evening. "I'm sorry I'm late," she said, and all the lights went up in Tiki's world and mine and we were ourselves again.

In those days Peppard Common could still be said to be in the country. A few houses were grouped around it and to the north the road that crossed the common disappeared towards Henley between tall elm trees, the village pond to the left and the seventeenth-century inn, The Dog, to the right. The entrance to Dog Lane could hardly be seen where it left the road beside the inn, and the two cottages in the lane hiding behind the inn could hardly be seen either. Dog Lane is very ancient, it was a Pack and Prime lane,

and is still called that when it reaches Henley. The men with
their pack-horses primed their pistols when they rode up from
the river to the wild common lands above. The two cottages
are called Primrose Cottage and Rose Cottage and have
been called by those names for perhaps three hundred years,
and so it was no good for me to complain that there are too
many Rose Cottages scattered over the countryside and that
letters would go astray—which they do—for Rose Cottage
it had to be. Dog Lane, of course, was perfect as an address.
It seemed to promise, and has had, a constant supply of
dogs in both cottages and at the Dog inn.

The village wheelwright had lived at Primrose Cottage,
and the Rectory coachman had been succeeded at Rose
Cottage by his daughter, whose friendly ghost seemed so
close to us when we moved in. It had remained empty after
she died and then my predecessors had found it and restored
it skilfully, but they lived here for only a short time and had
been able to do little more than dig up the wilderness of the
old garden, lay down two small lawns and plant sweetbriar
hedges. The old fruit trees had been there already, apples
and plums, and prizing privacy beyond rubies Jessie added
cherry trees, oak trees and innumerable tall flowering
shrubs, so that the place is now very green, shady and bird-
haunted, with climbing roses and clematis trained to grow
up the old trees.

Gardening in an old garden can be exciting. In the
wilderness at the bottom of the garden Jessie found remnants
of very old roses, Apothecary and Rosamundi, Maiden's-
Blush and Moss rose. Transplanted they have flourished.
They bloom only once a year, but they are worth all the
modern roses put together, they are so lovely and their
scent is so exquisite. Sports of the old primroses have
appeared, jack-in-the-green, hose-in-hose and galligaskin,
but though we bought plants of the old species and tried to
grow them again we failed. Jessie tried to bring back to the

garden plants it might have held originally, collecting all the
herbs she could and planting rosemary and lavender. And
we kept carefully the strange bits and pieces that were dug
up in the garden, bits of old crockery and china, ancient
buttons, and parts of implements whose original use it was
hard to identify.

5

It is the perfect garden for dogs, room in it for racing with
balls, yet with shady paths and hidden corners where bones
can be hoarded, and a dog can lie up in the heat or hide
wrapped in invisibility when wanted for a bath or some
other uncongenial purpose. There have been three Dandie-
Dinmonts in this garden, all three mustard dogs. Dandies
come in two colours, pepper (black and grey dogs) and
mustard (honey-coloured). The latter have the advantage
that they are easier to see at night or when they have hidden
themselves from justice or the bath.

Tiki lived out the average ten-year span of a Dandie's
life, a span that is cruelly short, and perhaps that is one
reason why they are not a popular breed; heartbreak every
ten years is hard to face when the years go by so quickly.
Tiki, so-called because I was reading *The Kon-Tiki Expedition*
when she came to us, was not beautiful. She must have had a
rough time of it in kennels before she came to us at seven
months old because she had an injured leg that could not be
put right. She was something of a ragamuffin, a gamin, but
she had guts and spirit, was a digger and hunter in spite of
her lame leg and could run at a fair pace after rabbits or
hares. But despite her gamin quality she had great perception. It was she who appeared to be aware of some ghostly
presence in the cottage and she who always knew when
Jessie was coming home. The exact hour of Jessie's return

from a holiday or a shopping expedition is always unpredict-
able, but when the car was half an hour away Tiki always
knew it. She would walk to the door and lie there patiently,
a dog carved out of wood. I would time it by my watch.
After half an hour I would hear the car turn in and the
honking of the horn, and Tiki would erupt into a maelstrom
of joy.

She was succeeded by Randa, our beautiful filmstar dog.
Randa (short for Miranda, since on a dark winter's night
we drove through a tempest of wind and rain to see her for
the first time) had had a comfortable start in life and was no
gamin but a fine lady who liked to pose on silken cushions.
'The Sybarite', Irene called her. Her hair was long and
silky and she had melting, sad dark eyes. She disliked getting
her feet wet and unlike Tiki was an indoor rather than an
outdoor dog. She was also a hospitable dog. She had learned
how to smile and would welcome people to the house (if
she liked them) with the broadest of smiles. If she did not
like them she remained courteous, but unsmilingly so. She
was very vocal. She would talk at length (alas that we
could not always know what she was saying) and when
Jessie and I had to go out without her she would welcome
us home both with smile and song. From the very beginning
she was always a good dog, larger than the other two as well
as more beautiful both physically and morally. She never
knew beforehand when Jessie was coming home but after
her death at ten years old her spirit seemed very much with
us in the house and I would hear her barking her, "Here I
am, and am I not beautiful?" bark and would answer her.
She had of course been an indoor dog. The spirit of Tiki the
outdoor dog never seemed to return to us. Set free from her
hampering body with its lame leg she must have been too
happy running like the wind in the spirit body to want to
come back.

Froda, happily, is only three years old and so I have every

hope that she will outlive me. She is an outdoor dog and more like Tiki than Randa, but she too had a happy beginning to her life and is not a gamin, but a fairy creature who darts lightly about her kingdom of the garden, appearing and disappearing like a gleam of sunshine, aloof and mysterious in her fantasy world. Almost the first thing she did when she came to us was to make a bower for herself inside a thick clump of honeysuckle. (Hobbits, Professor Tolkien tells us, like to live 'in tunnels and holes'.) Inside her bower all was darkness but through the round open front door her baby face could be seen faintly gleaming. The fairy quality in her is fitting for she was named after Frodo the hobbit in Tolkein's *Lord of the Rings*; only as Frodo is a boy and she is a girl the O had to be changed to A. Hobbits, as the vast company of Tolkien's lovers all know, are described by him as having 'the art of disappearing swiftly and silently'. This is true of Dandies also, and like the Hobbits they have large furry feet.

Dandies were originally Scottish badger dogs, trained to dig our badgers, and even foxes, for in former days a couple of Dandies were attached to every pack of hounds. They did not run with the hounds, being too small, but were royally carried on horseback. The dogs got their name from the farmer Dandie Dinmont in Walter Scott's novel *Guy Mannering*, a man not unlike a real-life farmer called James Davidson who owned a pack of terriers who were all called either Pepper or Mustard, according to their colour, a man whom Walter Scott called "the proprietor of all the Pepper and Mustard family, in other words, the genuine Dandie Dinmont". Walter Scott once owned a pack of twelve Dandies. He loved them dearly and when one little bitch, to whom he was especially attached, got lost in a wood he nearly went out of his mind during the harrowing hours of search.

Queen Victoria had a Dandie, but I think only one, and

she was wise, for one digger at a time in the family is enough. They dig everything, not only the garden but the carpets and the beds (if they are allowed on the beds) and the sofa cushions and even bare boards. They are also a bit obstinate and difficult to train. In fact they are more likely to train you than you them. Perhaps this untrainable quality, as well as the shortness of their lives, has helped to send them out of fashion. But they will surely come back into favour, for there are no more lovable companions in the world. They are true Hobbits.

6

Solid old tree trunks, heavy and hard as stone, hold the cottage together, with lesser beams that seem to be ships' timbers, since they have bolt holes in them. Old ships used to be brought up the Thames to just below Henley and broken up there, and ships' timbers are to be found in houses and cottages within easy reach of Henley. On a very hot day an aromatic scent comes from the beams. Spices? Were these beams once part of a spice ship? Soon after our arrival Jessie called my bedroom 'the captain's cabin' merely from the look and shape of it, and great was my joy when the same friend who had brought Jessie into my life gave me a copy of a poem she had seen framed and hanging on the wall of an old house in Devon. She had copied it out then and there because it evoked memories of Rose Cottage, where at night the open country beyond us seems to hold such a great depth of darkness; and where an old white horse, put out to grass in the fields below our windows, was one of the joys of our early years.

He generally had company, black and white cows, sheep and their lambs, and in the first years gypsy caravans and horses and the gypsies singing round their fire at night, but

sometimes he was quite alone in the field. There used to be a
big old hawthorn tree in the centre of the field, where he would
shelter from sun or rain. I have a clear picture in my mind
of the hawthorn tree white with blossom and the old horse
standing beneath it knee-deep in buttercups; and another
picture of hares dancing near the tree. In an apple tree in the
farm orchard at the bottom of our garden owls nested and
brought up their families year after year. The hawthorn and
the orchard are cut down now, and the old horse is dead, but
the owls have found another tree and are with us still. This is
the poem.

My room's a square and candle-lighted boat
In the surrounding depths of night afloat.
My windows are the port holes, and the seas
The sound of rain on the dark apple trees.
Sea-monster-like beneath, an old horse blows
A snort of darkness from his sleeping nose,
Below, among drowned daisies.
                           Far off, hark,
Far off, an owl, amid the waves of dark.

CHAPTER XV

Gratitude

I

IT IS DIFFICULT TO WRITE ABOUT THE LIFE OR THE EXPERIENCE that is actually yours at the moment. It is like trying to describe the physical body you are wearing, you are within it and cannot (generally fortunately) see it. The passing of years brings a static quality to one's memories, even though they are living things in a living past. They can be looked at objectively as one looks at a picture. Even one's past selves can be looked at in this way, so different are the past selves to the self one now is. I acknowledge that in all of us the basic temperament, formed by inheritance and upbringing and early experience, cannot be changed, however desperately we may long to change it. But what is built upon the unchanging foundation by our own seeking and struggling, by what happens to us and by the profound influence exerted over us by the people we meet and live with, or whose books we read, creates an ever-growing and changing personality. One looks back at almost a stranger: "Knowing myself, yet being some-one other."

Of all the great poems I have loved and learned by heart, and that have come through life with me as much loved as human friends, I think one of the greatest is T. S. Eliot's 'Little Gidding'. So much spiritual experience is held in such a small compass and yet is so perfectly described. He follows up his eerie meeting with the stranger who is his past selves with a description of the remorse that the end of life cannot fail to bring.

> . . . the conscious impotence of rage
> At human folly, and the laceration
> Of laughter at what ceases to amuse.
> And last, the rending pain of re-enactment
> Of all that you have done, and been; the shame
> Of motives late revealed, and the awareness
> Of things ill done and done to others' harm
> Which once you took for exercise of virtue.
> Then fools' approval stings, and honour stains.
> From wrong to wrong the exasperated spirit
> Proceeds, unless restored by the refining fire
> Where you must move in measure, like a dancer.

But he does not leave our old age stuck in the remorse, he brings 'the exasperated spirit' round through growth and purgation to the memories of childhood, to where the circle is complete, with the fragmented selves becoming the whole person, whole as the child who came into the world and ready for the renewal for which the other springs of our lives have been no more than prophecy.

T. S. Eliot speaks of 'The stillness between two waves of the sea'. Donald Swann said the same thing when he called his autobiography *The Space Between the Bars*. Both phrases hold a depth of meaning known perhaps only to poets and musicians, but on a more superficial level they can describe those quiet times in life when nothing much happens and yet when a great deal happens that cannot be put into words. Quiet times are growing times and I think that quietness is helped by living in a house that is very old. All old houses, unless too much haunted by human disturbance, have the serenity and acquiescence that old age should have. Both Jessie and I are aware of the influence of our small house and garden upon us. "What an atmosphere this home has," people say to me sometimes. "It is happy and peaceful." To this I have always to reply, "It has nothing to do with us. It was like this when we came."

Certainly it has nothing to do with me, since at regular

intervals I have continually insulted my lovely home by allowing waves of homesickness for Devon to sweep over me. My roots are still there, apparently, and nothing now can pull them up. Several times I have nearly succeeded in taking us back to them, but something always crops up to prevent the exodus. Jessie has borne these attacks of home-sickness with patience, knowing I hope that they are always frustrated and in time die away again. When they are over I apologise to the cottage, for though I find it difficult to love this countryside (beautiful, but too civilised and park-like, with no running streams, no high hills, no wilderness) this cottage is, after the Ely house, the dearest of all my homes.

The great and Christian virtue of hospitality is a rather weakly plant in myself and Jessie; it needs a lot of nurturing; but in the cottage itself it is so strong that the moment the front door is opened to a guest I can feel the delight that rises up from its hospitable old heart. I once entertained thirty writers in our sitting room and even above the noise of the thirty all talking at once I imagined I was aware of the contented cat-like purring of the cottage. It liked it. This cottage knows in its wisdom how much human beings need each other.

Often readers of my books tell me how much I have taught them about human nature. That is what they think. Actually it is the other way round. If I have any knowledge of human beings it is largely a reflection of themselves. So many people coming to see me over so many years, so many letters, often written in times of difficulty, or sorrow, all so revealing of their writers. If that cannot teach me something of human beings nothing can. I only realise now how grateful I am to them all, how much they have taught me, how much I owe to them. But about this I have one big regret, and this is a regret that I believe other writers feel too. For those who cannot work at all without periods of quietness there is not the time or strength for the people brought to us by our books and for normal social life too. The whole of the latter has for many of us to be cut out of our lives, and we feel apologetic to the point of guilt.

2

After we had settled into Rose Cottage I said goodbye to the old life by finishing a final book about Devon, begun while I still lived there, and then the cottage took charge of me and made me write about itself. *The White Witch* is Jessie's book, commemorating the spells she wove over the garden. Anyone reading the book would think that the writer was a very knowledgeable gardener; but no, I merely tapped Jessie's knowledge. I like the book, it is one I actually enjoyed writing.

I expect that no writer is a good judge of his or her work. I know which of my books I hate, which I can manage to tolerate, which I like and which for some personal reason I love. I love only three. The first is a book I wrote in Devon, a children's book called *The Valley of Song*, a mixed up, confused book liked by a few children (and how I adored those children) but otherwise a quickly vanishing failure. I wrote it very much under the shadow of death but so much seemed to come through to me from the shadow that I loved the book.

The quietness of the cottage produced the other two. By the time I came to write *The Dean's Watch* I had written about all the places where I had lived except Ely, the best loved, but the Ely book had always been at the back of my mind, waiting. And also waiting had been the two lovers into whose world I once looked very briefly but could never forget. When I was young my father's friend Dr Matthews and his wife took me to the Grey's Inn Ball, a most lovely sight in the great lighted hall, with so many men in eigh-

teenth-century splendour, with buckled shoes and lace
ruffles. We had not been dancing for long when the loveliness became concentrated for me in a woman who was
sitting alone, waiting. I can see her now. She was young
but not very young, with the poise of a beautiful woman
who is well aware of her beauty, a tall white lily of a woman.
She wore a dress of pale, soft orange, a floating dress. The only
bright notes of colour were her emerald-green feather fan
and her green shoes. I thought I had never seen anyone so
exquisite. I felt breathless, looking at her, enchanted as a
girl so often is by a lovely woman much older than herself.
No one asked her to dance. No one seemed to know her.
She did not mind but waited alone in her beauty, serene and
still, knowing that he would come.

At last he came, another impressive eighteenth-century
figure, with the lace and shining buckles. These great ones,
I imagined, must be the judges, for he looked like my idea of
a judge. He was much older than she was, tall and rugged,
with the saddest, ugliest, but yet I thought the most lovable
face I had ever seen. They greeted each other as a man and
woman do who are much in love but do not care to show it in
a public place. She glanced at him quickly to see that all was
well with him, then lowered her eyes. Their hands touched,
and a brief smile gleamed on his face, softening his ugliness
to tenderness. They moved out together to where the dancers
were, and joined them, she very gracefully, her soft dress
floating, he, so much older, doing his dignified best. They
did not seem to talk to each other; it seemed as though she
was afraid to look up at him lest she betray herself; and their
faces were not alight but merely quiet. Neither of them
danced with anyone else and soon they went away together
and were no more seen. But I never forgot them. For more
than thirty years they lived at the back of my mind with the
Ely book. At a time of special quietness at Rose Cottage
I knew I was now ready to write that book and I took it out

with the man and woman inside it. But why in the book did that woman so much in love change and become the (at first) loveless Elaine? I don't know. The man remained as I had seen him but in the interval Adam had possessed himself of much of my father's character, with behind him the background of some great Fen Cathedral (any of them, all of them) grey, rugged and strong as himself.

The third and last book I love is as much Jessie's as *The White Witch* since it has its roots in the beauty of Pembrokeshire, a part of the world I would never have seen had she not taken me one spring to stay for two months in her cottage on the coast, seven miles from Fishguard. Another place to grip the heart. Not in the least like Keyhaven, not like the Island, yet bringing back memories of both. Another old cottage possessed of its own particular peace, a fisherman's cottage this time, with stone steps leading up to the front door; a half-door upon which, having opened the top half, you can lean your elbow as upon a window-sill, and look out across the estuary to the bay, with the sea wind in your face . . . Birds . . . You go to sleep, listening to the eerie cry of the oyster-catchers, a fluting just heard above the wash of the sea. Looking out early in the morning you may be in time to see the herons standing in meditation beside the estuary, perhaps the swans and ducks, certainly every kind of gull and comic cormorant. For the fortunate the seals may appear; but you have to be fortunate for they do not appear for everyone. They do not appear for me. Behind the cottage the small garden slopes up to the apple trees, and when you look up there is the mountain and 'up the mountain' (a phrase used by the people of the place) mountain joy is to be found; the smell of wet moss, the sound of the streams coming down, the keening of the wind, the curlews crying, and behind it all the great silence that is always waiting behind the murmuring of these things. The sea is glorious but the mountain is better still.

Further along the coast is St David's Cathedral, one of the great shrines of the world, and further along still is Roch castle, where Lucy Walter, the secret wife of Charles II, was probably born and where she spent her early childhood. It was on my first visit to Pembrokeshire that I read a book about her written by one of her descendants. It is a rare book, now out of print, and giving a very different account of her from those given by the history books. It was lent to me by a friend who is one of the leaders in the fight to defend the beauty of Pembrokeshire from 'modern development'. She insisted that I must read it, and wanted me to write a novel about Lucy in keeping with this book. I had not got far with my reading before I was longing to write about this new Lucy, the girl of whom I was so conscious when I stood in the little church at Roch, beside the old font where she was perhaps baptized. And I wanted, too, to express the pent-up joy of the birds and the sea and the holiness of the Cathedral. That book, *The Child from the Sea*, like *Green Dolphin Country*, took years to write, and was beset by so many total interruptions that it too became too long. I doubt if it is a good book, nevertheless I love it because its theme is forgiveness, the grace that seems to me divine above all others, and the most desperate need of all us tormented and tormenting human beings, and also because I seemed to give to it all I have to give; very little, heaven knows. And so I know I can never write another novel, for I do not think there is anything else to say.

CHAPTER XVI

The End Of Our Exploring

I

WHAT DO WE ALL FEEL, AT THE END OF OUR WORK? NEAR the end perhaps, of our life? Much the same, I expect. If like myself we are one of the lucky ones, overwhelming gratitude. And mixed with the gratitude, shame; for living and working should all be done in obedience to whatever vision of God may have been given to us; and how we do fail our vision of him.

What do I believe about the vision of God, and about judgment? Our ancestors believed that all souls would stand before the judgment seat of God, and that many would be sent to a hell of lasting torment. Today our ideas are less concrete but more merciful. What do I believe myself about judgment? My own picture of these things is clear in my mind. It is only my own picture but I expect I share it with many others. With me it is, literally, a picture, for even in old age I cannot manage to grow up sufficiently either to listen to music, to think or pray without seeing pictures in my mind.

I believe that we are created by love and that sooner or later the persuasion of love will draw us up out of our darkness to stand in its exquisite light and see ourselves at last as we really are. The picture I see is of a seed deep in the earth. Somewhere, far up above the weight of darkness pressing upon the pitiful little seed, is the drawing and the calling of the sun. It seems an impossible journey towards something that has never been seen and cannot be known, but half unconsciously the blind seed puts out roots to steady itself, pushes an imploring hand upwards and starts the struggle. The poor mad poet Christopher Smart said, "the flower glorifies God and the root parries the adversary." The struggling plant knows as little about the flower he will presently be as he knows about the God he will glorify, but the flower calls to him too as he pushes up through thick darkness with the adversary clinging to his feet.

The picture of the soul now turns in my mind from that of a plant to a little animal, like a mole, scrabbling with his forepaws to make an upward tunnel, kicking out with his hindlegs at the adversary who tries ceaselessly to drag him back and down. Often he *is* dragged down, but he recovers himself and goes on and with each fresh beginning he is a little higher up; and always the pull of the sun is far more powerful than that of the adversary.

He is through at last and stands in the sun, and sometimes in my picture he is a little animal with trembling paws covering his face, and sometimes he is a shivering spike of a flower with a closed bud. The sun must woo the opened eyes to peep between the chinks of the paws, or persuade the closed petals to open a little way. It is enough. A little warmth, a little light, and the creature can know for whom, and for what he was made. For love, that he may love perfectly, and perfected be useful to the love that has loved him from the beginning and will love him to the end.

But meanwhile, what is he? It is the judgment. There is no judgment seat for the sun does not judge him; merely warms him and gives him light. He is his own judge and strengthened by the warmth he looks at himself in the light. What has he made of himself in the dark tunnel? What is he like? A dirty little animal. A shaky bit of stalk holding up a crumpled bud that has no beauty in it. The knowledge is agony, for with blind eyes down in the dark he had thought a good deal himself, and the agony is both his judgment and his inspiration. He cannot stand in the light like this. The paws go out in supplication in my picture, or the petals push away the calyx and take on the shape of praying hands. Do what you like with me. Whatever the cost, wash me and make me clean that I may be with you.

2

If one believes in a God of love what can one think about hell? To my sorrow I am not a thinker. Thinking, with me, is not much more than a sort of confused worrying, but trying to sort out one's confusion is a great help to worriers, even if it is not thought.

As reported in the gospels Christ said some frightening things about hell and I have spent miserable moments with them, for I was taught that we must not pick out from the teaching of Christ the things we happen to like and repudiate the rest. But I cannot see that anywhere in what are called 'the hard sayings' Christ says that any human soul will live eternally in hell. His chosen word to describe hell is 'fire'. Fire purifies and fire destroys, but never preserves a living thing plunged into it alive in an eternal unchanging state. So there would seem to be two fires, the purification fire in which a thing may be held for a time that it may be purged and annealed, and the fire that destroys utterly.

I believe that in the parable of Dives and Lazarus, Dives is in purgatorial fire, for in his concern for his family one can see the beginning of the death of self-love. But in the parable of the sheep and the goats it appears that the latter have finally rejected love, for they hear dreadful words, "Depart from me, ye wicked, into everlasting fire." This surely does not mean the eternal torment of a soul in the eternal fire but its destruction. This, Christ thinks, is fearful enough, since Saint Matthew's gospel reports him as saying, "Fear him who is able to destroy both soul and body in hell." And indeed it is fearful that any soul that God made for total love should be totally destroyed, but I cannot think that the destruction contradicts those greatest of all words, "I, if I be lifted up, will draw all men unto me." That sentence almost gives the definition of a man; a creature still capable of wrenching his eyes off himself and looking up, a creature (unknown to himself, perhaps) secretly longing for love and capable of it. If there should ever be a creature who had lost even the capability he would be no longer a man but a devil.

Christ said, "Everlasting fire." What did he mean by that 'everlasting'? God alone is everlasting, so did he say that the cleansing and destroying fires are God himself? Men have always looked up at the life-giving sun and seen in it a symbol of God, the best they can find to explain their idea of him. "Thou deckest thyself with light as it were with a garment, and spreadest out the heavens like a curtain," says the 104th Psalm. "The earth shall tremble at the look of him; if he do but touch the hills, they shall smoke." And St Francis says in his *Canticle of the Sun*, "Fair is he, and he shines with a very great splendour. Oh Lord, he signifies to us, Thee!" So if the two fires are two aspects of God himself, God the Purifier, God the Destroyer, then the hard sayings are hard indeed and divine love must be a terrible thing.

The true lovers of Christ have always thought so and have not shrunk from describing him in his terrible aspect. St John the Divine, describing his vision of Christ, said, "His countenance was as the Sun shineth in his strength. And when I saw him, I fell at his feet as one dead." St John the Baptist said, "Whose fan is in his hand, and he will thoroughly purge his floor, and gather his wheat into the garner; but he will burn up the chaff with unquenchable fire."

Gerard Manley Hopkins enlarges on that saying in one of
his sonnets.

> . . . O thou terrible, why wouldst thou rude on me
> Thy wring-world right foot rock? lay a lionlimb against
>   me? scan
> With darksome devouring eyes my bruised bones? and
>   fan,
> O in turns of tempest, me heaped there; me frantic to
>   avoid thee and flee?
> Why? That my chaff might fly; my grains lie, sheer
>   and clear . . .

Christians are sometimes accused of believing in the
eternal life of the soul because it is a comforting thought.
It makes them feel good because they think their virtue will
be rewarded with pie in the sky. But will it? Unless we are
saints (which is most unlikely) our scraps of virtue (if any)
are no more than filthy rags and what they will be rewarded
with is purgatorial fire. It would be much easier to be done
with it all at death, not to have to meet the result of what you
have done and been but to shelve responsibility and contract
right out. It would be much easier but, in the final end, less
glorious.

3

And so having let go of the horror of eternal punishment
what do I think about hell now? I believe that in the old
sense of the word there is no hell, but that we can use the word
in a new way. We can say that all that is contrary to the will
of God is dreadful enough to be called hell, in the sense in
which most people still use the word. Those who know what
it is like to be in such darkness of mind that they feel God
has forsaken them think they know what hell is. Those who

have been in concentration camps, and have had the whole power of evil concentrated upon them, and those who have endured pain so bad that it is practically beyond human endurance say 'it was hell'. And they are right, since these things are contrary to the will of God and their origin is not in his creative love.

But I believe they are not entirely right for to be imprisoned in evils that are outside his creative love is not to be separated from his redemptive love, since in Christ he experienced these things himself and so left something of love at the heart of each experience. It is possible that he may be found in these things, so often he is, but in any case he is there, and because he is there the eventual end of these agonies is freedom from them.

I would like to believe that no human soul ever becomes a totally evil spirit—a devil—that no human soul is ever destroyed. I want to believe that every single soul reaches God at last. And yet—love cannot compel. Love can draw the little animal up and up, perhaps fighting all the way, to the point where he is aware of the presence of the sun and feels its warmth embrace him. He cries out like Jacob, "What is your name?" and he knows the answer and what it means. But he has to be asked a question himself. "Now you know what I am, do you want me?" As it is almost inconceivable to me that love should have to ask such a question of any soul he has created, so it seems equally inconceivable that he would ever receive any answer except, "Wash me and make me clean that I may be with you." Yet I have to believe that the soul may refuse if he wishes. And what then? Not eternal torment since the sun is fire, but eternal death. . . . And yet, Christ conquered death.

One struggles with thoughts and words, and then suddenly they all fall down like the cards with which a child has laboriously tried to build a house, and lie there in chaos at one's feet. For we know nothing. The mystery of the universe and of our tiny breath of being is too great for us. And then one can feel something like the forbidden sin of despair. In this state it comforts me to remember that the great religions of the world have been called "Traditions of response". Certainly all true living all down the ages has been a condition of response; to mountains and trees and great waters, to music, poetry, to each other, to loveliness without end, and always it is the response of as much love as we are capable. And as response grows we are capable of more and more and more love. Growth is not sterile. Out beyond all these things must be the reality that speaks through them, and when our own thoughts and words crumble it helps to turn to the mystics who are lifted above our confusions, and to the old myths of the world, some of them almost as old as time.

When I think of what are called 'the last things' and wonder about them I often think of the Hindu myth of redemption. In the story the good and bad spirits alike longed to find the nectar of immortality that is sunk in the ocean of milk, and they made up their minds to churn the ocean in order to find it. They placed a holy mountain in the ocean and began to rotate it, the good people pulling one way and the bad the other, and the first thing they brought up from the depths was the most terrible evil. They were appalled, for the good and bad people alike realised that unless help came it would destroy them all. But help did come for Shiva the Preserver, who is also Shiva the Destroyer, had mercy on them. He took the evil from them and he swallowed it, and pictures of Shiva show him with a blue throat, excoriated by the evil he has taken into his own being. (Christians, reading this story, cannot help remembering the words of Christ, "This cup which my Father hath given me shall I not drink it?") After that redemption the good and bad people churned again and at last they churned up eternal life. They both had a good look at it, and the good people accepted it and entered into it but the bad people turned away from it and were destroyed.

The myth is like a gold coin with two sides to it. It can be the story of each one of us, filled with horror at the evil we find in the depths of ourselves but powerless to save ourselves from it, or it can be a cosmic story, the story of the universe. In any case it is the same story since love works out from the central point of the soul in ever-widening circles of redemption.

Here is a poem I love, taken from the *Bhagavad-Gita*.

When goodness grows weak,
When evil increases,
I make myself a body.
In every age I come back
To deliver the holy,
To destroy the sin of the sinner,
To establish righteousness.

He who knows the nature
Of my task and my holy birth
Is not reborn
When he leaves this body;
He comes to Me.

Flying from fear,
From lust and anger,
He hides in Me,
His refuge and safety.
Burnt clean in the blaze of my being,
In Me many find home.

The Hindu poet, who wrote these verses centuries ago, might have been writing for Christians today, for we would agree with nearly all of it, delighting in the way in which the great religions echo each other as the chimes of the church bells used to do on Christmas night. But for us, though we believe great sons of God walk the world in every age, only one of them is the supreme Son of God who fulfils all longing because he is "everything God asks of man, and everything man asks of God".

One's own words are poor things, so this book shall end as it began, not with my own fumbling. It began with Ben Jonson rejoicing in the beauty of creation and it shall end with Thomas Traherne rejoicing in the glory of love.

O God, who by love alone art great and glorious, that art present and livest with us by love alone: Grant us likewise by love to attain another self, by love to live in others, and by love to come to our glory, to see and accompany Thy love throughout all eternity.

Index